John H. Oak

CALLED TO AWAKEN THE LAITY

Translators

Rev. Sam Ko, a Korean-Canadian, served as the International secretary and assistant to Dr. John H. Oak. A Graduate of Westminster Theological Seminary, Rev. Ko has extensive pastoral experience in Canada, the United States and Korea. He has two sons with his wife Jennifer and currently serves as the senior pastor at the Korean Church of Queens.

Rev. Jerry Vreeman has been involved in international media ministries since he graduated from Calvin Theological Seminary. He has extensive experience in radio and television. He is an ordained minister in the Christian Reformed Church of North America. He and his wife Cori have four daughters, two sons and two grandchildren.

© John H. Oak

ISBN 978-1-84550-224-9

10 9 8 7 6 5 4 3 2 1

First published in 2003, reprinted 2004 as
Healthy Christians Make a Healthy Church
Revised in 2006, reprinted 2009
by
Christian Focus Publications,
Geanies House, Fearn,
Ross-shire, IV20 1TW, Scotland

www.christianfocus.com

Cover design by
Disciple Making
Ministries International Designer

Printed and bound by
Bell & Bain, Glasgow

Mixed Sources
Product group from well-managed forests and other controlled sources
www.fsc.org Cert no. TT-COC-002769
© 1996 Forest Stewardship Council

Contents

PART 4
MINISTRY METHOD – DISCIPLESHIP TRAINING

PART 5
MINISTRY FIELD – DISCIPLES

This book is dedicated
to all my brothers and sisters in Christ
who devoted their time, money and energy
for the sole purpose of making
true disciples
of
Jesus Christ

Foreword

How do you turn the members of your church into mature lay ministers? That is one of the most critical questions in church health and growth today.

It's not enough just to hope and dream that people will get involved in serving Jesus. Your church needs an intentional strategy for leading people to deeper commitment and greater service for Christ. At Saddleback Church, in Lake Forest, California we've been able to commission literally thousands of lay ministers through a strategy of consistent communication, a practical process, and a simple structure. Your church can use these same elements to mobilize your members for ministry.

First, continually teach what the Bible says about the church, about spiritual growth, about serving and about spiritual giftedness. Next, set up a process for uncovering your members' gifts and talents and finding the best place for each one to serve. Then organize the structure of your church in a way that minimizes maintenance and maximizes ministry. That's what this book is all about!

My good friend, Dr. John Oak has written an outstanding manual on discipleship and equipping. It is full of wisdom that comes from serving Christ for many years. What Pastor Oak shares in the book is not mere theory. It works! It had proven to be effective in SaRang Community Church. God has used the principles in the book to build a church that is both balanced and healthy, not just large.

The starting point in leading members to maturity, ministry and mission is to invest time in teaching your members what the Bible says about these issues. You must lay the biblical foundation. Teach it in classes, sermons, seminars, home cell groups, and every other way you can emphasize it. You should never stop teaching on the importance of every Christian having a ministry. This book can be your guide.

Jesus said, 'For even the Son of Man did not come to be served, but to serve, and to give his life as a ransom for many' (Mark 10:45). Serving and giving are the defining characteristics of the Christlike lifestyle. If we are going to be like Christ, we must learn to serve and to give. We must put the Word into practice, not just listen to it. My prayer is that God will use this book to produce an entire generation of believers who are committed to serving and sharing the eternal purposes of God!

Dr. Rick Warren
Saddleback Valley Community Church, California
Author: *The Purpose Driven Church*
and *The Purpose Driven Life*

Preface

Looking back in history, we discover that the church's existence has been like treading on ice, embracing the uncertainty and uneasiness of the times in which it lives. When the church has lost its influence, it has not been able to avoid self-reproach and suffering due to the tension of the era. Yet in times of revival, the church has been more concerned about the decay and secularization of the world.

We are now living in an age of instability. In order for it to function as salt and light in this evil world, I believe the Holy Spirit initiates a certain amount of unrest and turmoil within the church. As long as the church is alert to these things, there will be no danger of falling asleep.

There has been in recent years a growing number of those who have asserted the importance of recovering the proper role and position of the laity. This seems to show the uneasiness that pervades many contemporary churches, and could serve to warn the church against falling into complacency and maintaining the *status quo*. In order to transform contemporary society into the kingdom of God where God's name can be hallowed, the church must be willing to face the challenge and embrace the necessary changes.

In fact, the laity are emerging as a serious issue in the contemporary church. To put it positively, lay people are the best and the greatest potential the church has. To put negatively, lay people are a serious challenge for the church. The issue of which perspective will prevail – the positive or the negative – lies entirely in the hands of the church leaders. Rediscovering the biblical role of the laity demands a radical remodeling of the old framework of ministry. This can place a heavy burden on a church leader. Although many clergy have a great interest in the role of the laity they find it difficult to put their beliefs into practice because this issue cuts to the heart of pastoral ministry.

As we all know, reformation is not an easy process to initiate or complete The reformation of the clergy prior to that of the entire church is required in order to break away from the prejudice and ingrown thinking deeply embedded in many churches today, and to gain insight into the importance of the laity. In fact, throughout history, this has often been the case. It is almost impossible for reformation to take place in the church unless it first takes place in the heart of the clergy.

Hendrik Kraemer correctly points out the need for the reformation of the church as a perennial imperative that is always directly related to the life of the church:

> In this sense the imperative is equally imperious for every kind of Church; the flourishing and the decadent ones, the self-complacent and the despondent. In the light of this rule of the perennial, constantly valid law of renewal, the laity, as said already, gets its essential place and meaning, because the whole Church is constantly called to renewal.[1]

Part 1 of this present work focuses on the current issues facing the church. As all of us probably know, an accurate understanding of a problem is essential to solving the problem. For this reason, it is important that we honestly search for and acknowledge the problems existing in the church. In addition, we will briefly consider the concept of the laity in relation to the clergy.

---

1. Hendrick Crammer, *Theology of Laymen*, p. 92.

Part 2 explains why we should not view the church merely as a worshipping community. The church is also a witnessing community in which the lay people serve one another as those who have received a calling from God. For our purpose, it is necessary to discuss the apostolic nature of the church, the priesthood of all believers, and the concept of the body of Christ. We must verify that reclaiming the role of the laity is not a merely temporary theological trend, but a fundamental task that corresponds to the essence and calling of the church revealed in the Scriptures.

Why does the church exist in the world? What are the roles of the laity in the church and in the world? To answer these questions, we must turn to the Scriptures. Our ministry philosophy will depend on how we answer these questions. Our ministry philosophy is none other than a pastor's ministry conviction that has been shaped by his doctrine of the church.

Unfortunately, many of us have been brought up in an atmosphere that neglects the concepts of the apostolicity of the church and the laity. In order for us to become responsible leaders of the church, we must break out of the shell in which we have been unwittingly confined.

Part 3 is about discipleship. Discipleship is a fundamental biblical strategy that is essential for reconstructing the laity's self-image congruent with the essence of the church. Discipleship offers an ideal image of the laity. Discipleship is Jesus' answer to the question of the standard by which we must train and teach the laity. In this sense, discipleship provides a clear direction for rediscovering the lay people in the church.

Part 4 summarizes practical principles and methods of discipleship training for developing the laity. Once we establish a clear ministry philosophy and strategy, finding the most ideal method will not be difficult. We would say that discipleship training is the answer. The setting of the small group, as used by Jesus Himself, has been demonstrated as one of the most effective methods of education. It will indeed be helpful to examine the important features of His method and apply them to current ministry.

Part 5 visits a ministry scene at a local church where actual discipleship training takes place in order to develop the lay leaders. We will be able to observe what takes place and how it is done, and analyse both the strengths and weaknesses. It will be an opportunity to get a feel for the possibility of making lay disciples in the local church.

Part 1
TODAY'S CHURCH AND THE LAITY
INTRODUCTION

Part 2
MINISTRY PHILOSOPHY
ECCLESIOLOGY

Part 3
MINISTRY STRATEGY
DISCIPLESHIP

Part 4
MINISTRY METHOD
DISCIPLESHIP TRAINING

Part 5
MINISTRY FIELD
DISCIPLES

Chapter 1

What is the Problem?

Exponential Growth

The Korean church has been an object of worldwide attention since the middle of the twentieth century. The explosive growth of Korean churches has brought about numerous words of encouragement. South Korea is known to have some of the world's largest churches and most fervent believers. A former missionary to Japan referred to the revival in Korea as the great drama of contemporary mission.[1]

Horace Allen and Horace Underwood, missionaries from America, started their mission endeavours in Korea in 1884 and had their first convert two years later. Christianity in Korea grew from this small beginning, and a century later, approximately six hundred thousand believers were added in 1983 alone. According to one survey, the churches in Korea have seen an average membership growth of 13-15 percent every year. This is six to seven times higher than the national annual population growth rate, which is only 2 percent.

Since the mid-1970s, South Korea has witnessed an amazing proliferation of churches. Nearly four thousand new churches have been planted each year, which is equivalent to 10 new churches a day.[2] One hundred

1. Neil Brown, *Laity Mobilization* (Grand Rapids: Eerdmans, 1971), 78.
2. 'Monthly Econo-Political Culture', *Kyung Hyang Daily Newspaper* (Korean), February, 1984, 198.

years of missionary efforts in Korea have witnessed such marvelous achievements that we can claim one out of every four among the almost 50 million South Koreans is a Christian today. Thus we had a good reason to celebrate the centennial year of Korean missions in 1984.

There are several underlying causes for the rapid growth of the Korean church. Those causes are still prevalent today. The primary cause has been ongoing evangelization by evangelical mission organizations. Such efforts have helped to propel the church into the world of our alienated young people. For the last 20 years, mission organizations with only a Bible in their hands have ignited the flame of the gospel in the hearts of our youth. The gale of the Pentecostal movement that swept through Korea has also had a powerful impact on the churches in Korea, challenging them on the need for a spiritual awakening. These are some of the external causes for the rapid growth of the Korean church.

In addition to the above factors, social and political instability also made positive contributions. Korean churches have been purified through the furnace of suffering and trials. This process of purification has helped them to bear bounteous fruit. In the midst of suffering, the abundance of God's blessings was made clear. Thus we have to remember that the growth of the Korean church was not a coincidence.

Controversial Issues of Revival
On the other hand, the voices expressing concerns about the churches in Korea are increasing today. We have been growing apprehensive about the alarming symptoms that are observed today. In reality, Korean churches seem like a pile of bricks that have been stacked at random.

To be honest, we would like to have a positive perspective toward the church. A pessimistic outlook

16

on the future of the church could be considered as a sign of unbelief, since Jesus Christ has won the victory. Additionally, the growth of the Korean church has always been spoken of in a positive manner. 'Korean churches will be revisited by a second phase of revival. And for that purpose, God will allow economic growth as well in order to support the missionary enterprise.' Everyone would be encouraged to hear statements like this.

However, Korean churches have been focused only on quantitative growth for too long and thus are facing serious problems today. It is vital that we take time to evaluate the optimistic outlook associated with this situation. It doesn't mean that church growth has stopped or that new churches are closing their doors. Such problems would be comparable merely to the symptoms that a cardiac patient would feel. What concerns us is the disease itself, not its subjective symptoms. We are at a point where we must confess, 'Why doesn't revival happen in our days? The answer lies within the church. The church itself is the stumbling block that prevents revival.'

Although it may sound odd, the revival of Korean churches shares similar characteristics and patterns with the modernization movement that led to Korea's rapid economic growth. For many years, Korea has been idolizing economic growth under the slogan, 'Let us live well'. Thus the ends have become more important than the means, and ethics have often been compromised in order to meet the goal. As a result, Korea's reputation has been tarnished, and Korea has become known as one of the nations where bribery and corruptions are commonly practiced. According to 'The International Transparency Headquarters', a private corruption control organization, the 1996 International Corruption Index showed Korea's ranking to be 27th out of 54 countries. This is where we stand. We are now trying to overcome all the economic turbulence which has resulted from our high-speed development policy.

But how can we say that this is true only in the case of economics? Even in the church, there are similar problems. We have been considering revival only in terms of quantitative growth for so long that the numbers of those who attend, the size of the church building, and the amount of the offering have become our focus and even our idols. In order to achieve a quantitative goal, some church leaders have disregarded pastoral ethics, adopted secular marketing strategies without reservation, and even caused spiritual confusion by importing shamanistic elements in some cases.

By contrast, the Scripture reveals that revival consists of both aspects of quantity and quality. There cannot be true revival when this balance is lost. True healthy revival is possible only when quality determines quantity. We must realize that we have already deviated from the essence of Christianity when we allow quantity to determine quality.

Three Aberrant Phenomena

The most serious problems caused by quantitative growth are what I call the 'Three Aberrant Phenomena'. What are they? They are 1) false statistic, 2) bluffing, and 3) illusion.

False statistic refers to the misrepresentation of data in Korean churches. The fact that church leaders are the ones who ignore this statistical data most indicates the seriousness of the problem. What happens when you meet someone who bluffs about their income or size of their apartment they live in? We begin to wonder about them.

However, we seem to be quite content to exaggerate church attendance numbers and other important figures. Some would even make an excuse by saying that these numerical values will reflect the size of your faith. This may be true in some cases, but what is the real problem? The real problem is that we have lost our conscience – it has been contaminated by materialism. We want to show off. If unbelievers knew about this, who would want to believe in Jesus?

We tend to measure the success of church ministry by its size, which can be misleading. By this standard, only a few mega-churches, which make up less than 5 percent of Korean churches, would be deemed 'successful' churches. Here is a critical comment by an American pastor, Bill Hull, which has relevance to Korea also:

> Let me be clear: I don't expect to reach the upper 5 percent of evangelism. Highly talented and creative entrepreneurial pastoral models dominate the upper 5 percent. They are very effective. God greatly uses them to minister to the masses, and they can offer a few principles and hints that can assist others in their work. But as models, they do more harm than good. Most pastors would do better if they had never heard of or been exposed to the upper 5 percent. The upper 5 percent presents the average pastor with an unrealistic, unreachable, guilt-producing model that threatens his ministry. Pressure to be like them has destroyed many.[3]

To God, one soul is precious. True revival begins when we accept this truth. We should not forget that a true church is not determined by its size. Thus, Korean churches must make conscientious efforts to be transparent especially in recording correct figures on all aspects of ministry.

---

3. Bill Hull, *Disciple Making Pastor* (New Jersey: Revell, 1988), 24-25.

Bluffing refers to the lack of Christian influence in society. God has placed His people in various positions in society to fulfill His purpose. We should not be taking our professions for granted but rather should use them to glorify God.

A recent newspaper article stated that 67.8 percent of those who were appointed as government ministers from 1993 to 1997 were Christians. And yet our society has been going from bad to worse – mentally, morally, and even in matters of public order. Unfortunately pastors, elders and deacons are often mentioned in massive scandals. What does this tell us? It points to the fact that Korean churches are not influencing the society. If Christians cannot function as salt and light in the world, then we are merely bluffing. It is distressing to see when Christians are ineffective and lukewarm. If we desire to see the revival of the church, we must seriously consider how to put our faith into practice. This requires repentance and self-examination.

Lastly, *illusion* refers to when Christians are living inconsistently and as a result fail to be different from unbelievers. Many Christians fail to live out their faith. The key to Christian faith is transformation of one's character and life. Therefore, having faith implies actions.

Sadly, Korean churches are not perceived as being any different from the rest of the society. The great legacy of the reformers is its rejection of any dualism that separates personal faith from public life. Christians must pursue a balanced spirituality of being *in* the world, yet not *of* the world. To know God is to know ourselves. Knowledge of God that has no bearing on our understanding of everyday life is not the spirituality of the reformers.[4]

---

4. Alister E. McGrath, *Spirituality in an Age of Change* (Grand Rapids: Zondervan, 1994), 49.

If our Christian life is restricted to a church setting, then we are just being religious and running away from the world God has made. Faith is about restoring the relationship between God and His fallen creatures. Believers are the key to this process of reconciliation. Thus Christians' faithfulness, obedience, and love for God the Creator should be reflected in their respect for, interest in, and dedication to the world He has created.

In this regard, we must strive to better preserve the tradition of the reformers. Korean churches have failed to make disciples. Attendance is high and yet many are like the crowds that gathered around Jesus only to have their physical needs met. A crowd is a mere illusion. Thus, we must make disciples whose faith is reflected in their lifestyle and *vice versa*. This is the way to turn from illusion to reality in the church.

As Christians are becoming a mainstream of our society, people long to see the true character of the church. They want the church to solve their problems. They do not want the churches to merely hold international meetings and events, but instead want real, practical answers from Christian laity whom they encounter daily in their lives. But they continue to be disappointed. Just as the salt that loses its saltiness is thrown away, the church is increasingly becoming a target of criticism.

Numerical Growth Can Be Temporary

We see many young people leaving the church in great disappointment to find truth in other religions. Every Christian denomination is showing a decreasing growth rate. Ironically, it has been our strategy centred on church growth that seems to have caused the decline in church membership. Such a side effect has already become obvious among the churches in developed countries.

Michael Green's warning cited in *Christianity Today* presents a good example. He contends that although America is more advanced technologically, England is still ahead of it in the religious realm. He then uses England as an example to make a keen analysis of the current status of American churches.

> *Fifty years ago our English churches were full like your American churches are today. But we were satisfied with big congregations that focused on the pulpit, routine attendance in the pew ... and our shallowness. Consequently, people became disillusioned by an ineffectual church and indifferent to her message. And today our churches are empty. Your American churches are crowded with people today, but there is no Biblical or spiritual depth among your laymen. Religion is largely a sentimental Sunday affair which does not radically influence daily life. If something doesn't change, fifty years from now your churches will be empty as ours are today. If I were an American minister, rather than concentrating on the people outside the church, I would spend all my time seeking the conversion and deepening of those who are already church members.*[5]

We are well aware of the fact that Green's prophecy has been coming true in American churches within the last half century. There is no guarantee that Korean churches will not share the same fate as English and American churches.

Assuming that the crowds swarming into contemporary churches could also leave the churches someday, cultural anthropology professor Kil Sung Choi said the following:

> *I believe it was neither the unilateral endeavor on the part of the church nor proper indigenizing of the Christian spirit*

---

5. Howard E. Butt Jr., 'The Layman as a Witness,' *Christianity Today* (Vol. XII, No. 23), 11.

that caused the surprising growth of Christianity in Korea. Instead, the cause was the easy accommodation of Christianity by the believers rooted in shamanism. It would be correct to say that the revival phenomenon of the Korean churches has a strong possibility that the converts to Christianity would either return to their old religions or become secularized.[6]

The contents of an article by the Church Growth Research Institute, published in November 1997, shows that Dr. Choi's concern for Korean churches is not without grounds. Korean churches showed an annual growth rate of 41.2 percent during 1960–70, 12.5 percent during 1970–80, 4.4 percent during 1980–90, and the growth has continued to slow down since then. The growth rates of congregations during 1990–95 were as follows: Full Gospel Denomination 0.5 percent, United Presbyterian 0.45 percent, Methodist 0.4 percent, and Hapdong Presbyterian 0.06 percent. In the interests of accuracy, it should be noted that this growth index doesn't reflect an increase, but rather a decrease, if we take into account the illusory nature of church statistics.

Although true revivals witnessed in church history have not *always* led to quantitative growth, true revival does tend to result in numerical growth. Thus there is certainly nothing wrong with quantitative growth in itself, for the kingdom of God, like a mustard seed, will surely grow to fill the entire world.

However, there is a negative aspect to quantitative growth. It could blind church leaders with materialism and cause them to forget the worth and potential of a single soul. God is more interested in one lost sheep than in the remaining ninety-nine sheep in the fold. In some sense God is not pleased with multitudes (1 Cor. 10:5).

---

6. Kil-Sung Choi, 'Some Characteristics of Minjoong Faith', in *Monthly Chosun* (Korean) (Chosun Daily News Co., December 1982), 73.

He is not pleased with a multitude when men take the glory for quantitative growth and obscure His will. God was not pleased with David when he wanted to take a census of the population, and He is the same today (1 Chron. 21).

Hans Weber points out the difference between God's and man's way of accounting:

> The result of true evangelism may be the cutting down of the number of church members; discovering the cost of discipleship often results in a decline in church membership; mission in the New Testament is not connected with statistics, but with sacrifices. [7]

I believe Korean churches ought to pay heed to the warning.

In order not to demean the precious revival that Korea has been blessed with and in order to continue to move forward with a greater vision of the kingdom of God, the churches in Korea must be transformed. It is time to put away the desires of the sinful nature and clothe ourselves with the Lord Jesus Christ (Rom. 13:14). This is not something that will be accomplished by changing the architectural design of our church buildings, or sewing another red stripe on the pastoral gowns. I am convinced that there is no other way to solve this problem than to teach and train the laity. Lay people are the main body and the representatives of the church. They need to become disciples of Christ. This is a matter of life and death for the church. We can find solutions to the problems we are facing today when we return to biblical principles. Did not the problems facing the Jerusalem church become an occasion for producing great lay leaders (Acts 6:1-7)? God can turn our misfortune into blessings for us today as well.

---

7. Hans R. Weber, *Evangelization* (New York: Paulist Press, 1975), 64.

Chapter 2

Rediscovering the Laity

If there was an awakening that shed a new light into the church of the twentieth century, I believe it was the laity movement. After World War II, this movement surfaced everywhere. Many research dissertations on this subject poured forth on a torrential scale, and lay training manuals were stacked up in bookstores.

The rediscovery of the laity in the twentieth century has even been compared to the Protestant Reformation of the sixteenth century in its magnitude and intensity. If the significance of the Reformation was in restoring the true image of the church for God, it could be said that the significance of the laity movement is in restoring the true image of the church for the world.

Why such a sudden awakening of the laity? Kraemer gives two practical reasons. One is a strong effort to utilize the laity's potential as witnesses for Christ in a rapidly expanding contemporary society. The other reason is the ecumenical movement.[1]

However, to say that the awakening of the laity was caused entirely by the needs of the time is one-sided. The calling and role of lay people must be regarded first of all as a biblical mandate. This can be seen in many evangelical mission organizations that have no direct

---

1. Hendrik Kraemer, *A Theology of the Laity* (Philadelphia: Westminster Press, 1958), 65ff.

ties with the ecumenical movement. Evangelical mission organizations were convinced that God was calling lay people to go into the world. Our sole foundation for reformation is the Bible. When we realize how a biblical truth addresses the needs of real life under the guidance of the Holy Spirit, we then accept it as God's will and apply it accordingly. This is the point of contact between truth and the realities of life. The following statement by John Stott is indeed pertinent:

> *The real reason for expecting the laity to be responsible, active and constructive church members is biblical, not pragmatic, and is grounded on theological principle, not on expediency. It is neither because the clergy need the laity to help them, nor because the laity want to be of use, nor because the world thinks this way, but because God Himself has revealed it as His will. Moreover, the only way in which the laity will come to see and accept their inalienable rights and duties in the Church is that they come to recognize them in the Word of God as the will of God for the people of God.*[2]

The Pulse of Church History

When we look back into the history of the church, we will see that lay people kept their position intact in the beginning. During the first two centuries of the New Testament church era, the laity was the centre of the church. Adolf Harnack, a renowned historian of the early church, draws the following conclusion:

> *It is impossible to see in any one class of people inside the Church chief agents of the Christian propaganda...we cannot hesitate to believe that the great mission of Christianity was in reality accomplished by means of informal missionaries.*[3]

---

2. John Stott, *One People* (Downers Grove: InterVarsity Press, 1971), 11.
3. Quoted in Michael Green, *Evangelism in the Early Church* (Grand Rapids: Eerdmans, 1975), 172.

Although churches soon ceased to function properly and entered the Dark Ages, the torches of reformation that often shone in the Dark Ages were usually lit by lay people. This was true of the Wycliff movement in the fourteenth century. Luther's reformation was also an awakening movement supported by thousands of committed lay people. Reformation and revival were usually characterized by the restoration of lay people to their rightful place in the church, and the times of stagnation and corruption were usually characterized by the tyranny of the clergy.

Accordingly, a church with slumbering or stagnant lay members cannot be healthy. The less distinct the line dividing the clergy and the laity becomes, the greater the creative ministry of the Holy Spirit will be in the church. Although the following opinion may sound rather radical, we ought to think about it earnestly:

> *The first reformation took the Word of God exclusively out of the hands of the clergy and put it into the hands of the people. The second reformation is to get the ministry exclusively out of the hands of the clergy and into the hands of the people, where it rightly belongs.*[4]

It is very encouraging to observe that the number of leaders recognizing and studying the importance of the laity in Korean churches is currently on the rise. It is never too late to start awakening and equipping the laity, which will bring renewal and reformation to the church.

Rediscovering the laity should not be consigned to mission organizations or international bodies. We should not forget, not even for a moment, that awakening the laity is the calling and charge given to local church pastors who are labouring with sweat and tears.

---

4. Bill Hull, *Disciple Making Pastor*, 126.

If we continue to remain as clergy-centred churches in which multitudes are interested merely in liturgical worship, and if we continue to avoid the birth pain of making the laity into disciples of Christ, then we will once again face a shameful end of having quantity without quality. The result will be a stagnant church, which is not what Jesus Christ wants as the head of the church.

We cannot let the mob that disappointed Jesus in Galilee raise its voice once again in the church today. Pure Christianity is found in one or two spoonfuls of leaven rather than in large bags of flour. This, I believe, is one of the greatest lessons that we can learn from two thousand years of church history.

Thankfully, growing number of church leaders are beginning to recognize the importance of properly developing and fully mobilizing the laity. They have begun to realize that this is the most effective way for the church to function as leaven in our rapidly changing contemporary society. This indeed is a positive sign that promises a bright future for the church.

Chapter 3

The Laity

The Main Body of the Church

Laikos, the Greek word for the 'laity', is not found in the New Testament. However, it carries the same meaning as the word *laos* which does appear frequently in the Bible. This word simply means 'people', 'people group', or 'crowd of people'. In secular Greek, it referred to the citizens of the Hellenistic world. However in the Bible, it was first used to refer to the Jews in contrast to the Gentiles (Acts 4:10), and later in reference to the New Israel, including the Gentile converts to Christianity – in other words, the church in the last days (Acts 15:14).

There is, however, no instance in the Bible where the word was used to refer to a special group of people. It was always used as a general term referring to an entire group of people.[1] Therefore, we must keep in mind that the word 'laity' originally referred to the entire chosen people who have Christ in their hearts – saints, disciples - that is the whole church, the community of believers. We must also remember that the word 'laity' did not differentiate clergy from the rest of believers. As Stott points out, there is only one condition used to differentiate people in the Bible. It is the unique condition of being God's children set apart from the world.[2] In other words, there is no basis for differentiating the children of God within

---

1. John Stott, *One People*, 28.
2. Ibid., 28.

the church. Therefore, even the office of the clergy does not confer upon them a status different from the rest of believers.

In order to further verify this truth, we will consider several basic concepts of the church. The Bible offers several motifs to describe the character of the church – the people of God, the temple of the Holy Spirit, and the body of Christ. They all provide the reasons for designating each and every lay person as the principal body of the church, and explain why there is no difference in status between clergy and laity.

Let us first examine the concept of the church as the gathering of God's chosen people. Everyone who believes in Jesus Christ is one of God's chosen people. There can be no difference between clergy and laity. Both are God's chosen people, and everyone is equal before God who called them by grace. Thus, there is no room for allowing a special status or position within the church.

'The church is always and in all cases the whole people of God, the whole *ekklesia*, the whole fellowship of the faithful.'[3] Therefore, all believers are equal members of God's family. Without any exception, every believer is a chosen one, a saint, a disciple, and a brother or a sister.

Next is the concept of the temple of the Holy Spirit. All who believe in Jesus Christ have been set free from sin (Rom. 6:18-23). They no longer belong to themselves but to Christ who has set them free (1 Cor. 6:19). Therefore, a believer is a spiritual person filled with the Holy Spirit. The Holy Spirit has come upon the entire community of the church and upon each believer, thus making the entire church a new creation. In this sense, the church is the temple of the Holy Spirit, and all believers have become a holy priesthood, offering spiritual sacrifices acceptable to God (1 Pet. 2:4, 5). This sacrifice is not a

---

3. Hans Kung, *The Church* (New York: Image Books, 1967), 169.

material sacrifice but a spiritual sacrifice that offers the fruits of prayer, praise and thanksgiving, and repentance. The Holy Spirit dwells in every believer. Both the clergy and the laity are a holy priesthood offering spiritual sacrifices through the Holy Spirit, and there is, therefore, no difference between them. Accordingly, lay men and women are irrefutably the principal constituents of the church. They are the community of the church itself. And the clergy is also the principal body of the church only by the virtue of being a part of this church community.

Third is the concept of the body of Christ. Paul referred to the church as the body of Christ (Eph. 1:23). Christ is the head and believers are the body (1 Cor. 12:27; Col. 1:18). Believers participate in the body of Christ when they are baptized by the Holy Spirit (1 Cor. 12:13). Furthermore, they experience supernatural oneness within the body of Christ when they partake of the bread and the cup in communion (1 Cor. 10:16, 17).

The church as the body of Christ signifies the fact that each believer is important and has special talents and abilities. Each believer is endowed with gifts and dignity. Thus it is imperative that believers care for one another and serve with love, joy and thanksgiving. Could there be any difference between clergy and laity in this sense?

This distinctive organic quality of the body brings all believers into an interdependent relationship. This is so crucial that it would be difficult to maintain one's faith severed from the church community.

Faith does not exist by itself, but in the actual men who believe. And these men do not live as separate individuals, isolated believers... They have their faith through the community, which as a believing community proclaims the message to them and provokes the response of faith in them... It can be a relief as well as a burden to realize that despite our total

CALLED TO AWAKEN THE LAITY

individual responsibility, our faith is part of the wider and richer, old and yet young faith of the believing community that is the Church. [4]

Believers are in a profoundly dependent relationship with each other, and this assumes the necessity of mutual cooperation. They cannot survive unless they help one another. Not only should the clergy serve the laity, but the laity also must minister to one another in spiritual service. For this purpose, the Holy Spirit graciously gives gifts to each believer (1 Cor. 12:11). The gifts of the Holy Spirit are impartial, and therefore there is no exception or discrimination. Each member takes care of one another and brings unity to the body through these gifts (1 Cor. 12:24, 25).

As we have seen in the brief study of these concepts, there is no basis found in the Bible for assigning a higher status to the clergy over and against the laity. On the contrary, we have verified that the two are equal and there is no difference between them. Even so, in reality, lay members of our churches are often treated as if they are inferior to the clergy. It has become a common perception that the clergy are the most important part of the church. Many lay members behave as though they are mere servants existing for pastors. How seriously wrong we are! How can lay men and women recover their original status and fulfill their true role in such an environment? It is as though we have outwardly rejected the Roman Church's unbiblical elevation of the clergy, but have secretly adopted it. However, if we truly desire to awaken the laity and build a healthy church, we must no longer tolerate such an abnormal and unbiblical practice.

---

4. Ibid., 58.

What Does 'Laity' Mean?

The word 'laity' is commonly understood as referring to all believers excepting the clergy. Why is that? A quick review of church history shows how the distortion of the original meaning of the word 'laity' came about. When the Roman Empire officially recognized Christianity around the third century, churches began to grow at a rapid rate and inevitably became institutionalized. Naturally the concept of professional clergy was introduced to lead these institutions, and the distance between the clergy and the laity grew further apart. The answer was provided by Bishop Cyprian, who publicly began to use the word 'laity' to refer to the general population of believers, as distinguished from the clergy.

The use of titles such as 'clergy' and 'laity' began to separate those who were professionally working for the church and those who were not – as though their relationship was akin to that between the priests and the people in the Old Testament period. As a result, the word 'laity' soon deviated from its original meaning and became a word that classified believers into two groups. And it has remained thus for the last 1,500 years or so.

It is strange, to say the least, to persist in using the distorted word 'laity' in the church where all believers are equal as God's children. It is important that we do not stop at merely understanding the original meaning of the word. Instead, we must know how the word became distorted over time and reinstate its rightful meaning. Here is the reason why we still use the word. Over 99 percent of the churches are lay people. The visible church does not belong to a few professional clergy but belongs to lay people who are to give a concrete expression of the kingdom of God in and through their lives. After Pentecost, people in Jerusalem were able to observe lay men and women who lived transformed lives according to the apostles' teachings. And the church was comprised of the laity.

> *All the believers were together and had everything in common. Selling their possessions and goods, they gave to anyone as he had need. Every day they continued to meet together in the temple courts. They broke bread in their homes and ate together with glad and sincere hearts* (Acts 2:44-47).

The world comes to know the church by observing the laity. In other words, how the world sees the church depends on the laity. Whether the church appears like David courageously facing Goliath or like Saul shaking with fear - depends on the impression that the laity makes in the world. Thus, the laity cannot be mere guests of the church. They are neither mere spectators who attend worship services on a regular basis, nor are they mere patrons who contribute to the church's maintenance. And they certainly are not mere servants who grudgingly follow their master's commands. Lay people are the people of God and the principal body of the church. They are on a par with the clergy in the body of Christ. They, too, have received their call from the Lord, who is the head of the church. Furthermore, they all have received spiritual gifts as determined by the Holy Spirit in order that they may also do their part as the members of the body.

The Slumbering Laity

Unfortunately, the laity are slumbering in many churches. These giants with amazing potential are not using their power. Of course, every church has a small group of zealous and self-sacrificing lay people. The values and beauty of their service can be seen through the blessings that God has showered on churches worldwide. However, the problem is that even the ministries of these excellent lay members are limited to general institutional maintenance of the church. Furthermore, even those few exemplary lay members involved in more essential ministries of the churches are often considered as mere handmaidens waiting on the clergy. And this is not all. There are even more serious problems. The above functions of lay people are being monopolized by an exceedingly small number in the church, and this phenomenon is accepted by the rest of believers as a reasonable practice.

Some clergymen contend that the passive state of the laity is a natural outcome of the course chosen by lay members themselves and thus is not the clergy's responsibility. There is some truth to this contention. It has been an unfortunate habit of many lay people to make excuses for themselves whenever the church leaders sought to teach and train them. They say they don't have time. They think that evangelizing, teaching, and counseling are only for those with theological or seminary backgrounds. They think that since their life and work in the world are so demanding and difficult, it is okay for them to just do what they are told to do and keep the back seat of the church warm. Consequently, they give up the most fulfilling responsibility that God has given them, just as Esau hastily relinquished his birthright as the eldest son.

Let us reflect on the words of Sir John Lawrence, as quoted by Stott:

> What does the layman really want? He wants a building which looks like a church; a clergyman dressed in the way he approves; services of the kind he's been used to, and to be left alone.[5]

---

5. Quoted in John Stott, *One People* (Downers Grove: InterVarsity Press, 1971), 30.

Just look around and see how many lay people would agree with this statement. If a church leader yields to such erroneous demands of the laity, then he should consider his ministry a failure. Jesus, as the head of the church, will hold the clergy responsible for neglecting lay people and for their spiritual sickness. If the house is built with wood or hay that can be burned, the leaders and not the laity, will be held liable. Therefore, the excuses made by the laity do not justify the failings of the clergy. There may have been some shepherds who were eaten by lions, but there have never been any shepherds victimized by their own sheep. If the laity is in error, then the leader is at fault. Are lay members attending the church as mere guests or spectators? Are they slumbering and not waking up? If so, it is time for the clergy to remember the command of the Lord and tremble in fear.

Recovering the Identity of the Laity
Today, lay people are not raised to their fullest potential in regard to their identity, role and calling, and on how to be better equipped to serve the Lord. This is an ongoing mistake of contemporary churches. A report submitted by the Korean representatives at the World Mission Conference held in Lausanne, Switzerland in 1974 contains a statement to the effect that 'in relation to potential in manpower, resources, training, and spiritual vitality the Korean church is not lacking'.[6]

What I would question in the above statement is the part 'do not lack in … training'. The Korean representatives were probably speaking of the Early Morning Prayer meetings, high church attendance numbers, active home visitations, and other traditional ministries which are in-

6. Quoted in D. Douglas, *Let the Earth Hear His Voice* (Minneapolis: World Wide Publishing, 1975), 398.

deed the strengths of the Korean church. Surely, these are important tools for spiritual training. However, if we were to strictly evaluate these traditional ministries and point out their weaknesses, I am not sure if we could be content and infer that there is no 'lack in ... training'. Here I address the church leaders. Let us ask ourselves honestly. Are we providing concrete spiritual training for our lay members? And are we accepting them as active ministry partners?

A lay person named Madison made an unforgettable appeal to the leaders at the Lausanne Conference. We must not forget that similar appeals are being made around us as well:

What do lay people want? We want to participate in important ministries. And the clergy need to 'show' us how to study the Bible, how to pray, how to love, how to evangelize, and how to become like Christ... We need the clergy to lead and challenge us.[7]

In some ways, the Protestant Church did not clearly establish the identity of the laity as the principal body of the church. It can be seen as a kind of cancerous tumor that has been growing gradually since the beginning of the Reformation. We should pay attention to what Kraemer has sharply pointed out:

It (Calvin's Polity of the Church) was the most dynamic of Church orders which issued from the Reformation. His high conception of the excellence, indispensability and authority of the minister, necessitated by the need for a well-led Church, implied however involuntarily a neglect of the real significance and relevance of the laity.[8]

---

7. Ibid., 458
8. Hendrik Kraemer, *A Theology of the Laity*, 72.

Kraemer's criticism is not an overstatement. It is no secret that over the last 400 years, many church leaders who inherited Calvin's theology, while confessing and declaring the priesthood of all believers in public, behaved as if they were the priests of the Old Testament period. This overemphasis on the importance of the clergy has instilled a class distinction between the clergy and the laity, thus nurturing a dualism that separates spiritual life from the rest of life. It has also cultivated an inferiority complex in many lay members, causing them to think that they are somehow less holy than the clergy. Besides, the clergy fell into subtle, vain thoughts that their sermons were enough to satisfy the laity, and thereby neglected the task of training lay people to become powerful and productive ministry partners

We live in an age where courage and diligence are needed to revive the biblical image of the laity. To that end, we who are church leaders must put all our energy into this endeavour. The church whose lay members continue to slumber will degenerate into a powerless mob that cannot do anything for the world. We must recognize that awakening the laity is the only way for the church to become salt and light in the coming age of uncertainty.

Chapter 4

The Relationship Between
the Clergy and the Laity

Jesus Authorized the Office of the Clergy

If lay people are the principal body of the church, what should be the relationship between the clergy and the laity? This is a very difficult problem which is often ignored. Historically, the church has always wrestled with the dilemma of this relationship. In reality, it is very difficult to insist upon the special clerical role without falling into the temptation of separating its position and privilege from those of the laity. The clergy and the laity have a very close and yet a fragile relationship. Breakdown of this relationship often leads to strife between ecclesiastical authority and anticlericalism. As Stott has said:

> *The spirit of clericalism is to despise the laity, and behave as if they did not exist. The spirit of anticlericalism is to despise the clergy and to behave as if they did not exist, or rather, since they do exist, to wish they didn't.*[1]

Some say that ecclesiastical authorities themselves have caused this opposition, for the clergy has often surreptitiously suppressed and disregarded the laity. Therefore, the laity is now challenging the clergy, claiming that there is no difference between them and the clergy be-

---

1. John Stott, *One People*, 34.

fore God. However, the fact that lay members may have been hurt by obnoxious behaviours of the clergy does not entitle them to reject biblical church order and office. Viewed from man's perspective, anticlericalism may find some sympathy. However, one needs to bear in mind that anti-clericalism will not be able to win the case at the highest court – the Scripture. The office of clergy is an office solemnly appointed for the church by Christ himself. 'It was He who gave some to be apostles, some to be prophets, and some to be evangelists, and some to be pastors and teachers, to prepare God's people for works of service, so that the body of the Christ may be built up' (Eph. 4:11-12).

John Calvin, in his discussion on the importance of the clergy, saw the clerical system as an important key that brings all believers in the church together, as that which protects the church, and as an institution that is personally overseen by the Lord himself. Therefore, he concludes that opposing the clerical system itself is not acceptable:

> Whoever, therefore, either is trying to abolish this order of which we speak and this kind of government, or discounts it as not necessary, is striving for the undoing or rather the ruin and destruction of the church. For neither the light and heat of the sun, nor food and drink, are necessary to nourish and sustain the present life as the apostolic and pastoral office is necessary to preserve the church on earth.[2]

On the other hand, there is an important fact that we need to keep in mind as we recognize the biblical basis of the clerical system. As we all know the administration of the Word and Sacraments should be by and large limited to the clergy. As Stott quotes from Article XXIII of the Book

2. John Calvin, *Institutes of the Christian Religion* (Philadelphia: The Westminster Press), 110.

of Common Prayer, 'It is not lawful for any man to take upon him the office of public preaching, or ministering the sacraments in the congregation, before he be lawfully called, and sent to execute the same'. However as Stott points out, we must be clear that this is a question of order and not of doctrine.[3]

Church order cannot hold as much authority as doctrine. Before a person is called to the pastorate, he must go through theological training. This is a matter of order. We also know that there will be those who will cause disorder, confusion and havoc.

Unwholesome groups that cause such misunderstandings already exist. For example, some of the young people who took part in evangelical mission organizations in the past have become antagonistic toward the clerical system. There was even a group which started out by rejecting the office of clergy and ended up denying the church order itself. Fortunately, such phenomena belong to an extreme minority. However, there is a group that poses a greater threat. This is those who think that emphasizing the role of the laity and viewing them as ministry partners are threats to the clergy system. Thus they object and attempt to discard such threats by citing a small number of anticlerical mission organizations and a few radical individuals. They even use these examples to defend their own status and authority. They do not open themselves to discussing the biblical basis of the role and responsibility of the laity. Therefore, we must keep in mind that those who negate the role of the laity can fall into the same trap that those who oppose the ecclesiastical system fell into.

Does this mean that the clergy has no authority over the laity? Strictly speaking, the clergy does have an authority in ministry that the laity does not have. Not

3. John Stott, *One People*, 42.

all lay people can become pastors. Calvin expresses this pastoral authority as 'an uncomfortable authority', because it is not 'an authority of power', but rather 'an authority of submission'. In other words, a pastor is not God, yet he has a sacred authority that must not be handled lightly.[4]

The Meaning of the Laying On of Hands

It has been a church tradition to officially recognize ecclesiastical authority through the ceremony of laying on of hands. What does the Bible teach about this practice? The Bible shows four types of laying on of hands.

The first is when commissioning someone to a public office. Moses ordained Joshua as his successor by laying his hands on Joshua (Num. 27:23). The apostles ordained the seven deacons by laying their hands on them (Acts 6:6). Elders laid their hands on Timothy (1 Tim. 4:14).

The second example is the laying of hands on the sick (Mark 16:18). The third example is praying for those who want to receive the Holy Spirit by laying hands on their heads (Acts 8:17). The fourth example is laying on of hands to revive the gifts of the Spirit (2 Tim. 1:6).

From the above instances, we can conclude that laying on of hands was not limited exclusively to the commissioning of the clergy. However, there are several facts which we need to be aware of. Laying on of hands has been commanded by God, and thus has a divine origin (Num. 27:18, 23). Also it was not done privately in secret, but performed in public (Num. 27:19). Furthermore it was God Himself who designated the individuals on whom hands were to be laid.

---

4. Quoted in John R. Crawford, 'Calvin and the priesthood of all believers,' *Scottish Journal of Theology* (Vol. 21, No. 2), 152.

In this sense according to Calvin, the act of laying on of hands signified the dedication of the commissioned person to God. And considering the fact that the apostles continued to lay hands on such occasions, Calvin regarded it as a kind of ecclesiastical command. He described the spiritual blessings of laying on of hands as follows:

> *And surely it is useful for the dignity of the ministry to be commended to the people by this sort of sign, as also to warn the one ordained that he is no longer a law unto himself, but bound in servitude to God and the church.*[5]

Therefore, the authority of laying on of hands is found in publicly acknowledging those chosen and sent by Christ to take care of the sheep. Through this ceremony, the whole church can witness the personification of God's calling in that one person. Otherwise, it would be difficult to find another appropriate method to confirm and publicly recognize those who have been called to the pastorate. In this sense, the act of laying on of hands – that is, ordination – can be considered as an act of faith on the part of the entire church which confesses the spiritual authority of the clergy.

Authority Stems from Humility and Commitment

Even if a clergyman is ordained and becomes a leader in the church, his authority is not to dominate or control the church, but to submit to the entire church, including the laity. Stott explains that although God's call to the pastorate is indeed important, pastors do not stand above but below the church community composed of the believers chosen by God to belong to Him. As such, pastors cannot rule over the church. Rather they belong to the laity whom they have been called to serve.

---

5. John Calvin, *Institutes of the Christian Religion*, 127-128.

So if anybody belongs to anybody in the church, it is not the laity who belong to the clergy, but the clergy who belong to the laity. We are theirs, their servants for Jesus' sake. In the past, it was customary for a lay person to conclude a letter to his bishop with the words, 'I have the honour to be, sir, your obedient servant'. It would be more biblical, however, for a bishop (or any pastor) to sign himself as the lay person's obedient servant![6]

In reality, the idea that the authority of the clergy belongs to the laity could prove to be a stumbling block for many pastors in Korea and elsewhere in the world as well. The reason we cannot accept such statement with an 'Amen' is not because the statement is biblically unsound. Rather we cannot accept it because we are addicted to authority and power. We should ponder anew Paul's confession: 'For we do not preach ourselves, but Jesus Christ as Lord, and ourselves as your servants for Jesus' sake' (2 Cor. 4:5).

What is the main point of this verse? It is that a servant of the Lord is a servant of the laity. When we submit to this truth, then and only then, our authority as clergy and the glory of the laity as the principal constituents of the church will be seen.

> *Jesus said to them, 'The kings of the Gentiles lord it over them; and those who exercise authority over them call themselves Benefactors. But you are not to be like that. Instead, the greatest among you should be like the youngest, and the one who rules like the one who serves. For who is greater, the one who is at the table or the one who serves? Is it not the one who is at the table? But I am among you as one who serves'* (Luke 22:25-27).

The authority of the clergy differs from that of the world in that the authority of the clergy comes from serving.

6. John Stott, *One People*, 47.

As the apostles were pledging to return to their proper role, they said, 'And we will give our attention to prayer and the ministry of the word' (Acts 6:4). The Greek word used for ministry used in this passage is *diakonia*, which means 'to serve'. As we know, *diakonia* refers to serving as a servant or a slave. Even the ministry of the Word, which granted authority to the apostles, was seen as a way of serving the laity. If preaching and teaching are serving the laity, then what more can we say concerning other works?

As Paul looked back on his three years of pastoral ministry at the farewell service with the elders of Ephesus, he summarized genuine ministry as that which serves the sheep:

> *I served the Lord with great humility and with tears, although I was severely tested by the plots of the Jews. You know that I have not hesitated to preach anything that would be helpful to you but have taught you publicly and from house to house. I have declared to both Jews and Greeks that they must turn to God in repentance and have faith in our Lord Jesus* (Acts 20:19-21).

Paul did not speak of his poverty as that which made him a genuine servant (cf. Acts 20:33-35). Paul saw poverty as a means of service as Jesus did, but did not see poverty itself as a service. The true service of the clergy consists of guiding the laity to their rightful place and helping them to fulfill their role. If pastors fail to do this, they should be ashamed to be called servants of the laity regardless of the poverty they may have to endure.

As Oscar Feucht writes:

> *Calvin, with Luther, places the emphasis upon 'duties,' 'obedience,' 'services,' and 'functions' of the ministerial office rather than 'status,' 'power,' and 'dignity.'... These Reformation*

leaders did not sweep the minister or priest away, but they declared that the vocation of the layman was as deeply religious as that of the priest, in fact, it too is a priestly vocation.[7]

Pastors execute the functions of the priesthood that belongs to all believers. However, pastors fulfill the priestly functions *alongside* the lay members, not in place of them. Therefore, the importance of the clergy does not lie in representing or replacing the laity, but in helping and guiding the laity to exercise the privilege of their own priesthood.

Another thing we should be mindful of is that the clergy must set an example, especially in the area of servanthood. 'Not lording over those entrusted to you, but being examples to the flock' (1 Pet. 5:3). A demanding attitude is not compatible with service. Clergy must set examples of service, instead of lording over. When the clergy properly exemplify the life of service, the whole church will submit to them (1 Pet. 5:5). The authority of ordination will be honoured and respected when the clergy minister through exemplary service. If the clergy degenerate into an overgrown ecclesiasticism that oppresses the lay people with a sense of inferiority and inability, then they will be introducing an evil that injures the church and defiles the sanctity of the office of clergy.

If we want to maintain a proper relationship between clergy and laity, then we must be fully convinced of the fact that the laity *is* the church. Pastors are servants appointed by God to serve the church and do their utmost to help the laity to mature according to God's will. There is a need for the pastors in the contemporary church to humble themselves as servants of God. The laity should also recover their proper role as they humbly submit to the authority given to the clergy in order to serve them.

---

7. Oscar Feucht, *Everyone A Minister* (St. Louise: Concordance, 1977), 63.

Part 1
TODAY'S CHURCH AND THE LAITY
INTRODUCTION

Part 2
MINISTRY PHILOSOPHY
ECCLESIOLOGY

Part 3
MINISTRY STRATEGY
DISCIPLESHIP

Part 4
MINISTRY METHOD
DISCIPLESHIP TRAINING

Part 5
MINISTRY FIELD
DISCIPLES

Chapter 5

What is Ministry Philosophy?

It is rather surprising that many church leaders don't think deeply enough about what a true church is. Often the most they can reiterate are fragments of knowledge they retain from their systematic theology class or from their denominational constitution. Somehow we have become complacent in our limited knowledge. A pastor should continually ask, 'What is the church and its mission?' Otherwise, one can easily forget the spiritual mandate that clergy and church must continually reform and develop. We must not overlook the serious consequence this has on the entire ministry of the church. It may be more serious than we could ever imagine.

> The hope of the world, conceived in the mind of the all-wise God, comes off as irrelevant to real life. That's unthinkable. Services aimed at revealing truth about the Creator are called lifeless, boring, and predictable. That's the ultimate contradiction. People walk away from the church carrying a heavier burden than when they approached. That's a travesty of the Gospel. That's a modern-day tragedy.[1]

The leader who discovers such a contradiction in his own ministry will be obliged to earnestly search the Word and ask, 'What is a true church?' A pastor must ask every-

1. Lynne & Bill Hybels, *Rediscovering Church* (Grand Rapids: Zondervan, 1995), 58.

day, 'What is the church?', for his view of the church will determine the direction of his ministry. For example if a pastor views the church primarily as a place of worship, then he will probably prioritize matters related to the church building and worship service. On the other hand, if a pastor considers the church as a place where the wounded and abused gather together for fellowship and healing, then we can probably guess the direction that his ministry will take. So we must stop for a moment and answer the questions: 'What is the church? Why does it exist?' At the same time, we must verify and be convinced of our answers.

Rick Warren gave the following words of wisdom concerning the church:

> *Every church is driven by something. There is a guiding force, controlling assumption, a directing conviction behind everything that happens. It may be unspoken. It may be unknown to many. Most likely it's never been officially voted on. But it is there, influencing every aspect of the church's life. What is the driving force behind your church?*[2]

Ministry philosophy is the driving force that moves the church. It is not an overstatement to say that a key reason we experience frustrations and discouragement in ministry is the lack of a sound and unassailable ministry philosophy that tells us the direction that we should take, and why. The ministry philosophy of a leader is often hidden behind his methodology, and thus is not readily visible. This makes it easy to attribute the success of a ministry to a methodology, overlooking the philosophy or principle hidden behind it. However, a healthy church does not depend on methodology. Therefore, it

---

2. Rick Warren, *The Purpose Driven Church* (Grand Rapids: Zondervan, 1995), 77.

is of the utmost importance to establish a ministry philosophy.

We have a special interest in making disciples in order to awaken the laity. Making disciples of the laity is not some kind of temporary theological trend or methodology. We must understand that it is based on the Bible and is a fundamental task which corresponds to the essence and the calling of the church. Thus our ministry philosophy depends on how we answer the question of the church's identity and the reason for its existence. Our ministry philosophy in turn will determine our ministry strategy and method. In this sense, a pastor's ministry philosophy is none other than the ministry convictions issuing from his own doctrine of the church.

Let me emphasize once again. We must have a philosophy of ministry. To do so, we may have to study the doctrine of the church again. We must continue to ask ourselves 'What is the church?' until we gain an unshakable conviction about the need to awaken the laity.

A Neglected Subject
The subject of 'church' is one we all seem to be familiar with; yet at the same time, it is often a misunderstood subject. Everyone considers it to be well known, and very few take the time to wrestle seriously with the doctrine of the church. Consequently many carry on their ministry with mistaken perspectives.

Neglecting the doctrine of the church is not merely a personal issue. It is a matter of church history. A quick glance at church history soon shows that, compared to other doctrines, the doctrine of the church has rarely received direct and full attention. As we are well aware, topics such as the doctrines of Christ and the Trinity were already objects of particular interest by the 4th and 5th centuries due to the appearance of heresies that were threatening the church. As a result, such topics have been consolidated doctrinally. Soteriology (the doctrine of salvation) was the favourite child of Protestantism during the Reformation in the 16th century, and since then it has been firmly established as the cornerstone of Christianity. On the other hand, until the beginning of the 20th century, Christianity has hardly ever wrestled with the doctrine of the church. This is a fact that was publicly mentioned by Ploropsky at the first WCC conference in 1948. In his keynote speech, he hit the mark when he predicted that the present century would be the era of the doctrine of the church. During the past several decades, significant theses and books have been published on ecclesiology. However, it is regrettable that the doctrine of the church remained of little interest to Korean churches until the 1980s. Although we have spent much time in the church and worked for the church we have failed to retain the attitude of the reformers. We have not been asking the question, 'What is the church?' Consequently, we have been ministering without a concrete ministry philosophy.

A Clearly Defined Philosophy Will Move People

Many clergy would agree that in order to turn over the soil of their ministry so as to grow a healthy church, awakening the laity through discipleship training is the most effective method. However, this cannot be accomplished with vague ideas. Imitation of others does not offer solutions either. Those who try imitations will often give up, due to hardships and apparent lack of results. Who can guarantee that those clergy will not turn into ministry gypsies, snooping around here and there, always looking for something new?

Only those who, have a firm conviction about their newly discovered ministry philosophy and an inner fire that are too strong for them to remain silent, will be able to carry out discipleship training. At one point, Jeremiah found it so hard to proclaim God's Word to the perverse Israelites that he had even thought of giving it up. Then he bemoaned the fact that he could not quench the fire inside him (Jer. 20:9). Those who want to carry on discipleship training must be gripped by it to this extent. Borrowing Jeremiah's words, we should be able to shout: 'If I say I will not do discipleship training, it is like a fire shut up in my bones. I am weary of holding it in; indeed I cannot.'

A person with a philosophy, a fire in his heart, and a clear vision for tomorrow cannot remain still. Such a person cannot stop even if enormous sacrifices are demanded. Discipleship training will be almost impossible unless the pastor is totally committed and is ready to risk his life to the point of being considered a fanatic or obsessed. There are those who oppose discipleship training with all their might. Many are terribly afraid of anything that might disrupt and change their familiar routines and patterns of the Christian life. Moreover, adding discipleship training to the pastors' already jam-packed schedules could be a frightening thought. Even without it, they are struggling to meet the demands of already existing ministries such as preaching, visitation, administration, and more. How could those who consider discipleship training merely as an option even attempt to start the training under these circumstances?

Here is a question: do you really want to awaken and mobilize the laity? If you do, then you must become wild and crazy about it. Both Jesus and Paul were told that they were out of their minds. You must begin with the resolution that you are at a dead-end and discipleship training is the only way out. You must have the determination to even leave your ministry if you can't do discipleship training. For that purpose, we must first establish our ministry philosophy. The closer our ministry philosophy is to the essence of the church, the healthier and more balanced our ministry will be. When we hold fast to the essence, doors will open. Once our ministry philosophy is established, ministry strategy will emerge, and ministry methods will naturally become clear. Let us ask once again: 'What is the church? Why does it exist?'

Chapter 6

The Church

Definition of the Church
The most basic definition of the church is 'God's people called in Christ' (1 Cor. 1:1; 2 Eph. 2:19). This becomes clearer when we take a closer look at the meaning of the word 'church'. There are over 100 words, parables, and symbols used in reference to the church in the New Testament. The most frequently used Greek word is *ekklesia*. This word refers to the gathering of God's chosen people, or in other words, a congregation. Strictly speaking, this word includes the gathering process of the congregation as well as the community of people gathered in one place.[1]

God gave birth to his people (John 1:12-13). He made, called, preserved, and saved them. The church began with the emergence of those who, after Jesus' resurrection, confessed Jesus Christ as the Son of God. They are new creatures rescued from the power of darkness and brought into the kingdom of the Son of God (Col. 1:13). In that sense, the church is a chosen people and a holy nation (1 Pet. 2:9). The church is unlike any other gathering of the world because it is in God the Father. The church is also distinct from the gathering of the Jewish synagogue because it is in Jesus Christ (1 Thess. 1:1).

---

1. Hans Kung, *The Church* (New York: Image Books, 1967), 120.

The church is God's people called out of the world, and as such it can be viewed as a living, systematic, and public expression of God's reign, realized through Christ's incarnation. If the kingdom of God refers to the comprehensive domain of God's sovereign rule, then the church is the transitional institution of that reign. The church in the transition period should humbly and earnestly wait for the consummation of God's kingdom which will be perfected at the second coming of Christ. The church has not yet arrived at its final destination but is on its pilgrimage toward the eternal city. Thus the present church is a sign that announces the end and a billboard that reveals what is to come. The church will inherit the kingdom when the king comes, and the kingdom of God will be realized throughout the whole universe.[2]

The Calling Is Missing

The definition of the church as God's chosen people is a precious legacy of the doctrine of the church that has been inherited from the reformers. In a sense, this is a perfect definition with nothing more to add or subtract. Who could believe that this perfect definition has ironically contributed to handicapping our ministries today? Regrettably, however, this has been the case. The definition of the church as the gathering of God's chosen people includes both the invisible and the visible church. It cannot be denied that this definition, at its face value, gives more weight to the invisible church of the 'End Time' than to the visible church on earth. Accordingly, the visible church can be perceived as if it has already been perfected. One gets a sense that the church has already come home after a long journey and is resting in the Father's house. We may feel so enraptured by the glory that we have come to enjoy freely in Jesus Christ

---

2. Peter Kuzmic, 'The Church and Kingdom of God', *A Thesis from Wheaton International Evangelical Conference '83*, 22-49.

that we may even get the impression that all else can be forgotten. However, this image of the visible church is far from the truth. Why? Because the church that is in the world has a unique calling, which can be considered the very reason for its existence. That calling is to fulfill God's will, which is to save the world. Therefore, a definition of the church that does not mention this calling may be appropriate for the invisible church, but is not adequate to define the visible church.

Perhaps this might sound too far-fetched, and maybe it is. However, previous centuries have shown that churches that thought of the visible church simply as the gathering of God's chosen people and taught likewise fell into self-absorption and narcissism. Look around you with keen spiritual eyes. How many pastors are out there who seem to understand their ministry simply as looking after God's chosen people? How many lay people are out there who are content with their own salvation and therefore remain lukewarm or indifferent to God's work? They are all satisfied and think that lay people have no special calling.

Meanwhile, pastors do not seem to even attempt to correct and teach the laity, as if they want to parade the authority of the clergy as those with an exclusive calling. How ineffective the church has become in society as a result! How often does the church become a target of criticism! Most lay people believe simply in order to go to heaven. They lack a lucid, self-conscious desire to live out their Christian life in order to fulfill their calling. Although many in number, they are becoming no more than a mob.

We must reflect on how and why such unhealthy conditions have become prevalent. There may be other reasons, but we must admit that the chief cause is found in the traditional definition of the church that has confused the visible church with the invisible church. Any concept or ideology that dulls our thinking, no matter how slowly, will have an appallingly negative influence on our speech and conduct once it takes hold of us. The church is God's chosen people. Let us suppose that we continue to go around in circles on the periphery of such a doctrine of the church without ever opening our eyes to see the church differently. What would happen to our ministry? What would happen to the church?

A denominational supervisor once said, 'As I travel around the world, I see that churches with a Reformed theological background are not growing. Korean churches are no different. We talk a lot, but circle only around our issues without considering a bigger picture. We lack social awareness, and thereof social responsibility. I don't know what the solution would be.' When I told him that the problem seems to lie in our doctrine of the church, he agreed without any hesitation.

In order to awaken the laity, we must rewrite the definition of the visible church on earth. The visible church is not only given the privilege of being called out *of* the world, but is also given the calling to go out in*to* the world.

The invisible or heavenly church has no need to be sent into the world, and would have no reason to proclaim the gospel in the world. However, the visible church in which we minister remains in the world. We ought to be able to acknowledge our calling along with the privilege in our confession of faith. We should not be creating a crippled church that knows only its privilege but not its calling. Are you enjoying the privileges of being called? Then you must also obey the calling to go out into the world. Pastors must teach this and the laity must respond to the teaching in faith in order for the church to awake from its slumber and arise from obscurity.

The New Testament Church is the Local Church

As we discuss the definition of the visible church, there is another issue we must deal with: validating and affirming the identity of the local church. In the New Testament, the word 'church' does not refer to the collective sense of local churches of certain denominations. In other words, the New Testament does not use the word 'church' to refer to a gathering of the churches under the umbrella of a denomination. Nor is there any reference to a national church, such as the Korean church. In fact, there is no reference to the world church either. But the word 'church' is used to refer to the universal church or a local church. For example, *ekklesia* is represented by the Thessalonian church or the Corinthian church.

> *The Church is not a limited company or organization of individual communities; the* **ekklesia** *is not made by adding together the local Churches nor can it be broken down into them. Rather, the* **ekklesia** *of God exists in each place. There is not a Corinthian* **ekklesia** *(or an* **ekklesia** *of the Corinthians, or an* **ekklesia** *of Corinth), but: 'the* **ekklesia** *of God, which is at Corinth' (1 Cor. 1:2; 2 Cor. 1:1). Each* **ekklesia**, *each congregation, community, Church, however small, however poor, however insignificant, is a full and perfect manifestation of the* **ekklesia**, *the congregation, the community, the Church of God.*[3]

A local church is not a section of God's church, but is the church itself and a definite expression of its entity. And if each local church is a true representation of God's church, then we should take pride in serving a local church as its members. Unfortunately however, there are many among us who have been infected with the virus of inferiority. Such a virus is produced by comparing

---

3. Hans Kung, *The Church*, 120.

one church with another. Once a person is infected with the virus, he starts to see his small church as only insignificant crumbs under the table. In extreme cases, he thinks that his church is not a whole church. What a wrong perspective that is! Jesus, as the head of the church, does not measure His church by its size! Why is it that we often forget that Jesus is not interested in quantity but in quality of the people? Could it be because we do not know the true meaning of the local church?

Do you want to awaken the laity? You must have the conviction that even the few sheep God has placed in your care are God's complete *ekklesia*. We must know that the world will see that the kingdom of God is near through the small local churches we serve. When there is a paradigm shift in how we see our ministry field, we will be able to dedicate ourselves single-mindedly, with passion, to the task of making one soul into Jesus' disciple. A pastor who is always longing for a larger church will never be able to make disciples.

I am not denouncing large churches, but am emphasising the truth that the value of God's church is not determined by its size. A professor at an American seminary said the following to the graduates: 'I am going to give you one prophecy. No matter how hard you try in your ministry, 80 to 90 percent of you will spend the rest of your life in a small church. The remaining 10 percent might be able to serve at a large church.'

These are not necessarily encouraging words, but nevertheless this is the reality. One does not serve at a large church because he wants to, and one does not end up at a small church because he wants to. Each of us serves the church that God has given us according to His good will. Therefore, we must be certain of the fact that our church, regardless of how small or insignificant it may seem, is God's church.

So far, we have evaluated the traditional definition of the church. We have also briefly talked about the adverse effect this definition has had on the laity and their sense of calling. Then how should we define the visible church? It can be defined in the following way:

The visible church is the community of God's people called out of the world, and sent into the world as disciples of Christ.

Before agreeing to this definition, it is necessary for churches to examine and confirm their sense of calling as disciples sent into the world. How can we convince the laity of their calling? What is the biblical foundation and theological evidence? These are important issues which we will now address.

Chapter 7

Challenging the Traditional Doctrine of the Church

Common Criticisms

We have just considered that even a thorough definition of the church can work negatively in the ministry field. Let me mention one more thing. The traditional doctrine of the church's passive treatment of missions has weakened the mission awareness of the visible church. Consequently, churches with a Reformed theological background give the impression of being either passive or indifferent toward the world. It seems worthwhile to consider the validity of this view.

First, we will consider several criticisms of the traditional doctrine of the church.

> *What we need is a true doctrine of church. What we have today is insufficient. It may have been applicable during the Middle Ages. In those days, the main interest was on the external marks of the church.*[1]

This means that the traditional doctrine of the church framed by the reformers of the 16th century is no longer suitable for the present age. We are living in a different era. The reformers lived during the period of the Holy

---

1. Stephen C. Neil, *Creative Tension* (London: Edinburg Press, 1959), 112.

Roman Empire which was steeped in Christian culture. Therefore, there is a problem accepting and applying their perspective to our time without any adjustment, and there seems to be some validity to this criticism when we keep in mind the circumstances.

Here is another criticism:

The Great Commission was authorized and restricted to the apostles only according to the reformers and many theologians up to the seventeenth-century. When the apostles died, Christ's command died with them. This command was ineffective among the churches planted by the apostles.[2]

This might sound excessively critical. However it is not implying that the reformers never mentioned missions in their teachings. In fact, they often spoke of the need to take the message of salvation to the world. Then why is there such a criticism? It poignantly points to the fact that the reformers' doctrine of the church does not fully reflect the absolute calling of mission that the visible church has received from the Lord. Later, we will be able to verify through an example that this criticism is not without grounds.

There is another criticism that we should consider:

The difference between the Reformation and our time is that during the Reformation, the structures of society were for the most part static and fixed, whereas today these structures are fluid and dynamic. The problem is when the same static way of thinking is applied to the age in which we live.[3]

Though the Reformers' definition is as valid as it is, it is inadequate for Christians today, because it says nothing about mission [4]

---

2. Harry Boer, *Pentecost & Mission* (Grand Rapids: Eerdmans, 1975), 18.
3. John H. Piet, *The Road Ahead* (Grand Rapids: Eerdmans, 1970), 11.
4. Ibid., 12

Although the Reformers' definitions were founded in Scripture, we cannot deduce that they are completely biblical. The biblical doctrine of church presupposes the aspect of mission, whereas the Reformers' definitions arose from a given social context at that time. When the books of the New Testament were written, no notion of a Holy Roman Empire existed. What did exist was the dominating power of pagan Rome.[5]

Speaking of the social structure as 'static or dynamic' describes whether the circumstances surrounding the church are Christian or anti-Christian. In this sense, the social structure of the Middle Ages was certainly static. Consequently, it was difficult for the church to be aware of the urgency to proclaim the gospel of salvation to the world, for the whole world already seemed to be under the dominion of the gospel.

On the other hand, the early churches in the New Testament were in a situation in which the existence of the church could not be guaranteed unless they proclaimed the gospel, risking their lives. That was clearly a dynamic situation. The churches in the New Testament had this type of dynamic background. On the other hand, although the reformers were men of eminent spirituality, they were used to static situations. In other words, they had a limited understanding of the church because they lacked the situational basis to sense the urgency to proclaim the gospel.

The scholars who have challenged the traditional doctrine of the church are all from the evangelical circle with backgrounds in Reformed theology. These scholars are not saying that the doctrine of the church inherited by the reformers is wrong, but that it is insufficient to instill the mission mindset to the visible church. They are concerned that such a pristine doctrine will hinder

---

5. Ibid., 28.

the church from effectively evangelizing contemporary society.

It is very interesting to see how Luther's and Calvin's comments on 1 Corinthians 12:28 validate such criticisms. The following is Calvin's comment on the text:

And in the church God has appointed first of all apostles, second prophets,....For the Lord created the Apostles, that they might spread the gospel throughout the whole world, and he did not assign to each of them certain limits or parishes, but would have them, wherever they went, to discharge the office of ambassadors among all nations and languages. In this respect there is a difference between them and pastors, who are, in a manner, tied to their particular churches. For the pastor has not a commission to preach the gospel over the whole world, but to take care of the Church that has been committed to his charge.[6]

Luther makes a similar remark:

That the apostles entered strange houses and preached was because they had a command and were for this purpose appointed, called and sent, namely that they should preach everywhere, as Christ had said, 'Go into the world and preach the gospel to every creature.' After that, however, no one again received such a general apostolic command, but every bishop or pastor has his own particular parish.[7]

These two very prominent scholars, used greatly by God, gave a succinct interpretation of the differences between the apostles and pastors. However it is surprising that they explained the solemn command 'to make disciples of all nations' which the apostles received directly from

---

6. John Calvin, *Commentary on the Epistles of Paul the Apostle To The Corinthians* (Grand Rapids: Baker Book House, 1979), 414-415.
7. Quoted in Harry Boer, *Pentecost & Mission*, 19.

Jesus as being applicable only to the apostles. Whatever their intentions were, it is no mere coincidence that succeeding generations of pastors who have inherited the reformers' doctrine of the church adopted a passive attitude towards equipping the laity with the call to mission.

The reformers' doctrine of the church provided sufficient justification for succeeding generations of pastors to think idly that shepherding their churches fulfil their pastoral task. Therefore, we must not take lightly the rather harsh criticism that the reformers have neglected missions.

The Purity of the Church
Although the reformers may have neglected the church's call to missions in their treatment of the doctrine of the church, we cannot lay the total blame on them. They lived in their own unique historical circumstances. From 395 AD to the period of the Reformation, the church and the government had become so closely affiliated that anyone who seceded from the church could be arrested and punished by the government. It appeared as if the whole world was steeped in Christianity. In this kind of environment, mission simply did not appear as a significant issue. Naturally, the reformers' doctrine of the church was influenced by these historical circumstances. The following words of Hans Kung are significant:

> In any age, the church retains an image of the period and is shaped by the historical circumstances. During the first three centuries, the church and pagan nations were antagonistic toward each other. Then there was a truce. During the sixteenth century, the two were separated again. Each stage helped to form the image of the church.[8]

8. Hans Kung, *The Church*, 120.

During the Reformation, Calvin and Luther focused on the purity of the church. In other words, their pressing issue was differentiating the true church from the false church. Exposing the difference between them clearly, using the Bible, was the most important matter which required their immediate attention. As a result, the three famous marks of the true church took an important place in their doctrine of the church. They declared that the church of Jesus Christ maintains its purity by 1) the proclamation of the Word, 2) the administration of the sacraments, and 3) the discipline of the church.

This is a priceless historical legacy we have inherited from the reformers. However, their perspective seemed to imply that a true church should distance itself from the world. Although Calvin boldly taught that God's sovereignty must be over the whole world, he failed to teach that the church must be a witness of the gospel for that purpose. This is one of the reasons why the reformers' doctrine of the church is criticized as being static. Consequently the church gradually fell into self-centred parochialism, and took on the defensive image of stubbornly emphasizing only worship and piety. Thus, to idolize and hold up the reformers' doctrine of the church as perfect and faultless is to be guilty of indolence, renouncing the spirit of reformation that the reformers passed down to us. It is not to say that their doctrine of the church is entirely wrong. Instead, it is to say that their doctrine is neither perfect nor complete. One of the greatest legacies that we have inherited from Calvin and Luther is the spirit of reformation. In order to reform the age in which they were living, they gave all their energy to testing and applying the principles of the Bible, and to finding the solutions to their problems. We should also take over the same spirit and face the contemporary church with new eyes.

As Francis Schaeffer has warned, we must not confuse the absolute standard for the church recorded in the Bible with provisional standards absent from the Bible. In every age, the church has the freedom to tackle the demands of the time according to the guidance of the Holy Spirit within the boundaries sanctioned by the Bible. If the church were to renounce this freedom to continue on with the Reformation and keep its eyes closed, then today's church would bring upon itself isolation and death.[9]

Therefore, if the doctrine of the church that we have inherited does not adequately reflect the calling to go out to the world and is incapable of awakening the laity to their calling, then we must cast off the awkward cloaks belonging to the Middle Ages. Instead, we must put on a new cloak essential for the present age in which depraved secular culture constantly threatens the church.

In order to accomplish this, we must re-examine the apostolicity of the church which has received inadequate treatment from the traditional doctrine of the church. A deliberate neglect of the apostolicity of the church in Reformed theology has contributed to the emasculation of contemporary churches. The circumstances facing the twenty-first century church bear a closer affinity to the time of the early church in the New Testament than to the time of the church preceding the Reformation. The number of converts to Christianity today is not keeping up with natural population growth. The church is surrounded by pagan cultures that are becoming increasingly anti-Christian. We are facing a civilization which is changing at such a rapid rate that it is impossible to foresee what will happen three years from now. It is a matter of urgency that contemporary churches recognize

9. Francis Schaeffer, *The Church of the Late 20th Century* (Korean Translation) (Seoul: Word Press, 1972), 95.

the great potential the laity has for missions. The church must equip the laity as witnesses of the gospel like the disciples in the early church in the New Testament. For that purpose, we must open our eyes to the importance of the apostolic nature, or the apostolicity, of the church. Rediscovering the theological meaning of the apostolicity of the church will be the path to solving the problem concerning the laity in the contemporary church. Indeed, it will become the crux of developing the doctrine of the church.

Chapter 8

The Apostolicity of the Church

The Most Fundamental Nature of the Church

Those who desire to awaken the laity to fulfill their calling through discipleship training will need to look for the basis of their conviction in their doctrine of the church. They need firm biblical evidence in the doctrine of the church that the laity also have received a calling to go out into the world, as the apostles did. Unless they can prove it, they will not be able to mobilize the laity. However, as they start to research, they will soon discover that Reformed theology's traditional doctrine of the church does not offer a satisfactory answer. From that doctrine, we learn at best that the essence of the church is holiness, unity and universality. The apostolic nature of the church is occasionally mentioned; however it receives only partial treatment, often with reduced significance.[1]

It is easy, therefore, to fall into the trap of thinking that awakening the laity is just a pastor's personal priority, and that discipleship training is an alternative solution that has been successfully carried out especially among the parachurch organizations. However, if disciple-making ministry is not the very essence of the church, then there is no need to insist on discipleship training even if it appears to be a good thing.

---

1. See F. L. Cross, Oxford Dictionary of the Christian Church (London: Oxford University Press, 1958), 74-75 ; also, R. B. Kuiper, The Glorious Body of Christ (London: Banner of Truth, 1967), 68.

I was deeply convicted when I was studying in the United States. One day at the seminary bookstore, I found a book called *The Church* by Hans Kung, a Catholic theologian who enjoyed a favourable appraisal from many Protestants.[2] Through Kung's doctrine of the church, I became convinced that the visible church has inherited from the apostles a calling to go out into the world. I learned that awakening the laity is a command of the Lord, for the church in its essence is built on the foundation of the apostles. I will borrow from the words of Kung to explain the apostolic nature of the church more specifically:

---

2. There is no question that I have been greatly influenced by Hans Kung, especially in the area of the apostolic nature of the church. His main points – 'all Christians are called' and 'all Christians are called into the service of God' – are the two most important contributions that he has made to me personally. However, I also see some dangers in his theology. First, while emphasizing God's people as God's priests in the New Testament era, when it comes to the topic of the position of the pope, he is not very strongly opposed to it as he is about Catholicism in the rest of his discussion. He said in his book, *The Church*, 'the enormous burden of responsibility, of care, of suffering and anxiety which weighs upon the Petrine ministry – provided that Peter's successor is truly a rock, key-bearer and pastor in the service of the whole church' (Kung 1967, 605). 'For the Catholics this "specialty" is the pope. But in a sense they are not alone' the orthodox Christians too have their 'pope'; their 'tradition'; and the Protestants too have their 'Bible'... (Kung 1967, 609). Despite making some critical comments regarding the authority of pope, statements like these indicate that Kung still has come limitations in regard to his position on the pope. Secondly, in his discussion of the church as the creation of the Spirit, he commented that 'the Spirit of God, if domiciled in the church, is not domesticated in it. He is and remains the free Spirit of the free Lord not only for the Catholic city, not only of Christians, but of the whole world' (Kung 1967, 223). There is no question that he seems to indicate the possibility of salvation outside of the Christian faith, by non-Christian religions of the world.

The apostolic nature of the church was confirmed by the Council of Nicea in 325 CE as one of the four fundamentals of the church. Since then, much time has elapsed, with obvious instances of apostasy in the church. This happened, sometimes, in the name of apostolic succession. By claiming that the papacy is the legal successor to Peter the apostle, the Church of Rome camouflaged its false doctrines as tradition, and used the apostolic nature of the church as a necessary and essential prop to justify Catholicism. As a result, the word 'apostolic' has become a term that has naturally been authoritative to the reformers of the church. They understood the meaning of 'apostolic' to be the authority of the papacy. In their fight against the Church of Rome, which insisted that it was apostolic, the reformers themselves did not properly address the apostolic nature of the church, as they should have done. As a result, even many Protestant scholars have taken the position that there is no need for apostolic succession. If not adamantly denying it, some still went only as far as admitting with Luther that, 'apostolic' means truth concerning Christ.[3]

Consequently, they took the apostolic nature of the church merely to mean inheriting the teachings of the apostles.

What is Apostolicity?
What then is the true meaning of 'apostolicity'? The apostolicity of the church begins with the establishment of the church on the foundation of the apostles whom Jesus sent into the world: 'As the Father has sent me, I am sending you' (John 20:21). It is 'built on the foundation of the apostles and prophets, with Christ Jesus Himself as the chief cornerstone' (Eph. 2:20).

The apostles were the first eyewitnesses of the risen Lord, personally commissioned by Jesus to spread the

3. Jong Sung Lee, *The Doctrine of Church I* (Korean), 164.

gospel to all nations. The church was built on the testimony and ministry of these apostles. In this sense the apostles were the beginning and the permanent foundation of the church. Based on this fact it could be said that the church is apostolic in essence. Kung viewed apostolicity as being the most fundamental among all the attributes – such as unity, universality, and holiness – that determine the essence of the church. He states:

> In our search for unity in diversity, catholicity in identity, holiness in sinfulness, the question of a criterion must always be in our minds. How far can the Church be one, holy and catholic? What is true unity, true catholicity, true holiness? The crucial criterion is expressed in the fourth attribute of the Church: the Church can only be truly one, holy, and catholic if it is in all things an apostolic Church. What is in question is not any kind of unity, holiness and catholicity, but that which is founded on the apostles and in that sense is apostolic.[4]

The church is holy because it is separated from the world and because it is a temple of the Holy Spirit. It is universal in the sense that it is one, transcending times, cultures, and borders. It is united because Jesus Christ alone is the head of the church. However, if the church is not founded on the gospel proclaimed by the apostles, then it cannot be God's church. If it is not built on the foundation of the apostles, then even the other attributes of the church lose their meaning. The Unification Church calls itself a church, but we do not recognize it as a church because it is not founded on the teachings of the apostles. In this sense apostolicity is the most fundamental attribute and is the standard by which other attributes are evaluated.

Kung has demonstrated a great insight in seeing the apostolicity of the church not simply as one of the at-

---

4. Hans Kung, *The Church*, 443-444.

tributes of the church, but as the most fundamental attribute of all. Surely this is premised on the fact that Kung has removed himself from the traditional Roman Catholic position and has given a correct and biblical definition of the apostolicity of the church. If this were not the case, his use of the word 'apostolic' would be just another false doctrine of the Roman Church and would not merit any consideration. As long as a church has been built upon the teaching and the ministry of the apostles, it is certainly apostolic. And if it is an apostolic church, then it is a church that corresponds to the Bible. There is no authority apart from the Bible to verify the apostolicity of the church. In this sense, an apostolic church means a biblical church. How then is apostolicity inherited? In other words, what is biblical apostolic succession?

Apostolic Succession
Apostleship is unique and cannot be repeated. Only the twelve disciples who saw Jesus after His resurrection and were personally appointed by Him had the privilege of holding the apostolic office. Paul is the only exception, since he was called after Jesus' ascension. Thus no one can replace or represent the Apostolate any more. It is a great fallacy on the part of the Roman Catholic Church to assert that an individual pope or a systematic succession can inherit the office of the apostles. The apostles, in a narrow sense, do not exist anymore. Only the apostles' teachings and their ministry remain. Then who are the present successors of the apostles? Here are the words of Kung:

> There can only be one basic answer: the Church. The whole Church, not just a few individuals, is the follower of the apostles. We do, after all, confess an apostolic **Church**. The **whole** Church is the new people of God, gathered by the

*apostles through the preaching of the gospel of Jesus Christ. The **whole** Church is the temple of the spirit, built on the foundation of the apostles. The **whole** Church is the body of Christ, unified by the ministry of the apostles... This succession must be understood in terms of substance, not just of history; there must be a real inner continuity. This continuity cannot simply be created for the Church by itself, it is something that is granted to it by the Spirit of God and Christ, the Spirit which filled the apostles and their apostolic witness, and moves and encourages the Church to follow them. The Church has only to be open to the Spirit in faith, and it will find the necessary obedience to the apostles and their witness. In this sense apostolic succession is a thing of the spirit. Apostolicity, too, is a gift and a requirement at the same time.*[5]

These are very important words, and thus it is worthwhile to explore them further. The church is composed of God's people, called without any distinction or discrimination. Thus, no single individual or a special group can be put forward above others to succeed the apostles. Anyone who belongs to the church, including both laity and clergy, is qualified to succeed the apostles. In this sense, it is correct to say that the whole church is the sole successor of the apostles.

Then the issue of the basis of the succession can be raised. The pope presents a genealogical record and claims to be the legitimate successor of Peter. However, the church neither has a genealogical table from the apostles nor considers it important, for all believers are God's children born of the Spirit of God. Kung contends that apostolic succession is validated by the Holy Spirit. The Holy Spirit who had inspired the apostles to become the gospel witnesses is now in the church and leads the saints of God to believe and obey the gospel passed down

---

5. Ibid., 458.

from the apostles. The invisible inner continuity goes on without ceasing.

As the apostles were of the Spirit, we also are of the Spirit. We are thus qualified to be their successors. Is there any lay man or woman who could be excluded from this succession? No, there is none, for anyone who does not have the Spirit of Christ does not belong to Christ (Rom. 8:9).

Inheriting the Apostolic Teaching

Now we will consider the way in which the church continues to carry out the apostolic succession.

First, it inherits the apostolic teaching when the church accepts by faith the entirety of the living testimony of the apostles handed down in the New Testament. This signifies that the church follows and abides by the apostles' faith and confession. The apostles were the first eyewitnesses and the ministers of the Word. It is the apostolicity of the church that inherits the gospel passed down by the apostles, which makes it possible for all believers to become one in their faith and knowledge of the Son of God. (Eph. 4:13; Luke 1:2). The church cannot directly hear the inspired words of Jesus; it hears only through the testimony of the apostles. Kung describes it in the following:

> *Of course, the Church must not simply listen to the apostles. Through their witness the Church must listen to the Lord Himself, and allow him to speak in the midst of the Church through their witness; he who hears them, hears the Lord. The reverse is also true: he who does not hear the apostles, does not hear the Lord. There is no route to the Lord which bypasses the apostles. The Church can only know him through their witness...Apostolic succession is therefore a question of a continual and living confrontation of the Church and all its members with this apostolic witness; apostolic succession*

is fulfilled when this witness is heard, respected, believed, confessed and followed.[6]

Accordingly, the way to achieve unity and fellowship for all the churches in the world does not lie in a system or in artificially orchestrated movements. Instead, it is found in believing and confessing the apostles' testimony, namely the New Testament, that has been handed down to us.

All Protestant churches agree and practice the apostles' beliefs and teachings and so conserve the apostolic heritage. Churches must teach and proclaim the New Testament in its entirety without adding or subtracting anything, and also must instruct the laity to accept the Word as their spiritual food. Unlike the ancient Church of Rome, we do not keep the laity away from the Word of God. Rightfully, we can say that all Protestant churches are apostolic in nature.

Inherits the Apostolic Ministry

Secondly, the entire church inherits the apostolic ministry. This means inheriting the commandments that the apostles received from Jesus, and obeying them. Kung comments eloquently on this point:

> *Apostolicity is never an unchallenged possession, a secure piece of property which the Church has at its disposal. Apostolicity can never mean power through which the Church might rule. It is not a question of others submitting to the Church; the Church must itself submit by accepting the authority of the apostles and of the Church's and the apostles' Lord. By following the apostles, the Church can learn what real submission and real service mean. Apostolic succession entails a confrontation of the Church with the testimony of the apostles, in a living*

---

6. Ibid., 458.

continuation of the apostolic ministries, with all their various forms of expression. The apostolic Church least of all can be an end in itself. Everything the Church does must be directed towards fulfilling its apostolic mission to the outside world; it must minister to the world and to mankind. To be a Church and to have a mission are not two separate things. To be itself, the Church must follow the apostles in continually recognizing and demonstrating that it has been sent out to the world... This makes it clear that apostolicity, like unity, holiness and catholicity, is not a static attribute of the Church. Like them it is an historical dimension, a dimension which has constantly to be fulfilled anew in history. Apostolicity too must continually be achieved afresh, must be a recurring event in a living history which occurs between the Church and the apostles, between the Church's preaching and the apostles' witness, between the Church's ministry and the apostles' commission... Apostolicity is not something that can simply be stated and proved in theory. The Church must share in this history in order to recognize and understand, to experience and discover what the apostolicity of the Church means. As an individual Christian, I must become a true successor of the apostles, I must hear their witness, believe their message, imitate their mission and ministry. I must be, and always become anew, a believing and living member of the apostolic community.[7]

Korean churches do not seem to have properly and theologically established the important fact that the laity, as the whole church, have inherited the great commission, which is the call to mission the apostles received directly from the Lord. A climate that speaks of this calling as belonging only to a special group of people has prevailed in Korean churches until now. Needless to say, pastors and missionaries certainly have a special calling to ministry that the laity do not have. However, it

7. Ibid., 459-460.

is a grievous error to neglect and abandon equipping the entire church with apostolicity, which is a fundamental essence of the church, in order to emphasize the special calling given to those few. When the essence of the visible church is apostolic, how can the lay people, who form the principal body of the church, be free from the apostolic calling?

Many churches try to motivate their members to evangelize by using the rationale that the Lord will be pleased when they can reach their annual growth goal. This causes rather critical members of the church to feel that their pastor is being very ambitious. They may even entertain rebellious thoughts, wondering how many more members the pastor needs in order to satisfy his greed. Why does this happen? It results from the failure to teach lay people that they are the true successors of the Apostle Peter who received the command to proclaim the gospel to all nations and who was martyred while obeying this command. It is not wrong to ask for the laity's commitment under goal-oriented slogans of national or world evangelism. The laity, however, must be awakened and given the understanding of their calling as the successors of the apostolic ministry before being asked to commit themselves. Otherwise, it will be like sending a young man to a battlefront to defend his country without giving him a clear sense of his identity as a citizen belonging to that country.

The Will of God
In order to substantiate further how essential it is for the visible church to inherit the apostolic ministry, it is necessary to consider God's will revealed in the New Testament. After thoroughly researching the concept of the will of God (*thelema*) as it appears in the New Testament, Gettlob Schrenk draws a significant conclusion:

The plural form is almost completely absent from the New Testament – God's will is expressed in the singular because the concept is shaped, not by individual legal directions, but by the conviction that the will of God is a powerful unity.[8]

Why is this so? It is because there is a distinct unity between God's will and His plan of salvation. In other words, the singular form of the word 'will' signifies that God's will points to only one objective. That objective is to complete His work of salvation of redeeming the world through Jesus Christ.

Herein lies the reason why Jesus said after saving the Samaritan woman, 'My food is to do the will of Him who sent me and to finish His work' (John 4:34), and was filled with the joy of the Holy Spirit when the seventy reported back after their mission trip (Luke 10:21).

The Apostle Paul declares that the church renders glory to God when everyone in heaven and earth confesses Jesus Christ as Lord. This is God's will directly related to His glory (Phil. 2:10-11). Carl Kromminga has pointed out well the relationship between God's glory and the work of mission:

When the doxological motif is isolated from the missionary, the universal expanse of God's saving purpose and the significance of the gift of the Spirit to the church are not given their due. The greater glorification of God's grace and love is obstructed if the doxological motif is not complemented by the missionary.[9]

Therefore, the church must prioritize the endeavour to align itself with the will of God, who desires that all people be saved and come to the knowledge of the

---

8. Gottlob Schrenk, *Theological Dictionary of N.T.* Vol III, 54.
9. Carl Kromminga, *Bring God's News to Neighbors* (Nutley: Presbyterian & Reformed, 1976), 110.

truth (1 Tim. 2:4). 'An important purpose of the church's existence is to proclaim the gospel to all nations. Other functions of the church such as service, sacraments, doctrine, and worship also are incidental and exist for the purpose of evangelism.'[10]

The church does not exist in order to be saved. The church has already crossed over from death to life and exists with a new identity that possesses eternal life (John 5:24). Therefore, the goal of the church should not be what it will *be* but what it will *do*. When the Great Commission that Jesus gave to the apostles has been inherited and fulfilled by the church, the world will come to an end and the visible church will be replaced by the New Jerusalem that will come down from heaven. If the church desires for the gospel to be proclaimed to all nations and aspires to inherit the universal kingdom which will be realized with the return of the King of Kings, then there is no other work that is as important as spreading the gospel to the world and sealing it with love.

Disregarding the apostolic call to the world is to renounce the hope for the return of the King and the realization of the eternal kingdom. 'And this gospel of the kingdom will be preached in the whole world as a testimony to all nations, and then the end will come' (Matt. 24:14). It has often been observed that churches forfeit their spiritual power when they abandon the call to proclaim the gospel. The reason is that they have stopped obeying God's will and have lost their hope in the consummation of God's future kingdom.

The Relationship Between the Holy Spirit and Apostolicity

The church exists in order to inherit the ministry of the apostles as is clearly seen in the work of the Holy Spirit

---

10. Stephen C. Neil, *Creative Tension*, 9.

who was given to the church by our Lord. The apostolicity of the church has an inseparable relationship with the
Holy Spirit. The Holy Spirit calls the chosen people of
God to accept, believe, and confess the testimony of the
apostles. And He causes those who have already come
to faith to respond to the call to share the gospel with
others in need of salvation. To this end, He equips them
with power. Thus the world encounters a new kind of
people who, being clothed with Christ, live and speak
through the Holy Spirit. These are the lay people of the
church, namely the community of witnesses. 'When the
Counselor comes, whom I will send to you from the Father, the Spirit of truth who goes out from the Father, He
will testify about me; but you also must testify, for you
have been with me from the beginning' (John 15:26-27).

The relationship between Jesus, who came to fulfill the
will of God, and the Holy Spirit, who descended upon
him at Jordan, illustrates both the relationships between
the apostles and the Holy Spirit and between the church
and the Holy Spirit.

> As Jesus Himself had been anointed at His baptism with
> the Holy Spirit and power, so His followers were now to be
> similarly anointed and enabled to carry on His work. This
> work would be a work of witness-bearing-a theme which is
> prominent in the apostolic preaching throughout Acts.[11]

When Jesus was baptized and filled with the Holy Spirit,
God finally broke His long silence and began to speak
again. As long as the Holy Spirit who descended upon
Jesus is in the church, there must be no more silence. The
book of Acts, which has been also called the Acts *of the Holy
Spirit*, mentions the words 'witness' or 'testify' over 30
times, because the early church could not remain silent.

---

11. F. F. Bruce, *The Book of the Acts* (Grand Rapids: Eerdmans), 39

From this we can discern that the most important objective of the coming of the Holy Spirit was to empower the disciples as witnesses of Christ. The Holy Spirit did not come only to comfort them, but to equip them as missionaries. In this sense, the Holy Spirit makes the eschatological church into an apostolic entity. This is the key that explains why the characteristics of the church in the New Testament differ so much from the church in the Old Testament. The church in the Old Testament revolved around the sacrificial system. In contrast, the church in the New Testament does not offer sacrifices. Jesus Christ has offered the eternal sacrifice for sin and has made sinners righteous forever. Consequently, the church no longer needs to offer sacrifices for sin (Heb. 10:12-18). What remains for the church is to boast of the cross of Jesus Christ who has offered the eternal sacrifice for sinners (1 Cor. 2:2). The Holy Spirit came and transformed the nature of the church to become a fitting tool to do His work. As a result, the New Testament church took on the character of a witnessing community from the first day of its appearance in the world. It has become a church that confesses, proclaims, and praises its Lord.

The dramatic phenomenon that appears in the second chapter of the book of Acts teaches us an important truth. The first thing that happened with the coming of the Holy Spirit was that people began to speak with a new tongue as the Spirit enabled (Acts 2:4). In other words, the Holy Spirit opened the mouth of the church. Why did He open its mouth? It is because the visible church has been called to go out into the world and spread the gospel. On this point, the Holy Spirit did not distinguish the apostles from the rest of the disciples. The Holy Spirit came upon all 120 who were in the upper room, and they all obeyed the Spirit and opened their mouths (Acts 2: 3, 4). Their words were not groanings that disappeared into thin air. These words were loud enough for the people in Jerusalem to hear and to draw their attention. The people who had heard them testified, 'We hear them declaring the wonders of God in our own tongues' (Acts 2:11). It is still hard to guess the specific content of the words spoken in different tongues. However, we have the sermon preached by Peter as the representative spokesman. Peter spoke of the death and the resurrection of Christ and that Jesus Christ became the Lord and Christ of the world (Acts 2:14-36).

The speaking with other tongues (by the prompting of the Holy Spirit) dramatically demonstrated the witnessing character of the Church; Peter's sermon set the pattern through which that witnessing character finds normal and continuing expression.[12]

The Holy Spirit opens the mouth of the church, but Satan closes it. Opening our mouth is to obey God, but shutting our mouth is to obey Satan (Acts 4:17-20). From this we can conclude that the supreme purpose of the coming of the Holy Spirit on the visible church is to open the mouths of all believers to proclaim the gospel to the world.

So far, we have discussed the theological basis for awakening the laity to their calling in this age. A church based on the Bible must be apostolic. In order for the church to become apostolic, the whole church, including all lay people, must believe that it is the successor to the apostles. The church must believe and confess the testimony of the apostles in order to be the apostles' successor. At the same time, the whole church must confess the apostolic calling and obey the command to spread the gospel to the ends of the earth as did the apostles. It

---

12. Harry Boer, *Pentecost & Mission*, 103.

is the Holy Spirit who confirmed the apostolicity of the church beyond a shadow of doubt, and broke the silence of the church by opening its mouth from the moment He came upon the apostles and the rest of the believers. Awakening the laity, therefore, means teaching the laity to confess that each of them has been called to inherit and fulfill the apostolic ministry.

The apostolic task has not yet been completed. It will remain incomplete until the end of the world. The apostolic ministry has not been consummated, for it is a work that embraces all peoples of the earth. Therefore, the church must always remain in the world, confessing Christ, witnessing to and serving others as the apostles did in the world. This is the fundamental and biblical mission that determines the existence of the church.

Pastors in Korea must accept responsibility for failing to equip the estimated twelve million lay Christians. We ought to reflect and examine together who is causing the laity to slumber and think they have no calling since they are 'just laymen'.

Chapter 9

Why Does the Church Exist?

We have already considered that the church has been called to go out into the world as the apostles' successor. This is not to say that mission is the only work of the church in the world. The church has other ministries connected with the call to spread the gospel. Thus without equally emphasizing all ministries, it would be difficult to see properly the true character of the church. For this reason, we will now explore more specifically the reason why the church exists in the world.

The usual response given to the question, 'Why does the church exist?' is 'to glorify God'. This is probably the most concise and accurate answer. There is no doubt that all things will bring glory to God when the church exhibits its fullness over all creation. However a drawback of the expression 'to glorify God' is that it is somewhat abstract and lacks specificity. It does not explain how and with what the church glorifies God. Thus it is necessary to explain what it is that the church needs to do to bring glory to God. As a matter of convenience, we will examine this under three headings.

Worshipping Community

First of all, the church exists to worship God. God called the church out of this world for His name's sake, for rendering the glory that befits His name (Acts 15: 14). Therefore, the first priority of the church is to worship

God. The first thing that the people of God must learn is to worship the God who has set them apart. God has given us the privilege of entering into His holy sanctuary to worship Him. Christian worship is unique in that it is a sacrifice of the total person. Through Christ, the people of God became one body as the church and a holy priesthood, offering their bodies as holy sacrifices, pleasing to God (Rom. 12:1; 1 Pet. 2:5).

Above all things, church worship is based on the character of God. We must first know who He is and worship Him properly (Ps. 29:2; Rev. 4:8). Worship must be founded on what God has done for the church in creation and redemption. The elders surrounding God's throne give glory, honour, and power to God for His work in creation (Rev. 4:11). The angels worship the lamb that was slain (Rev. 5:12). The redeeming grace that has saved us from eternal death is the basis of worship. This explains why the worship of the early church expressed gratitude for Christ's presence through the breaking of bread in the Lord's Supper. Calvin and Luther both wished the church to retain these spiritual and physical characteristics of worship. These reformers believed that God is pleased to accept the worship offered in His Son's name through the means of the Word and sacraments.[1]

There is a question that we must ask when discussing worship: What constitutes true worship? Worship leaders concede that this is a rather difficult question that cannot be satisfied by a simple answer. A new era has arrived in Christ. Therefore, neither the Old Testament form of worship nor any form cemented in tradition can bind or satisfy us. [2] Jesus summarized the worship of the church in the last days as worship in spirit and in truth. This is

1. Robert E. Webber, *Common Roots* (Grand Rapids: Zondervan, 1978) 84-90.
2. S. C. Farris, *Dictionary of Jesus and Gospels*, 892.

not to say that there are only one or two ways to worship God in spirit and in truth, as the terms 'spirit' and 'truth' imply profound spirituality and diversity of worship.

When reading the four gospels with the subject of worship in mind, the scarcity of the teachings on worship makes us wonder. Not only that, it is difficult to find specific instances of worship. At most, we read that Jesus and His disciples occasionally visited the temple and the synagogues. The disciples at the time were confessing that Jesus is the Son of God and the Christ, and were following Him. But there are no examples of any kind of formal worship given to Jesus in the gospels. Nor is there any instance where Jesus required the disciples to worship in a certain way.

The epistles also do not contain any passages that refer to any kind of worship formats. They only give instructions regarding the basic elements of worship such as praise, thanksgiving, prayer, and the Word. The epistles do not demand forms of worship with which we are familiar. Furthermore, they assert that one of the most important ways to worship is to render to God the spiritual worship of offering our bodies as holy and living sacrifices (Rom. 12:1). More interesting is the fact that the responsibility to lead worship is not mentioned as one of the purposes for appointing pastoral leaders in the church. It is written that He gave some to be pastors and teachers to prepare God's people for works of service and to build up the body of Christ (Eph. 4:11, 12). This is rather surprising when we consider the contemporary reality that gives the impression that pastors exist in order to lead worship.

The point here is not to demean the importance of worship or to negate the need for worship formality. No one can deny the fact that one of the reasons the church exists in the world is to glorify God through worship. A concern I have is that freedom in worship in the Korean church is excessively constrained. It gives the impression that the church is restricted by a few worship formats and is unable to break out of it. Even just a little change in worship becomes a target of criticism. My concern is that the worship which should be offered in spirit and in truth might degenerate into legalism.

In extreme cases, there are those who do not consider sharing the Word in a small group setting as worship. They argue that Bible study and worship are different things. Is this true? In the Colossian church, it was when lay believers gathered together to share the Word of God that they were able to truly praise God and offer thanks. They did not have separate times of worship and of sharing the Word. To be sure, they did come together officially on the Lord's Day to take communion together. However, they do not seem to have insisted on a certain format as being the only way to worship (Col. 3:16, 17). Thus, a separation between the vertical and the horizontal dimensions of worship must not be allowed. Teaching to build up the believers around you and worshipping the God who is above, are two sides of the same coin. To make disciples of lay people is to worship God. Therefore, separating worship and Bible study is tantamount to restraining worship under the yoke of formality.

There is another point that needs to be made. As stated above, pastors are often seen as those who prepare and lead Sunday worship services. Any meeting with a pastor always starts with a fixed form of worship. Even visitations focus on worship. Moreover, anyone who attends Sunday service on a regular basis is considered faithful. Consequently, lay people think they are fulfilling the requirements of spiritual life by simply attending Sunday worship services. Thus, our ministry has become lopsided, revolving excessively around worship.

Why is that a problem? It is a problem because such a lopsided ministry plays a huge role in weakening and causing the laity to slumber. Because pastors see the most important role of the laity as coming to Sunday worship service, they hastily conclude that anyone who faithfully attends worship service is a healthy Christian. On the other hand, the laity regards any demands or requests other than attending worship services made by the clergy as being excessive. This makes the task of thoroughly training the laity enormously difficult. If such conditions persist over a long time, how can the church ever awaken the laity?

True worshippers are not produced in a vacuum. True worshippers are made. Thoroughly training the laity to make disciples of Christ signifies the creation of true worshippers. Lopsided ministry that concentrates only on Sunday worship services frustrates the effort to create true worshippers. In certain instances, it even leads to the hypocritical idea that it is unnecessary to generate true worshippers.

To Save the World
The church exists to save the world. The church is the gathering of believers who have been called by God and sent out into the world as the witnesses of Christ. Spreading the gospel to the ends of the earth is the most important responsibility of the church. The entire church, including both the clergy and the laity, has been called for this task. Every member of the church, as a part of the body, has been given gifts to carry out this task. There is no exception.

The greatest ministry to which the laity are called is witness to Jesus Christ, evangelism, which means spreading the good news about Him.[3]

---

3. John Stott, *One People* (Downers Grove: InterVarsity Press, 1975), 44.

This point has already been thoroughly discussed in the previous section on the apostolic nature of the church. However, it is a very important point for those of us who want to awaken the laity. Thus in order to nail this truth down, we will briefly review the doctrine of the priesthood of all believers.

All believers are a royal priesthood (1 Pet. 2:9). A priest has at least four glorious privileges. First is the privilege of appearing directly before God's presence. Christ has completed the perfect work of intercession through His sacrificial death and opened wide the veil into the Holy of Holies (Matt. 27: 51). As a result, anyone who believes can approach the throne of grace directly by faith. Accordingly, there is absolutely no need for a human mediator other than Jesus.

Second, there is the privilege of offering spiritual sacrifices. All believers under the new covenant have the responsibility to offer holy and living sacrifices to God (1 Pet. 2:5). The Bible identifies various sacrifices that can be offered to God. Proclaiming the gospel (Rom. 15:16), praise, helping others (Heb. 13:15-16), martyrdom (2 Tim. 4:6), prayers of the saints (Rev. 8:3), and more are mentioned as spiritual sacrifices. The distinctive feature of these sacrifices is that the one who offers the sacrifice offers oneself. Moreover, these include not only worships offered in church, but also all that has to do with everyday life. There is no distinction between the sacred and the secular.

Third, there is the privilege of proclaiming the Word:

The priesthood of all believers includes not only the witnessing with actions, with one's whole life spent in loving self-sacrifice, but also the specific witnessing with the word.[4]

---

4. Hans Kung, *The Church*, 481.

Proclaiming the Word is not a task entrusted to a few in the church but given to all believers who are called a royal priesthood. Why has God called believers a royal priesthood? It is to declare the wonderful grace and goodness of God (1 Pet. 2:9).

The fourth privilege is intercession. The priesthood of believers is not just for them to approach God's throne and remain there, but to serve others both in and outside the church. This priesthood is not only about the vertical relationship with God, but includes horizontal functions such as praying for and serving others through spiritual sacrifices. Believers are the priests for the world. In faith every believer can approach God freely and pray for other brothers and sisters.

> *The priesthood of all believers consists in the calling of the faithful to witness to God and his will before the world, and to offer up their lives in the service of the world. It is God who creates this priesthood and hence creates fellowship among believers. Each one knows that he appears before God on behalf of others, and knows that others appear before God on his behalf. Each is responsible for his fellow men, called to share in his struggles and in his difficulties, called to bear his sins with him and to stand by him in everything. The priesthood of all believers is a fellowship in which each Christian, instead of living for himself, lives before God for others and is in turn supported by others.*[5]

Reviewing the privileges of the priesthood of all believers reveals the heavy responsibility every lay person has toward the world. Why do we have to go directly to God? It is to intercede for the world. Why do we have to spread the gospel? We have to proclaim the gospel because it is our spiritual worship, holy and acceptable to God.

---

5. Ibid., 487.

The tendency to apply the word 'priest' exclusively to the clergy seems to increase with the development of church hierarchy. As a result, lay people lose interest in the concept of their own priesthood. Contemporary churches have a pressing task before them to restore the basic spirit of the priesthood of all believers. In order for the church to recover its apostolic nature and allow lay people to fulfill their role in their proper place, the entire church, not just a few members, must become an ecclesiastical community that directly approaches God to offer spiritual sacrifices, proclaims the gospel, and serves its neighbours. Let us bear in mind that limiting the glorious office of priesthood to those few who have been called into the pastorate is an aberration from the biblical truth that can never be permitted by the Word of God.

Nurturing Mother
Lastly, the church exists to nurture and train believers. This is the central focus of Calvin's doctrine of the church. According to Calvin, God gave us the church in order to compensate for men's flaws caused by indolence and ignorance. Believers as God's children are placed in the bosom of the church, and until they reach the goal of faith as mature Christians, the church must provide motherly care. Therefore, believers should never leave the community of the church, because they are inherently weak. [6]

As Jesus was leaving the world, he commanded His followers to teach others to obey all that he commanded.

Only then would disciples be made. The Apostle Paul emphasized the importance of a particular gift when he was discussing the qualifications of the overseer. That

---

6. John Calvin, *Institutes of the Christian Religion*, 110.

gift was the ability to teach (1 Tim. 3:2). This signifies that a leader must be able to teach the Word in order to nurture believers. According to the epistles, there are three things that Jesus, as the head of the church, gave for the ministry of making disciples of believers. He gave pastors as the teachers of the Word (Eph. 4:11), the Bible as the teaching content (2 Tim. 3:16-17), and an excellent model as a teaching method (Col. 1:28-29).

Therefore, if our ministry fails to thoroughly teach lay people to become Christ's disciples, we greatly disappoint Jesus who entrusted the church to us and asked us to 'take care of my sheep'. Perhaps it could be said we have been doing so far the ministry of 'teaching to obey'. However, we all admit that the result has not been satisfactory. We must seriously question whether or not so many worship services, so many sermons, and so many Bible studies are transforming the laity and building them up as a people with a mission.

In order for the church to fulfill the role of a mother, we must examine the whole of our ministry that seems to be running only on inertia. And we must show the resolution to correct the wrong and supplement what lacks. Only then will the church raise Christ's disciples like a swarm of bees.

Inseparable Relationship

So far we have discussed the reason for the existence of the church under three headings. It is important to bear in mind that these three cannot be separated into independent parts. They are closely connected to each other. Failure in one part will cause a breakdown of the whole. Thus we should not neglect any one of these three – worship, evangelization, and training. Only when they find a balance in our ministry, can we expect the utmost result – the glory of God.

Evidently the church has always suffered from focusing on only one of the three parts as the reason for its existence. This is due to its own incomplete nature. Some theologians speak of the church as existing only for God. For example, Herman Bavinck said the following, insisting that the glory of God is the most important reason for the church's existence:

> *Above all, the church exists to praise God through its speech, conduct, prayers, and worship. Glorifying and praising God are of such importance that it must form a nucleus of the church.*[7]

However recently, there have been increasing numbers of theologians who insist that the church exists for the world. Thus, putting forth the thesis 'The church is mission', Kraemer insists that the church exists for the world and by no means for itself, and presents it as the basic law of the existence of the church. In his view, mission is not a part of the church but is the essence itself.

> *The church is the community of the sent, just as she is the community of witnesses. She is sent to and into the world* [8]

However, the church must not neglect any of the three parts mentioned above. God wants to receive honour through the glorious worship of believers. He wants to receive glory through the celebration of the return of the lost sheep. And He wants to receive glory through the maturity of His children who have attained to the whole measure of the fullness of Christ. To lose sight of any one of these is not His will for us.

---

7. J. H. Bavinck, *An Instruction to Science of Mission* (Philadelphia: The Presbyterian & Reformed Publishing, 1960), 68.
8. Hendrik Kraemer, *A Theology of the Laity*, 147.

The church appears to be losing its equilibrium today. It is neglecting the basis for its existence. Traditional doctrines of the church have overly emphasized worship, generating the misconception that the church is not responsible for the rest of the world. Mission is considered as an exclusive possession belonging to a small number of special people. The laity has been reduced to an incompetent mass that come to church simply to worship and satisfy their self-centred spiritual needs. Worship is there, but it lacks living testimonies. Teaching is there, but training is absent. The church is neglecting the responsibility to train the laity to live according to their calling and fulfill God's will in the world. Many lay people have fallen into a dualism that separates God's work from secular work. And many feel guilty about being engrossed in the affairs of this world, and fear standing before the judgement seat at the end of their life.

We have verified the church's call to missions by examining the apostolicity of the church and the reason for the church's existence. Therefore, we must supplement our doctrine of the church with the call to missions. Only then will we be able to blow the trumpet with the power to awaken the slumbering laity.

Chapter 10

Strategic Merits of Training the Laity

Confusing Terminology

Nowadays the terms 'disciple' and 'discipleship training' are being used as fashionable catchwords. Although these terms are sometimes misused, the trend seems to indicate that many pastors are gaining interest in discipleship, thereby displaying a strong desire to explore discipleship and apply it to their ministry. Indeed, such an attitude is spreading widely, and there are quite a number of ministries that are bearing much fruit through discipleship training.

When asked to define 'disciple', each person comes up with a different answer. There still seems to be some confusion about this concept. Some think that it is just a title of some Bible study materials. Then there are those who criticize the tendency to emphasize discipleship, questioning the relationship between the words 'believer' and 'disciple'. Some who have been deeply influenced by Dietrich Bonhoeffer's ideology tends to interpret discipleship as a radical ethical motif.[1] On the other hand, some mission organizations have a parochial understanding of discipleship. In other words, they think of discipleship as a kind of product that they manufacture from a unique mold of their organization.

---

1. James A. Todd, *'Participation,'* Encounter, (Winter 1973).

It is Jesus who commands us to go and make disciples. Thus we need to correctly understand the concept of 'disciple'. It is not wrong to use this word frequently. However, the more we use it, the more important it becomes for us to clearly establish its biblical definition and character. We must not underestimate the harm that results from a flawed understanding of this important concept. Already there are those who view discipleship training with a critical eye due to those leaders who teach erroneously. Some have even said derisively, 'If that is discipleship training, then I would rather take a nap at home'. Why is this happening? It is because of the leaders who tried to teach without properly understanding the true meaning of the word 'disciple'.

It is true that churches have been blind to the concept of disciple for a long time. They understood the command to make disciples as applying only to evangelism. However in the early 20th century, Dawson Trotman, the founder of the Navigators, 'saw the light' while reading the Great Commission (Matt. 28:18-20). Since then the discipleship movement began to spread rapidly, both in evangelical mission organizations and also in churches. The eyes of Christian leaders were being opened to the truth that Jesus' command to make disciples means more than just 'to evangelize' or 'to proclaim the gospel to the ends of the earth'. The impact that Trotman has had on Christianity during the last century has indeed been tremendous.

The word 'discipleship' does not appear in the Bible. Nor does the Bible define or explain the word 'disciple'. Instead, the Bible is full of stories and incidents that portray the character and life of those called 'disciples'. Thus it is not difficult or ambiguous to explain discipleship. Discipleship is not so much a concept that needs to be defined, as one which needs to be understood through practical living and character formation. In other words, discipleship is a believer's lifestyle, a process to walk through, and a goal to be aimed at to the end. Discipleship is the sum of the church's ministry itself. Pastors with the responsibility to awaken the laity and develop them into disciples of Christ must open their Bible, and learn discipleship taught by Christ in order to have a proper understanding of their task.

Discipleship is a Ministry Strategy

Discipleship can be understood as a biblical and foundational strategy that reconstructs the laity's self-image to correspond to the apostolic nature of the church. The strategic value of discipleship lies in that it provides the goal and the standard for training the laity who have been called to go out into the world. In other words, the answer Jesus would give to the question 'What kind of laity do you want?' is 'disciples'. Before they even realize it, pastors could make disciples who are pleasing only in their own eyes. Or they could train the laity without any standard at all. This is a great tragedy. We must make disciples of Christ, and we must teach them to obey the goal and the standard that Jesus has shown us. 'All that I have commanded you' (Matt. 28:19) is contained in discipleship. Therefore when we train the laity, we must not run aimlessly or fight as one beating the air (1 Cor. 9:26).

Although it is true that the advocates of the ecumenical movement were the first to see the importance of the laity, they have not followed the strategies outlined in the Bible. Their strategy consisted of participation and secularization. Participation means that the church leaders open wide the ministry doors for any lay person to take part. Secularization means encouraging the laity to actively and boldly take part in all areas of society, excepting sin, so that their voice could be heard in the world. On the other hand, the leaders of the evangelical mission organizations that seemed to have a feeble beginning in America, adopted discipleship found in the Bible as their strategy. In other words, the ecumenical movement had its strategic priority in practical actions, but mission organizations had their strategic priority in character formation.

Who was right? Jesus' principle was to equip a person first, and then give him a task. This is the basic principle of discipleship. Christ's way is to put people first before work and action. In other words, a strategy that assigns ministry or work to someone without prior preparation of the person is not a strategy that Jesus taught.

What has been the result? After several decades, the lay movement in the ecumenical camp has left the impression of having ended as a mere theory, while mission organizations are still gathering its fruit on a worldwide scale. Paul Schrotenboer evaluates it in this way:

WCC is faced with mission crises in its character and strategy. However, the evangelical mission organizations that are promoting the discipleship of the laity are growing rapidly.[2]

In some ways, the strategy of making disciples could be seen as a movement to create an elite laity. As Ezra Bounds has commented, the world looks for a better method but God looks for a better man. Discipleship contains all the important principles of making the people that God seeks.

It seems as though churches both in Korea and the western world have for a long time neglected the task of making disciples of Jesus. Thus, now churches seem to be

---

2. Schrotenboer, 'The Unity of the Church in Mission,' *A Lecture for Reformed Missions Consultation* (Grand Rapids:Calvin Theology Seminary, 1976), 8.

paying a high price for their failure to awaken the laity. The waves of the world such as secularism, communism, heretical doctrines, shamanistic ideologies, the New Age movement, unwholesome Holy Spirit movements, formalism, and moral laxity are pouring into churches, because many of them lack strong walls to withstand those waves.

In addition, due to natural increases in population and overcrowding in the cities, churches in some areas are suffering from quantitative obesity, which hinders further the work of forming a 'quality' laity. Now is indeed the time to pay attention to the following warning once again: 'The continued expansion of the churches without profound teachings will weaken the churches in the future.'[3]

It is a well known fact that the basic strategy of communism and many cults is to make a small number of core leading members first. Before putting people to work, they make a huge investment in developing individuals. Before focusing on the masses, they devote all their energy to preparing a few who will have a pivotal influence on the masses.

Isn't disciple making Jesus' strategy? It is as though, when the church abandoned its work of making disciples, Satan snatched the secret and developed it into a powerful weapon to attack and destroy the church. We cannot even fathom the extent of the harm that the church has suffered as a result. Now is the time for us to return to the place of repentance and learn why Jesus has commanded the church to make disciples.

---

3. Carl Wilson, *With Christ in the School of Disciple Building: A Study of Christ's Method of Building Disciples* (Grand Rapids: Zondervan, 1976), 8.

Chapter 11

Jesus and His Disciples

When Jesus was beginning His public ministry, the first thing He did was to choose disciples. Unlike traditional Jewish leaders, He did not wait for disciples to come to Him, but took the initiative and searched for a few men who suited His purposes. Jesus chose twelve disciples to embody and model His teachings.[1] Within and through them, the gospel was to be sustained and proclaimed to everyone. Thus they became apostles, the 'sent ones' (Luke 6:13). 'They ultimately became his apprentice.'[2]

The twelve were especially chosen from among many other disciples (Luke 6:13). Jesus chose them with care. He spent a whole night in prayer for this task (Luke 6:12). Jesus gave the twelve the privilege of being always with Him and learning of and from Him (Mark 3:14). They had to know Him and become His men before they could do anything for Him. Because they were given to Jesus by the Father (John 17:6), they had to inherit every word of truth that Jesus had received from God (John 17:14). They were sanctified through the Word (John 17:19). Thus Jesus explained to the disciples in detail the mystery of the kingdom of heaven which He had spoken to the crowd only in parables (Matt. 13:10ff.).

---

1. William Barclay, *The Mind of Jesus*, 89.
2. Ibid., 92.

He revealed Himself as the Messiah to the twelve and demanded their confession of faith, while He hid His true identity from the public. And He was satisfied with their confession and promised that He would build His church on it (Matt. 16:16-20). As His end was drawing near, Jesus devoted Himself wholly to the twelve. He avoided the crowds in order to examine and pray for His disciples, just as a great artist would add final touches to his painting before an exhibition (John 13–17).

Although the disciples were mostly fishermen from Galilee and had come from various backgrounds and experiences, Jesus had a keen insight to penetrate into the infinite potential hidden behind their ordinary lives. He did not hesitate to nurture the radiant dream of the kingdom of heaven with these ordinary men. Although the disciples demonstrated unbelief and betrayal at the scene of the crucifixion, Jesus did not give up on them. Instead, after His resurrection, He shared once again with these failures the blueprint of the glorious kingdom that was to be constructed through them. He was able to foresee that, although they could not follow Him at the present time, they would soon be able to do so (John 13:36). And He was confident that they would not only do what He had done, but that they would do even greater things (John 14:12).

Although Jesus saw the immaturity and unbelief of the disciples before His ascension, He decisively made the most authoritative farewell proclamation: 'As the Father has sent me, I am sending you' (John 20:21). He also entrusted to them the Great Commission to make disciples of all nations, baptizing them and teaching them His words (Matt. 28:18-20). While He was in the world, Jesus did not leave any diary or stone monuments by which to commemorate Him. The only inheritance left by Him was a handful of ignorant and ordinary disciples who had learned from Him. That's how much Jesus valued the making of a small number of disciples, and He devoted His whole life to this task.

Chapter 12

The Concept of Disciple in the Four Gospels and the Book of Acts

In the New Testament the word 'disciple' appears only in the four gospels and in the book of Acts. It is used approximately 250 times. Examining the way it is used in each book will give a better understanding of the concept of 'disciple'.

Disciple in the Four Gospels

Except for two instances, Matthew always uses the word to refer to the twelve disciples. Only in Matthew 27:57 and 28:19, does the word 'disciple' refer to those other than the twelve. Although the word 'disciple' in the above two verses appears as a noun in some translations like the Korean Bible, it is in the form of a verb in the original text. It means 'to become a disciple' or 'to make a disciple'. Some people claim that since the word was not used as a noun in these two verses, Matthew used the word 'disciple' in a narrow sense only; that is to refer only to the twelve disciples. However, I believe this is too restrictive. Although it is in the form of a verb, it still contains the root of the noun 'disciple'. When Jesus gave the command 'to make disciples' (Matt. 28: 19), He had undoubtedly foreseen that His disciples would include not only the twelve but also many who would become God's people through them. Thus Matthew is teaching that all believers, whether they are pastors or lay persons, must always remain as disciples of Jesus Christ, who is the one and only Lord.[1]

Mark in his gospel uses the word in a narrow sense without any exceptions. He does not call anyone a disciple other than the twelve.

The Gospel of John uses it in both a narrow and a broad sense. John calls many people disciples other than the twelve (John 6:66). Moreover, John shows the way to become true disciples to all the Jews who believed in Jesus. In that occasion, the word 'disciple' was used in a broad sense to mean that all who abide in His Word are His disciples (John 8:31).

It was Luke who played the most innovative role in using the word 'disciple' in its broad sense. Especially in Acts, he does not hesitate to call whoever believes in Jesus a disciple. In other words, Luke uses the word 'disciple' to describe believers who have entered into a new community of faith called the church. Only two instances (Acts 19:1; 9:25) serve as exceptions. At that time, there were a great number of believers who had not personally seen Jesus but were still called 'disciples'. In the beginning of Acts, 'believers' and 'disciples' are used interchangeably to refer to the new believers. However as the book progresses, the former term disappears and only the latter term remains (Acts 2:44; 4:32). Furthermore, as the Gentile mission begins to take place in earnest, the disciples in Antioch are given a beautiful nickname 'Christians' (11:26). This was an honourable title given only to those whose character and life embodied the power of the gospel of Christ.

---

1. Mark Sheridan, 'Disciples & Discipleship,' *Biblical Theology Bulletin* (October 1973), 255.

Silence in the Epistles

The word 'disciple' suddenly disappears when we come to the epistles. What is the reason for this? Some claim that the writers of the epistles avoided using the word because they did not want Christianity to be misunderstood as a mere philosophical movement in a world dominated by the Hellenistic culture. Others say that although 'disciple' was an appropriate term to be used during the earthly ministry of Jesus, it was no longer a suitable term to refer to the community of believers formed after Jesus' ascension. Hence, other words replaced the word 'disciple'.[2] It is hard to see immediately which opinion is correct. However, considering the fact that the teachings in the Bible form a unity under the inspiration of the Holy Spirit, it seems reasonable to conclude that there are other words that contain the meaning of discipleship used in the epistles.

Consider the use of the word 'perfect' or 'mature' (1 Cor. 14:20; Eph. 4:12; Col. 1:28; 2 Tim. 3:17). The original Greek text uses two to three different words to connote these terms. When we compare Ephesians 4 verses 12 and 13 side by side, it is rather easy to discern that 'a mature or perfect person' is closely related to a 'disciple'.

*To prepare God's people (**katartismos**, v. 12) was originally used to mean putting a bone back in its place. Accordingly, it implies the act of preparing people with appropriate qualifications. 'Become mature' (teleios, v. 13) follows after and it denotes reaching the goal, or maturity.*[3]

Although there is a slight difference in their meanings, the fact that these terms were used in the above verses to

2. Michael J. Wilkins, *Following the Master* (Grand Rapids: Zondervan, 1992), 281-289.
3. Barth, *A Linguistic Key to the Greek NT* (Regency, 1980), 531.

convey an identical message shows that their meanings coincide. Seen from this perspective, verse 13 explains in detail what it means to prepare, equip, or perfect God's people. Paul explains what it means to become perfect by using a metaphor, 'the whole measure': 'become mature, attaining to the whole measure of the fullness of Christ' (v. 13). 'The whole measure' here refers to a grown-up person. Accordingly, 'the whole measure of the fullness of Christ' signifies becoming a mature adult like Jesus. It contains the nuance of a little child saying 'I want to become like my Dad someday.' Therefore, becoming a mature person means to become like Jesus and to live like Jesus; in other words, a disciple. In these contexts, it seems reasonable to conclude that the word 'disciple' used in Acts has been replaced by 'mature or perfect person' in the epistles.

'Become mature' refers to the two stages of spiritual maturity pursued by all God's children who have received new life. The first is the stage of maturity that can be achieved in this life. This refers to the maturity of believers who are becoming more and more like Jesus. It is the signpost and the goal toward which every believer must press on. A growing faith (Heb. 6:1, 2), maturing character, and victorious life (2 Tim. 3:17), are all included in this stage. The second stage of spiritual maturity denotes being glorified with Christ at His second coming (Phil. 3:12-14).[4]

Occasionally, there are people who argue that it is not right to burden the laity with the idea of becoming perfect or mature, because it is impossible in this world. Thus they criticize discipleship training, which teaches the laity to be like Jesus and live like Him, as an extreme ministry method. However, we should keep in mind that

---

4. W. W. Klein, *Dictionary of Paul and His Letters* (IVP, 1953), 459.

this kind of attitude becomes a catalyst for secularizing the church. When lay people are not given specific goals and standards by which they ought to live, their spiritual life naturally heads downward instead of up. We should always be cautious of such thinking. We must also be wary of those who claim that there is no need for discipleship training since the instruction to 'make disciples' cannot be found in the epistles.

Many think that they become disciples by simply confessing their faith in Jesus. However, the believers in the early church were not called 'disciples' out of courtesy. They were called disciples because they followed Jesus wholeheartedly. We must guard against perverting the spirit of discipleship by the misuse of the word 'disciple'. Read the gospels and observe the character and the life of Jesus who commanded others to follow Him. Observe carefully the transformations that took place in those who were called disciples in Acts. Surely we will find distinctive features that are often absent among the believers in the contemporary churches.

Why do the disciples in Acts seem so different? They were indeed true Christians who were worthy to be called disciples. Jesus did not tell the disciples to 'make church members' of all nations but 'to make disciples'. He wanted the citizens of His new kingdom to be like Him without any exceptions.

Chapter 13

Are All Believers Disciples?

As local churches show more interest in discipleship training, we often encounter misunderstandings around the question, 'Who is a disciple?' Some of the churches that have implemented discipleship training program regard the program as a kind of gauge that separates disciples from those who are not. They seem to be comparing the program to Jacob's staff that separated the spotted sheep from those without spots.

Even in SaRang Church, it is not difficult to meet those who say, 'I'm not a disciple yet, because I have not received the training'. Pastors often seem to think similarly, perhaps subconsciously, despite knowing well how erroneous such thinking is. Thus they unknowingly end up treating some as disciples and some as just one of the crowd. When that happens, naturally one group will act as if they are the privileged few and others will shy away.

It is not just the program itself that causes misunderstanding and confusion regarding who is a disciple. Confusion and misunderstanding are also found in problems that pastors wrestle with. Honestly speaking, what we call discipleship training cannot really be compared to the content and method that Jesus used to train His disciples. We do not literally follow Jesus' methods of discipleship training as recorded in the Bible. For the most

CALLED TO AWAKEN THE LAITY

part, we apply the principles we have derived from the Bible to our own times. Thus, I fear at times that perhaps our discipleship training not only falls short of the biblical standards, but does not even come close to a cheap imitation. Realistically, our environment does not allow us to demand more vigorous and sacrificial discipleship from the trainees. Consequently, we naturally end up wrestling with the question, 'Is it possible to make disciples in this way?' When we fall into this kind of self-reproach, it is possible for us to end up saying, 'There is still no one who can be called a disciple of Christ in our church'.

Whether the misunderstanding regarding who is a disciple is caused by the training program or the pastor's apprehension, we cannot afford to ignore it. It is contrary to the true nature of the church, and it attacks the identity and independence of the laity. Thus, we must first give a clear answer to the question, 'Who in the church can be called a disciple?', and then start discipleship training. It is not just the pastors or the trainees who need to know the answer. All members of the congregation must know the answer. We examined earlier those who were called disciples in the four gospels and in the book of Acts. Although we have already found the answer in a sense, I think it is still necessary to make it a little more precise and clear. We must not forget that the devil's favourite bait to a church that is implementing discipleship training is the divisive debate which asks who is a disciple and who is not. With such bait, Satan always looks for an opportunity to rip apart the body of Christ.

A disciple of Christ is not a title used to refer to a person who is receiving discipleship training in the church. Neither is it a title given to those who have completed the training, nor is it a name given to those lay leaders who sacrifice more than others. It is not a medal reserved for those who have entered into a higher stage of spiritual maturity. And it certainly is not a nickname given to clergy or missionaries with a special calling for ministry. Then whom does 'disciple' designate? For the answer, I think it would be most appropriate to borrow Michael Wilkins' opinion. In his masterpiece, *Following The Master*, which was written from the conviction of his heart and soul, Wilkins has given an excellent treatment of these easily misunderstood problems concerning 'disciple' and 'discipleship'.[1]

The path of discipleship, which Jesus requires, applies to all believers. It is not something that one can choose depending on one's spiritual maturity. It is not something for which the dedicated believers pay the price, and from which those who are not quite yet dedicated are exempted. The path of discipleship does not require all believers to pay the same price. However, Jesus expects all who have come forward to believe in Him to walk on the path of discipleship. In Acts, we find that everyone who confesses Jesus as Lord and Saviour – whether male or female, Jew or Samaritan, or even foreigner, and whether a leader or a lay person in church – is called a disciple. This aligns with the Great Commission of Jesus to make disciples of all nations. Therefore, discipleship is a path that is and must be walked by everyone who believes in Jesus. We must not forget that discipleship is not something that can be chosen or rejected by programs or by the level of one's devotion or maturity.

Although all believers are disciples as we have seen, there can be degrees of difference in the lives of disciples. According to the Great Commission, in order to make disciples, we are to go and witness, baptize, and then teach them to obey the Word. If this is the case, then a newly converted believer is a disciple, one who has been

1. Michael J. Wilkins, *Following the Master*, 24-47.

baptized and is living a proper spiritual life is a disciple, and one who is learning and trying hard to mature spiritually is a disciple. However, there is a difference in the level of their spiritual maturity. It cannot be denied that normally believers who have been taught and trained to obey the Word are spiritually ahead of those who have just been baptized and have not yet been trained in the Word. Thus, believers who confess Jesus as their Lord do not receive training in order to become disciples, but they receive training because they are already disciples.

The twelve disciples also went through several stages of a developmental process in following Jesus. There was the beginning stage of believing in which they accompanied Jesus occasionally (John 2:12; 3:22). In the second stage, they abandoned their secular occupations in order to follow and have deeper fellowship with Jesus (Matt. 4:18-22). Then there was the last stage in which the twelve disciples were appointed as the apostles and received a special training for this. It should be noted that in every stage, they were disciples of Jesus. We must make sure that the laity do not doubt that they are disciples of Christ as long as they confess Jesus as their Lord, no matter what stage of spiritual maturity they are at. We must constantly teach that all – new believers, devoted believers, and the clergy – are disciples.

There will always be something lacking in the completion of discipleship, for in this world a disciple is always in the process of discipleship.[2] Therefore, the church should constantly emphasize that those who have been called to be disciples must not stand still, but continue to grow and mature. We have to continually remind them that discipleship is a lifestyle and the process of spiritual growth. We are to run unceasingly toward Jesus. Those who remain idle and refuse to press

2. Ibid., 235.

on must surely know that they are throwing away their precious status as disciples of Jesus to the pigs. In this sense, discipleship training is more of a program for those who wish to run in order to be like Jesus, than a course created to make a special group of quality people within the church. Furthermore, it should challenge new believers to feel the need for training in the Word in order to become more mature disciples. When this is done, we will be able to avert futile misunderstandings and confusions about discipleship training and the question, 'Who is a disciple?'

Chapter 14

Personal Commitment

The concept of 'disciple' contains several important elements underscored by Jesus in His teaching and example: personal commitment, witnessing, and servanthood. 'Discipleship' is a word that expresses these three basic elements in one concept.

There are not many examples in which Jesus personally explained or specifically defined discipleship and its elements. Instead, He called the disciples and trained them by living with them. Discipleship, therefore, is living truth embodied in real lives rather than a term to be defined.

Because the three elements of discipleship are absolutely related to the character of Jesus, their meanings and characteristics cannot be understood apart from Him. Furthermore, they are not separate elements that can be understood independently of one another, but are mutually related, compound elements. Discipleship cannot exist devoid of personal commitment. Without the element of witness, it forfeits its ultimate vision. And unless discipleship is followed by the element of servanthood, it loses its flavour.

The Meaning of Commitment
Discipleship involves a personal trust by which we commit ourselves wholly to Jesus. A study of the New Testament shows that one cannot be called a disciple

unless he has entrusted his life to Christ. The Gospels of Matthew and Mark state that anyone who does not completely trust and follow Jesus is not worthy of Him (Matt. 10:37ff.; 16:24; Mark 8:34ff). Luke wrote, narrating the same episode, 'he cannot be my disciple' instead of 'is not worthy' (Luke 14:26, 27, 33). The exact reason why the gospel writers used different expressions is not known. Presumably Jesus spoke more than once on the subject. He probably used different expressions depending on the occasion - in order to better explain and to make clear His teaching, being mindful of its importance. Thus it is possible that the gospel writers chose particular expressions that they deemed best. And there is no doubt that the Holy Spirit guided them in their decisions.

Rudolph Bultmann, a proponent of textual criticism, compared Matthew's 'not worthy' with Luke's 'cannot be a disciple' in order to find out which was closer to Jesus' actual statement. He concluded that the Gospel of Luke is closer to the actual words of Christ.[1] We cannot agree with Bultmann's method of questioning which is a more genuine message of the Lord in the Bible. We can, however, reaffirm the fact that the total trust of giving up everything and taking up one's cross to follow Jesus is indeed the most basic element of being a disciple of Jesus.

Completely committing ourselves to Jesus begins with the Lord's call to 'follow me' (Matt. 4:19; Mark 1:17, 20). This call assumes that anyone who follows Jesus must decide to give up everything. There is no instance in the gospels in which, upon hearing Jesus' call, someone followed Jesus without giving up everything. One who would not give up could not follow Jesus (Luke 18:18-30).

1. Rudolf Bultmann, *The History of the Synoptic Tradition* (Basil Black Well: Oxford 1963), 160.

The three verbs in Mark 8:34, 'come after me', 'deny himself', and 'take up his cross', signify denying oneself by giving up everything. In Greek, these verbs are in the simple past tense, which indicates events or actions that occur once. One who wants to follow Jesus must decide at once and put his decision into action. Denying oneself and taking up one's cross to come to Him is not a repeated action, but is a decisive event that takes place once. When that is done, one can follow Jesus continually. The verb 'follow' in the passage is in the present tense, which implies an ongoing action. This conveys a profound truth. It shows that following Jesus is a lifelong undertaking that is intrinsic to the life of a disciple. The passage teaches us the truth that, like a farmer who puts his hand to the plough to work the soil, we must not look back once we have committed our lives to Jesus.

Jesus' disciples, who are to devote themselves as faithful witnesses of the gospel for the new kingdom of Christ in this world (Matt. 10:32-33; Mark 8:38), must first count the cost. This is not a simple matter that can be treated carelessly. Jesus did not hide anything from the crowd when He talked about the requirements of following Him. He used the most transparent and honest expressions possible (Luke 14:25ff). It is sensible to count the cost of construction before building a tower. A king who does not consider the war expenditure and the odds of success before going out to war cannot be expected to win. Likewise, Jesus says that only those who first count the cost are fit to follow Him.

The Price That Must Be Paid

A price that a disciple of Jesus must pay is that of being involved in battle (Matt. 10:34-36). At times, it becomes impossible to avoid discord with a close family member (Matt. 10:34-36). This does not imply giving up proper family life. It means that family should not become a hindrance to following Jesus.

> Our love and commitment to our family should not hinder our loyalty to the Lord. If they do, we need to overcome them courageously.[2]

Another price that must be paid by a disciple of Jesus is sacrificial choices (Matt. 10:38). The demands of circumstances do not always correspond to the will of God. There might come a solemn moment when you have to choose between Jesus and your family. When John Bunyan was at the crossroad of either forsaking the faith for his family or going to jail for Jesus, he wrote that the agony of giving up his family was like tearing off flesh from his bones. The great martyrs of the Korean church also paid this kind of sacrificial price for choosing Christ.

> *Once again, this terrible choice will come very seldom; in God's mercy to many of us it may never come; but the fact remains that all loyalties must give place to our loyalty to God.*[3]

Another price that must be paid by a disciple of Jesus is taking up his cross (Matt 10:38). He must abandon the desires, the comforts, and the dreams that he had cherished until now. A disciple cannot do only what he wants to do. He must do what pleases Jesus. In some cases, he must be prepared to endure much suffering. 'Now if we are children, then we are heirs – heirs of God and co-heirs with Christ, if indeed we share in his sufferings in order that we may also share in his glory'

---

2. John Calvin, *Commentary on a Harmony of the Evangelical Vol 1* (Grand Rapids: Baker, 1979), 471.
3. William Barclay, *The Gospel of Matthew Vol I* (Westminster Press, 1958), 407.

(Rom. 8:17). Jesus has walked the path of suffering and of the cross, and therefore, His disciples cannot deviate onto a different path. Jesus' suffering is a model for His disciples. 'To this (to suffering) you were called, because Christ suffered for you, leaving you an example, that you should follow in his steps' (1 Pet. 2:21). 'In Christianity there is always some cross, for Christianity is the religion of the Cross.'[4] Carrying the cross, however, is not a curse. Didn't the great men of God who went before us joyously express that, 'At first I carried the cross, but later the cross carried me'? [5]

Yet another price that must be paid by a disciple of Jesus is the adventure of losing his life (Matt. 10:39). Personal security in the world cannot be the first priority in the life of a disciple who follows Jesus. A disciple of Christ has been called out of the world to serve God and his neighbours just as his master did. To reach this goal, he must be able to gladly give up his life. He must believe that true happiness is found in losing his life, for that is the way to possess and enjoy his life eternally. 'However, I consider my life worth nothing to me, if only I may finish the race and complete the task the Lord Jesus has given me – the task of testifying to the gospel of God's grace' (Acts 20:24). 'This is how we know what love is: Jesus Christ laid down his life for us. And we ought to lay down our lives for our brothers' (1 John 3:16).

When we understand that becoming a disciple of Jesus involves a total trust or total commitment by which we give up things that hinder us from following Jesus, we often experience enormous confusion. Frankly speaking, it creates a dilemma for our faith, for we cannot confidently claim that we have completely entrusted our lives to Christ. There is a great chasm between Jesus' demand

---

4. Ibid., 408.
5. John Calvin, *Commentary on a Harmony of the Evangelical Vol I*, 472.

and our response. Can we still be called disciples? We get a glimpse of such confusion in the confession that Marvin Vincent makes in his comment on Matthew 10:37-39, which speaks of the cost of discipleship:

> *These words – the discipleship words of the Synoptic Gospels – and others like them, have always been either a fascination or an embarrassment to the Church. For the hermit or the monastic, for the prophet and even for the mystic, they have exercised an irresistible attraction. For some of the greatest names in Christian biography – Benedict, Francis of Assisi, Jacob Boehme, William Law, Soren Kierkegaard, Dietrich Bonhoeffer – here lay the key to the mystery of Christian existence. But for the Church in general, they have always constituted a problem. If the words are to be taken literally, then there can be but few who can be disciples. If they are to be taken symbolically or spiritually, then they plainly mean something different for us than they meant for those who were first called.*[6]

We probably will not be able to completely avoid confusion or contradictions when we speak of discipleship. However, an undeniable fact is that becoming a disciple denotes the process of becoming like Jesus. This process may always include some anxiety due to the things that still remain to be accomplished. Furthermore, this process may be accompanied by suffering which results from our present state of imperfection. This is not at all strange. In its essence, becoming a disciple does not mean achieving perfection and a flawless life in this world. If a person is happy to be in the process of becoming like Jesus even in the face of his incompleteness and imperfection, then he is a disciple who has totally entrusted his life to the Lord.

---

6. Michael J. Wilkins, *Following the Master*, 25.

Returning to the book of Acts, we can see that the early church believers who had been called disciples were consistent followers of Jesus. However, this is not to say that they simply gave up everything and followed Jesus. Were they like the twelve disciples who accepted Jesus' words literally and gave up their families and careers? Except for a few, they did not do that. Despite this, they were those who totally trusted the Lord. They always believed that obeying the will of God was the most important thing and acted accordingly. The means of obedience depended on individual circumstances and thus differed from person to person. It was a matter to be decided by the leading of the Holy Spirit. However, none gave up the path of discipleship because of the inconsistency or confusion they sometimes experienced. Jesus was their only master, and their hearts were simple and childlike toward Him.

Unique Personal Relationship

The relationship between Jesus and His disciples was based on personal trust. In other words, the personal element gave it a unique character that cannot be found in the Old Testament period. The relationships between Moses and Joshua, or Elijah and Elisha, were not that of a teacher and a disciple. K. H. Rengstorf explains that the teacher-disciple relationship is not found in the Old Testament, because God Himself was the sole Teacher and Lord in the Old Testament era.[7] No one was able take God's place as a teacher. They were simply God's instruments used to reveal His will to His people.

Consequently, Moses and the prophets could not proclaim their message based upon their personal authority. In other words, they themselves could not

---

7. K. H. Rengstorf, *Theological Dictionary of the N.T. Vol. IV*, 427-431.

become God. No one was qualified to call others to follow him.

In the New Testament era, Jesus Himself was both God and the Word (John 1:1). He was a perfect man. The words that came out of His mouth were the words of God Himself. God was in Him, and He was in God. Therefore, only Jesus could be a true teacher who commanded others to follow Him and to entrust everything to His person. Only He had the authority to command others to give up everything. Truly He was the sole teacher with the authority to demand an absolute obedience. 'You call me teacher and Lord, and rightly so, for that is what I am' (John 13:13).

Accordingly, the concept of disciple in the New Testament was distinctive in that a disciple was personally united to the teacher who redefined his entire life. There is no instance in the New Testament where the word 'disciple' was used in the absence of a personal relationship. The focus was on the character of Jesus who was the teacher. Jesus was the one who called the disciples, and it was Jesus who provided the method and the content to consummate His relationship with the disciples.

The uniqueness of the personal relationship between Jesus and the disciples can be seen in the state of the disciples after Jesus' death on the cross. Jesus' teachings and the memory of His miracles could not become a bond that tied the disciples together after His death. When Jesus died, they were bereft of their relationship with Him. This can be seen in Luke's Gospel in which the word 'disciple' disappears after the story of Gethsemane. (Luke 22:47b). When Jesus was arrested, the disciples' personal relationship with Him was severed. They were no longer suited to be called 'disciples'. They were in a condition in which Jesus had to call them once again after His resurrection.[8] Although we do not have to agree totally with this view of Rengstorf's, it cannot be denied that the disciples' personal relationship with Jesus became at risk during the Passion Week. It is readily observed that their faith in Jesus began to crumble from its foundation.

To make disciples of the laity is to produce those who would entrust their life to Jesus and obey Him in the context of a personal relationship. Partial trust or commitment is impossible for a disciple. Such a relationship is bound to break sooner or later (John 6:66). 'For none of us lives to himself alone and none of us dies to himself alone. If we live, we live to the Lord; and if we die, we die to the Lord. So, whether we live or die, we belong to the Lord' (Rom. 14:7-8). A great illustration of such personal trust can be seen in the story of Ruth, a widow who followed her mother-in-law, Naomi. Read Ruth's famous confession again, replacing the word 'you', which refers to Naomi, with the word 'Jesus'. Then you will no longer need a further explanation. 'Don't urge me to leave Jesus or to turn back from Jesus. Where Jesus goes I will go, and where Jesus stays I will stay. Jesus' people will be my people and Jesus will be my God. Where Jesus dies I will die, and there I will be buried. May the Lord deal with me, be it ever so severely, if anything but death separates Jesus and me' (cf. Ruth 1:16, 17). If Ruth was able to follow her old mother-in-law with this kind of commitment, why can we not follow Jesus the Son of God with even a stronger passion and commitment?

Unfortunately, there are too many people in the contemporary church who are called disciples yet who lack the element of total trust and commitment. It is sad to hear people say that total commitment applies only to a select few with a special calling and that it is a biased view of some radical clergy to demand total commitment from every lay person.

---

8. Ibid., 446.

In addition we must remember: not to be a disciple of Jesus means to be a disciple of the power of darkness. And to be a servant of the world and of sin costs incalculably more than to be a disciple of Jesus – the price is the loss of the highest happiness in this life and darkness and affliction of soul throughout eternity. How insignificant is the price of self-renunciation in His service in comparison with the price to be paid for rejecting Him![9]

Most Critical Moment

Discipleship training is the process of transforming a lay person into a place of total commitment. In my experience, nine out of ten trainees live their lives far from being totally committed. And the most difficult moment in discipleship training comes in the lesson on total commitment. Much pain and tears will be involved in the process as the Holy Spirit works powerfully with and through the Word. Although it might be slow coming, this change will open up a glorious new world. However, if this critical moment is not overcome properly, discipleship training will continue to face difficulties to the end. It is disheartening to see leaders who consider discipleship training as just plodding through a few Bible Studies. But that is not discipleship training. Discipleship training entails the labour pains of childbirth through which lay people totally commit themselves to Christ. Let's reiterate. What is discipleship training? It is labouring to give birth to those who will give up everything to follow Jesus and obey Him, in spite of the fact that the result may not be totally satisfactory. Discipleship training is the work of reshaping a person who will do his best to pay the necessary price to follow Jesus.

---

9. Norval Geldenhuys, *Commentary on the Gospel of Luke* (Grand Rapids: Eerdmans, 1968), 399.

Chapter 15

Witness to the Gospel

The Disciples' Ultimate Mission

Strictly speaking, the ultimate commission Jesus gave to His disciples was to bear witness. He called people out of the world to be His witnesses. In the Gospel of Luke and in Acts, the words 'witness' or 'to testify' are often used inseparably with the calling of the disciples. Luke uses the word 'witness' in two instances: first to refer to the witnessing of the apostles who were the eye-witnesses of the death and resurrection of Jesus, then to refer to the witnessing done by those who believed in Jesus as a result of hearing the message of the apostles.[1]

Just before His ascension, Jesus commanded the disciples to proclaim the gospel. Setting forth the premise that repentance and forgiveness of sins will be preached in His name to all nations beginning at Jerusalem, Jesus declared to the disciples, 'You are witnesses of these things' (Luke 24:48). He also prophesied that 'when the Holy Spirit comes on you ... you will be my witnesses' (Acts 1:8). This prophecy was fulfilled in the witness of the apostles at and after Pentecost (Acts 1:22; 2:32; 3:15; 5:31; 10:41).

However, the ministry of witnessing was not limited to the apostles. When Jesus said, 'You are witnesses of these things' in Jerusalem, the apostles were not the only

---

1. H. Strathmann, 'martus,' *T.D.N.T. Vol. IV*, 492.

people present. We know that other disciples were also there among them (Luke 24:33). The Lord's command was given to all who were present at that place. Later, all 120 disciples who were gathered in Mark's upper room became Christ's witnesses. Stephen was also a witness for Jesus (Acts 22:20).

It is necessary to note that Stephen was called to be a witness even though he had not been with the apostles to personally observe all that Jesus had said and done. Soon afterwards, he became a martyr. Both words, 'witness' and 'martyr', are derived from the same root. In those days, witnesses of Jesus had to be prepared to lose even their lives. It was not Stephen's martyrdom that made him a witness; rather he became a martyr because he was a witness.

We can see the closeness of the relationship between 'disciple' and 'witness' by looking at the frequent usage of the verb 'to send' (*apostello, pempo*) together with the word 'disciple' in the gospels and in Acts. 'To send' is used as many as 215 times, most often in the context of Jesus sending out the disciples as witnesses. Luke's use of the title 'apostle' to refer to the twelve disciples also strongly supports the fact that 'disciples' are 'witnesses for Jesus'. This is because the word 'apostle' (*apostolos*) contains the meaning of 'being sent'. A disciple is one who is sent, not one who sends. There is no instance in the Bible where the word 'apostle' is used to indicate the act of sending.[2]

Inner Urgings of the Holy Spirit

It is not difficult to find out how passionate the thousands of male and female disciples of the early church were in witnessing for Jesus. They were not coerced or commanded to be bear witnesses for Jesus. It is amazing

2. K. H. Rengstorf, *T.D.N.T. Vol. IV*, 421.

that there is no record in the Bible of any instance in which the apostles command them to witness. Like the apostles, they were compelled by an inner urge: 'For we cannot help speaking about what we have seen and heard' (Acts 4:20). This explains the courage and passion with which the believers in the early church proclaimed the resurrection of Jesus; they could not be dissuaded by anyone.

What motivated them to speak thus? Was it some kind of external pressure to remember and obey the Great Commission of Jesus? There is no indication of this, or that they considered such obedience to be a burden.[3] Only the Holy Spirit could have supplied their inner drive. They all belonged to Christ by the power of the Holy Spirit. People with the Holy Spirit possessed an inner witness that corresponded to the apostolic nature of the church to which they belonged.

Whenever the apostles faced a crisis as witnesses of the resurrection, they repeatedly experienced the fullness of the Holy Spirit. This was something God did for them, to reaffirm publicly and unequivocally the presence of the Holy Spirit, who was always at work in them to bear witness (Acts 4:8, 31; 6:8; 7:55; 13:9).

If witnessing or confessing Jesus takes place through the inner urgings of the Holy Spirit, then this should be seen as a general phenomenon that can be expected of all believers universally. The Holy Spirit is a gift given to all who are called by God (Acts 2:39). When the Holy Spirit comes, all receive power, and all become witnesses for Jesus (Acts 1:8). This demonstrates that a witness is made by the Holy Spirit, and not by men.

We often hear people say that evangelism is a spiritual gift. This is not a completely valid perspective. A spiritual

---

3. See Harry Boer, *Pentecost & Mission* (Grand Rapids: Eerdmans, 1975), 118-130.

gift is a gift that the Holy Spirit in His sovereignty gives to each person as He determines, for the purpose of serving others (1 Cor. 12:11). We do not interpret the coming of the Holy Spirit on the disciples at Pentecost as a spiritual gift in a narrow sense. Certainly there was an element of spiritual gifting in the event; however the coming of the Holy Spirit at Pentecost had a greater significance.

If evangelism is exclusively a spiritual gift, then the Holy Spirit must be held wholly responsible for our inability to evangelize. Furthermore, people will think that evangelism is an exclusive task given to those special people with the gift of evangelism. Insisting that evangelism is only a spiritual gift limits the basic purpose of the Holy Spirit's coming on the church and violates the apostolic nature of the church that He has established.

There is one passage in the Bible that speaks of evangelism as a spiritual gift. It is Ephesians 4:11, which contains the word 'evangelist'. This could appear as meaning that not everyone can proclaim the gospel, but only those who have been qualified through a special spiritual gift of evangelism. However, this verse should not be seen as a proof that evangelism is only a spiritual gift. Paul is dealing here with the duties of ministers who were called to serve the church. The roles of the apostles and prophets were callings as well as offices appointed by God (1 Cor. 12:28). Evangelist was also one of the offices appointed by God. Appropriate spiritual gifts are given along with an office. A person with the office of evangelism may have a special gift of evangelism that others do not have. However, this should not be applied generally to all believers. We must distinguish between the inner prompting to bear witness that is in everyone who has the Holy Spirit and the gift of evangelism given to those who have been called specifically for the task of evangelism. This can be likened to the difference between the faith that leads to salvation and the gift of faith given to carry out a particular task (1 Cor. 12:9).

Why Is There No Command to Witness?

We cannot help but marvel at the apparent lack of any command in the New Testament given to the laity to evangelize. 2 Timothy 4:2 which we frequently quote – 'Preach the Word; be prepared in season and out of season' – is, strictly speaking, a command given to Timothy, who was a pastor. The New Testament is strangely silent on the subject of evangelism. The same is true concerning the assembly of the church. Apart from Hebrews 10:25, there is no other passage where believers are encouraged to gather together diligently. Evangelism and assembling together are vitally important to the life of the church. Voltaire, who was an ardent opponent of Christianity, advised the king that he should get rid of Sunday if he wanted to wipe out Christianity. If the church were to neglect or abandon evangelism and meeting together, it would only be a matter of time before Christianity would disappear from the face of the earth. Then, why is it that the Bible is excessively economical in its commands to evangelize and to meet together? Isn't this in the same vein as the command to 'pray unceasingly'? Here once again we can only be amazed. The fact is that despite the scarcity of these commands in the Bible, the early church was incredibly dedicated to evangelism and meeting together.

The key to understanding this phenomenon is the inner urgings of the Holy Spirit: 'We cannot help speaking about what we have seen and heard'. Witnessing for Jesus is an instinctive matter for those who belong to the Holy Spirit. 'Instinctive' means that it does not wait to be commanded. Instinct does not need a command. The urge to speak of what has been seen and heard precedes the command.

> There is no direct command of evangelism mentioned in the New Testament because of the power of the gospel and its self efficacy. After Pentecost, people voluntarily began to witness. There was no need of a commandment to evangelize.[4]

If we truly believe that the Holy Spirit has come to mold the eschatological church into a community of witnesses, and that He will be with the church till the end of the age in order to continue on with the work, then none of the expressions such as 'self-evident', 'natural', 'inner urge', or 'a new instinct' should feel awkward. The Holy Spirit is still in the church today, making His church apostolic. Yet, why is it that today's lay people do not seem to experience the inner urge to witness? Believers' lives as witnesses correspond to the essence of the church. Why is this not clear?

Verbal Witness
There is a problem that we cannot afford to overlook as we consider the relationship between 'a disciple' and 'a witness'. It is the fact that evangelism, as mentioned in the gospels and in the book of Acts, was always carried out by verbal proclamation. The disciples, as witnesses, were to speak about the gospel, and not simply to make an impression on others through their good deeds. Thus, some even claim that there is no indication in the New Testament that the early church understood discipleship from the vantage point of the moral act of imitating Christ.[5] This is indeed an interesting insight. Why

---

4. Robert Recker, *Witness in Word and Deed* (Grand Rapids: Baker, 1975), 375.
5. K. H. Rengstorf, *T.D.N.T. Vol. IV*, 455.

were these believers in the early church more intent on proclaiming Jesus as the Saviour and Lord of the world than on imitating Him as their ideal ethical model? Why did they prioritize the prayer, 'Now, Lord, consider their threats and enable your servants to speak your word with great boldness' (Acts 2:29)?

As we all know, the Lord heard their prayer and instantly filled them with the Holy Spirit so that they might become bold witnesses of the gospel (Acts 4:31). When a persecution broke out in Jerusalem, they were scattered everywhere and preached the gospel wherever they went (Acts 8:4). They so dedicated themselves wholly and single-mindedly to proclaiming Jesus with their mouths that they even appeared as though they were not interested in the moral aspect of imitating the perfect character of Jesus. They were persecuted because of their words, and not because of their good deeds. Good deeds rarely bring about persecution for the gospel. Strictly speaking, good deeds alone cannot be considered as a complete witness. Therefore, witnessing without the spoken words of the gospel cannot save the world. Now and then, there are those who think that they are witnessing for Christ through their good deeds. However, unless they open their mouths, the Jesus they think is being revealed through their deeds might not be the same Jesus who died the redemptive death on the cross.

For hundreds of years after the death of the twelve apostles and their successors, the Christians in the early church did not give up witnessing for Christ with their mouths even in the midst of persecution.

There were no missionary societies, no missionary institutions, no organized efforts in the ante-Nicene age, and yet in less than 300 years from the death of St. John, the whole population of the Roman Empire which then represented the civilized world was nominally Christianized.... Every congregation was a missionary society, and every Christian believer a missionary, inflamed by the love of Christ to convert his fellow-man... Every Christian told his neighbor, the laborer to his fellow-laborer, the slave to his fellow-slave, the servant to his master and mistress, the story of his conversion, as a mariner tells the story of the rescue from shipwreck.[6]

There are a good number of people around us who secretly scorn verbally bearing witness to Jesus, contending that it is more important and productive to witness through actions rather than through words in this contemporary age. However, let us refresh our memories here. Witnessing without words is not the witnessing the Bible speaks of. 'And how can they hear without someone preaching to them?' (Rom. 10:14). Why can't they hear? It is because witnessing without words lacks the concrete and specific gospel of Jesus, no matter how beautiful and good the deeds may be.

We are not repudiating witnessing through deeds by saying that true witnessing is done through words. Deeds are as important as words. Denial of either words or deeds in witnessing leads to serious problems. The fact that evangelising with words prevailed in the early church reminds us of the words of the sage, 'Even a live dog is better off than a dead lion' (Eccles. 9:4). It must be borne in mind that continually emphasising only witnessing through deeds could lead to promoting ourselves as good, instead of Jesus Christ who is the only proper object of the invitation to 'come and see'.

Training a lay person to become a disciple of Christ involves making him into a witness who confesses and

---

6. Philip Schaff, *History of the Christian Church Vol.II* (Grand Rapids: Eerdmans, 1967), 20-21.

testifies of Jesus in all spheres of his life. One of the ways to diagnose the health of discipleship training is to observe how much each trainee wants to speak about Jesus. Healthy discipleship training produces witnesses who cannot suppress the inner urgings of the Holy Spirit. Discipleship training helps the laity to be filled with Jesus Christ who lives in their hearts. Then not only will they joyfully boast of and confess Jesus, but their lives and characters will also emit the fragrance of Christ.

One of the problems that pastors are facing today is that we have too many lay people whose deeds stink because their mouths are sealed. Have you seen anyone who proclaims Jesus with his mouth but does not try to be like Jesus in doing good deeds?

Chapter 16

The Servant

The Example of Jesus

In the New Testament, being a disciple of Jesus and serving others went 'hand in hand'. The words 'servant' (*doulos*), which is a noun and 'to serve' (*diakoneo*), a verb, appear frequently as a pair in the Bible (Matt. 20:27-28; Mark 10:44-45; Luke 12:37). The word 'servant' indicates one's status, and thus refers to the kind of person one should become as a disciple of Christ. 'To serve' emphasizes function rather than identity or status, and thus teaches how a disciple who has Christ as his master should conduct himself in life.[1]

A disciple of Jesus must become a servant who serves. This is not incidental but a necessary and vital matter. This is a matter of essence and thus no one can be exempt. Why is that? Disciples of Jesus cannot evade servanthood, because it is the example that Jesus has shown us. Jesus came into this world, taking on the very nature of a servant (Phil. 2:7-8). And He lived in this world as a servant. 'But I am among you as one who serves' (Luke 22:27b). His whole life was a process of sacrificial devotion in which He gave Himself unsparingly for the world that He loved. During the Last Supper, Jesus served the disciples by washing their feet with His own hands. By that act, Jesus was teaching the disciples, whose necks were

---

1. T. F. Torrance, *Service in Jesus Christ* (Grand Rapids: Eerdmans, 1975), 1-2.

stiff with pride, that a true disciple is one who serves. 'Now that I, your Lord and Teacher, have washed your feet, you also should wash one another's feet. I have set you an example that you should do as I have done for you' (John 13:14-15). The sacrifice of His life on the cross as the sacrificial lamb was the final confirmation of Jesus' true servanthood. 'For even the Son of Man did not come to be served, but to serve, and to give his life as a ransom for many' (Mark 10:45).

A disciple who totally commits himself and follows Jesus cannot help but learn from, and imitate the example shown by his teacher. If he hesitates in becoming a servant, then he is a fool who thinks that a servant is greater than his master. Foreseeing that people with the title 'disciple' can easily fall into such danger, Jesus warned them in advance, 'I tell you the truth, no servant is greater than his master, nor is a messenger greater than the one who sent him. Now that you know these things, you will be blessed if you do them' (John 13:16-17). Blessing for a disciple lies in knowing that he is a servant and that he is not greater than his master, and in acting accordingly. Honour will follow disciples who do not forget that they are only unworthy servants, no matter how much they serve. 'So you also, when you have done everything you were told to do, should say, "We are unworthy servants; we have only done our duty"'(Luke 17:10). To such a humble servant, the master finally bestows praise and honour: 'Well done, good and faithful servant! You have been faithful with a few things. I will put you in charge of many things. Come and share your master's happiness!' (Matt. 25:21).

In order to join Jesus in His servanthood, a disciple must be prepared to suffer. To Jesus, there was no difference between being a servant and dying on the cross. A disciple's mission cannot be accomplished without being prepared to lose his life. The place where Jesus sends His disciples is an evil world controlled by the prince of the world.

Thus, a servant must drink from the cup of his master (Matt. 20:23), and be prepared to face calamities along with his master (John 16:33). In this sense, Bonhoeffer was not exaggerating when he said, 'When Christ calls people to become disciples, He is calling them to die.'[2]

Therefore, from the servant's standpoint, giving up one's life is to live and saving one's life is to die (Matt. 16:24-25).

> *The aim of Jesus and his disciples is not to set up a human order in this world. Their concern is with the kingdom of God and the age of glory. But they must pass through suffering and death to reach this goal. This determines at once the attitude of all whom God calls to His kingdom. The point of suffering is to be found in the service therein accomplished. This is what makes suffering sacrificial.*[3]

In other words, it means that servanthood and suffering have an inseparable and functional relationship. Servanthood is not just a part of the character and life of a disciple who follows Jesus, but the core of the character. It is not something to be carried out occasionally but continually. Suffering as a servant is a written guarantee of discipleship (John 15:19).

The Necessity of Witnessing and Confessing
Disciples cannot evade servanthood, because the gospel demands it. The subject of their proclamation is Jesus Christ (Mark 1:1). God's love is concentrated in Jesus,

---

2. D. Bonhoeffer, *The Cost of Discipleship* (New York: Macmillan, 1975), 79.
3. H. W. Beyer, 'diakonia.' *T.D.N.T. Vol. II*, 85-86.

and that love spreads from and works through His sacrificial death. On the cross, He has opened the springs of righteousness from which the whole world can drink. 'This is how God showed his love among us: He sent his one and only Son into the world that we might live through him' (1 John 4:9).

To Jesus, love was a matter of will and action, because in God's law of love, love is always expressed through action. God's love becomes visible and flows into the hearts of people through the sacrifices of a servant. There is a profound truth in the fact that the word *agapao*, which denotes 'agape love', is almost always used only in passages associated with Jesus. Jesus never showed or spoke of hypocritical love devoid of the sacrificial act of a servant. Therefore, a disciple of Jesus Christ must become a servant in order to be a witness. Together with his words that testify of Christ, his actions must show Jesus Christ who sacrificed Himself in love. It is impossible to become a witness for Jesus without becoming a servant. The life of a disciple must be thoroughly constrained by the gospel that he proclaims. In order to proclaim the gospel, a disciple must love his neighbour as himself (Matt. 22:39). Love must be given away (Matt. 5:42), and serve gladly (Mark 10:42-45; Luke 22:24-27). Only then, can we become consistent and trustworthy witnesses for Christ.

Jesus' love had a purpose. We are His disciples, and thus our love must have the same purpose also. The purpose was to find the lost sheep. In the parable of the Good Samaritan, Jesus taught the disciples three points about His mission (Luke 10:33ff). First, to whom should they show their agape love? To a traveller who was mugged by robbers and left half dead. Second, what is the purpose of loving him? To save his life. Third, how are they to show the agape love? By serving him with the readiness to even give up their lives if needed. The Apostle John solemnly declares the servanthood of discipleship in the following: 'This is how we know what love is: Jesus Christ laid down his life for us. And we ought to lay down our lives for our brothers'(1 John 3:16).

> But self-sacrifice is not just a revelation of love to be admired; it is an example to copy. We ought to lay down our lives for the brethren, or our profession to love them is an empty boast. We ought to do this, as a definite Christian obligation, because we belong to Christ, just as we ought to follow His example in all things and walk even as he walked (1 John 2:6).[4]

Volunteering

We should not forget that servanthood in discipleship is voluntary. A disciple is not forced to become a slave. He becomes a servant of Christ with joy. In the Old Testament, there were slaves who loved their masters and thus volunteered to serve them for life. Their ears were pierced with an awl to show that they served their masters not grudgingly under compulsion, but joyfully with love (Exod. 21:5-6). A disciple of Christ is like one of these servants. He does not serve grudgingly under compulsion.

As we have seen so far, to become a disciple of Christ means to become a servant. This implies following Jesus' example, and pledging obedience and allegiance to the Lord. Not only that, it denotes serving in this world to the point of giving up one's life. A disciple of Jesus knows that the message he proclaims is not so much a teaching but a promise by which he pledges to serve gladly with love. And it becomes a law in his life by which he cannot deny that he is a disciple of Christ. A disciple of Jesus is someone who willingly binds himself to the law

4. John Stott, *The Epistles of John* (Grand Rapids: Eerdmans, 1975), 143.

of love through the words of his mouth. But he does not consider this a heavy burden. Rather, he is filled with thanksgiving, for he considers it a joy and a blessing to follow the Lord.

Discipleship training in the church is to teach the trainees the character and life of a loving servant who resembles Christ. Discipleship training is not about explaining servanthood, but about helping the trainees to live out the life of a servant. Here, a leader must bear in mind that Jesus did not merely talk about his life as a servant, but demonstrated His servanthood through his actions. The power of love was in His actions, not just in His words. And this is the principle of the incarnation. Without emptying Himself by taking on the form of a servant, the victory on the cross would not have followed. Words alone do not bring any changes. As a person does not change by putting on a beautiful garment, a servant of love is not produced by beautiful words. We ought to learn that leaders must teach by exemplifying their servanthood in their actions before the trainees. As such, Paul always lived his life as an exemplary model:'Follow my example, as I follow the example of Christ' (1 Cor. 11:1).

I am afraid that we give a lot of lip service to being loving servants who follow the example of Christ, but secretly trample it under foot. There are many who would like to be first and be served in the church. The clergy seem especially vulnerable to this. What is the reason for becoming so stiff-necked and stubborn once a person becomes an elder? Many seem to be ignorant of the principle of God's kingdom that the greater one is, the lower one should become. Many forget that authority in the church comes from serving, and not from being served. A person who has been a believer for a long time, who is known for his strong faith, and who prays much from early morning on, should be more like Christ, who was a servant to others. But the reality seems to show otherwise. When the principles of the world replace the principles of the kingdom of God then the church reeks of human guile.

What is discipleship training? It is about healing such chronic ills. It is a ministry of the Holy Spirit that brings both the clergy and the laity to a place of lowly servanthood.

We have discussed three basic elements of discipleship. The world will see Jesus in a person who trusts, who witnesses, and who serves through his character and life. The zenith of discipleship training will be reached when Christ is reflected in and through our lives. In other words, the world needs to see the reflection of Jesus in the transformation and maturity that take place in us. Is this not the most pressing ministry for the laity, who must daily live and work in the world with so many unbelievers?

Chapter 17

The Nature of the Church Will Change

For the contemporary church to recover its apostolicity and discipleship, it will have to undergo fundamental changes. Discipleship is the self-image of the laity that corresponds to the apostolic nature of the church. Many unhealthy symptoms of the churches we see around us demonstrate the urgent need for reformation in the basic nature of the church. This is certainly more urgent than revival.

If we continue to seek numeric growth of the church prior to reforming its basic nature, the church's life and spirituality will face a crisis. If we were to implement the ministry philosophy of making disciples of the laity in our local churches, what changes would take place? Let me suggest a few fundamental changes that can be expected to take place.

A Renewed Image of the Church

It has been stated earlier that the church is a community of the chosen people who have been called by God to worship, to grow, and to witness. Contemporary churches, however, seem to be abusing this definition of the church. There is a tendency to fall into narcissism, engrossed in the privilege of being a community of the chosen and called people. Many in the church are under the illusion that they are already the raptured bride of Christ. Their attitude is like that of the Judaism of Jesus' time: insisting on its privileges while being oblivious to its mission. But if the visible church is the people of God called out of the world, then it is also the disciple of Christ sent into the world. With privilege there is responsibility. Why isn't this fact taken seriously? Jesus' summon to the disciples, 'Follow Me', assumes the secondary command, 'As the Father sent me to the world, I also send you'.

The image of the gathering church also contains the image of a dispersing church. Being called and being sent are not two separate notions. They are two sides of one coin. When a church rediscovers its apostolicity, it will clearly reflect this twofold nature. Then the church will not remain fixated on the gathering of the church as if that is an end in itself. Instead, gathering together will be seen as a means to accomplish the ultimate goal of the church. God can receive glory just through the sheer existence of the church, because he has purchased it with the blood of his Son. However, he is more glorified when the church becomes the body of Christ that serves the world. The church has to become a school where the people of God receive spiritual training, a workshop for God's laborers, a barrack to equip the soldiers of the cross for battles, a refuge for the tired and oppressed, a lighthouse that offers the last hope to those facing the storms of life, and a power plant that lights the lamp of the individual life and supplies the spiritual power for society through the life of believers. We believe and expect that such an image of the church will become all the more evident through discipleship training.

A Healthy Self-image of the Laity Can Be Recovered
Reforming the nature of the church depends a great deal on how lay people see themselves. If the lay people think of themselves as mere guests of the church,

then they will always be content with remaining under the protective umbrella of the clergy. They will be like lethargic children who always respond passively. This is not fitting for the church flying the flag of Jesus Christ who has won the victory. Unfortunately however, many churches are producing lay people who think of such a morbid self-image as normal. Discipleship is a biblical strategy that can change a lay person's way of thinking. What amazing transformations would take place if those who confess Jesus as their Saviour in contemporary churches could identify themselves with the disciples in the book of Acts! This might not be as hard as we think.

It is heartbreaking to see many churches looking to other areas in order to reform the nature of the church. However, reform cannot be achieved by changing programs or by renovating the church environment. A pastor in America was obsessed with the compulsive idea that there was no hope for the church unless there was a change of some sort. So one day, he suddenly moved the pulpit to the middle of the sanctuary and decorated it like a boxing ring. He then had the congregation worship around the pulpit. He was hoping that this would change the cold and passive attitude of his members. However, within a month, more than a half of the members left the church. This might be an extreme example, but it is no different from a woman who foolishly expects her marriage to improve if she rearranges the bedroom furniture. We must not commit such follies. Apply discipleship to change the self-image of the laity. Then the nature of the church will change beyond belief. If you find this difficult to believe, visit the churches that have been blessed through discipleship training. Do so until you are convinced.

Converting Guardianship into Training Ministry

A pastor is a shepherd. The words 'shepherding' or 'ministry' have come from Jesus' command 'take care of my sheep'. Taking care of sheep contains a very active meaning. It is 'teaching them to obey' (Matt. 28:20). 'To obey' denotes an active ministry that continues to lead believers to experience transformation of their characters to become more like Christ and carry out God's will in their lives. We replaced 'teaching them to obey' with the word 'training'. Ministry that sets forth training as a premise has a specific goal. Training without a goal does not make any sense. What is that goal? It is to bear much fruit. It is for the sheep to produce many offspring and thereby please God our master.

Therefore, the best ministry is to strengthen the sheep through training in order for them to self-produce. Guardianship ministry weakens lay people. They will always wait to be spoon-fed, and will only think of themselves. Instead of planning big things, they argue and clash with one another about little things. Because of their narrow perspective, they are not able to break away from the perimeter of the 'us only' attitude. What can the Lord do with such a church? A ministry focused on protection of the sheep is bound to petrify the nature of the church. Discipleship training can eradicate such ills. Lay people can become strong and productive through discipleship training.

The Whole Church Can Recover Cooperative and Dynamic Relationships

Once discipleship training that encourages cooperative ministry among the laity reaches a certain stage, various kinds of organic relationships will develop. These organic relationships facilitate the unity among believers to share their spiritual life and serve one another in love. Once the church members cease to see themselves as independent entities but as belonging to the body and existing to serve other members, the church will be healed of the many ills that have been caused by barren and lifeless organizations in the church. Discipleship training educates the laity to become functional people who can serve the body of Christ through cooperative ministries in the church. It also creates various conditions necessary both in and outside the church for such cooperative ministries to bear fruit. As a result, mutual relationships between believers will develop through special spiritual fellowships mentioned in the Bible (Col. 3:16; 1 John 1:3-4). This is *koinonia* that believers experience by sharing the Word in the Holy Spirit and serving one another with love. This fellowship has totally different characteristics from mere functional or organizational fellowships that form for a period of time in order to complete a task.

Try discipleship training. Within two to three years, you will observe the church changing from an organizational malfunctioning entity into a properly functioning organic and cooperative body.

From Clergy-Centred to Lay-Centred

Some theologians lament that although it has been almost 500 years since Luther proclaimed the priesthood of all believers, the church structures still deny this doctrine.[1] Although on the surface there seem to be many churches saying that there is no difference between the clergy and the laity, many of them conduct church affairs as if only the clergy are priests. This is an aberrant phenomenon observed in many churches. The authoritarianism of the clergy and their desire to monopolize power erodes the ground upon which the laity can stand as priests.

---

1. Lawrence Richards, *New Face for the Church* (Grand Rapids: Zondervan, 1970), 38.

155

Changing this chronic state of the church might be as difficult as the Reformation of the Middle Ages. But if we understand correctly what a lay-centred church is, then the outlook is not as dismal as it appears.

It has already been pointed out that this is in no way condemning the clergy system. A lay-centred church is a church in which the clergy serve the lay people, enabling them to find their rightful place and fulfill their role as the principal body of the church. In order for this to happen, the clergy must seek a lower place and humble themselves. However, this does not have to be understood as there being a greater and lesser position. When lay people find their rightful place, the position of the clergy will be modified accordingly. Discipleship training can change a church - in which the laity exist to serve the clergy - into a healthy church where the clergy exists to serve the laity. When this succeeds, I believe both the clergy and the laity will thrive.

Lay Leadership in Ministries Will Increase
One of the greatest anguishes for a pastor is the sense of loneliness stemming from the thought that there is no one else to work apart from him. Consequently, he carries a burden beyond his ability and eventually faces a burnout crisis whereby he loses his energy and desire. In the end, he unwittingly becomes a victim of the peace-at-any-price mentality. This is not an unusual phenomenon. Just as Moses at one time thought he could by himself take care of all the lawsuits brought by the people and did not try to raise leaders who could share the burden, many pastors are unwilling to train the lay members to partner with them in ministry and share the burden.

The kind of ministry that I refer to here is not that of being an usher or the head of an evangelism department. I am referring to pastoral and spiritual ministry that nurtures others through the Word and prayer. It's about sharing the gospel with neighbours and spiritually healing the sick and the wounded. It signifies sharing with the trained lay people the ministry that Jesus did while He was in the world – that is, the ministry of preaching, teaching and healing. Which church will harvest more: the church where only the pastor works or the church where the pastor works together with 50 other lay leaders? There is no other way to produce lay leaders than through discipleship training. If you are a pastor, do not hesitate, but begin today. The sooner the clergy and the lay leaders work together, the better it will be. I once saw an American church in Los Angeles introducing itself in a Christian magazine as a 'Church with 900 Pastors'. How enviable it is that they can boast in such a manner when there is only one ordained clergyman in that church!

Consistent Church Growth

When the number of lay leaders increases through discipleship training and the church members continue to be nurtured through those lay leaders, an impetus for church revival is generated. The daily life of the lay people becomes their mission field. Their conversations can function as a pathway that leads to the gospel. Everything they do can be used as both direct and indirect opportunities for saving souls. From this, revival and continuing evangelism can be expected in the church. We should not think of church revival as a result that follows some kind of event. Growth or revival should be viewed as a matter of the nature of the church. Desirable growth happens naturally and continuously. When discipleship training takes root, the church will be able to grow even without taking unnatural and unwarranted measures. How could it not be full of sheep when they are constantly giving birth?

A few more things about church growth will be said in addition since this is of major interest to all pastors. It is strange that there are many who think that it is unreasonable to expect the church to grow through discipleship training. Of course, there are various ways for the church to grow. Only those who are ignorant of the wisdom of the Holy Spirit and the diversity of God's grace would insist that discipleship training is the only way for church growth. However, it is also an immense misunderstanding to see a huge gulf between discipleship training and church growth. In a nutshell, when discipleship training is anchored in the very heart and nature of the church, then a healthy growth can be expected. Neither a sudden growth nor a prolonged stagnation is desirable. A healthy child does not have to worry about growing. Likewise a healthy church does not have to suffer from growth neurosis. Go ahead and carry out discipleship training. The nature of your church will be transformed for healthy growth.

There is something that must be kept in mind. Discipleship training should not be used only as a means for growth. If church growth is the only desired result of discipleship training, then it will deteriorate before long. Discipleship training does not have much to offer pastors who want instant and hasty church growth. However, it has much to offer pastors who desire a natural and enduring growth. It will first of all transform the pastors' sermons into messages that speak to the audience. Not only will pastors themselves be blessed as they lead discipleship training, they will also learn the spiritual needs and the language of the lay people. How can such pastors' sermons remain unchanged? Furthermore, pastors will get to develop a new paradigm for leadership by doing discipleship training. Traditional leadership that asks what can be done *for* the laity will be transformed into a leadership that asks what can be done *with* the laity. Discipleship training demands much from the laity. It challenges the trainees to read the Bible, pray unceasingly, witness, be a good spouse, and be committed, and so on. All these challenges may cause some pastors to worry that some lay people might leave the church. However, it is more likely that the opposite will happen.

Roger Finke, who has analysed and diagnosed the growth and decline pattern of the American churches for the last 200 years, reached a very encouraging conclusion. According to Finke, the mainline denominations have declined at a rapid rate since the latter half of the sixties, mainly because the clergy demanded too little from the laity in an effort to please them. On the other hand, evangelical churches shone in their growth because the clergy demanded much from the laity. Based on this analysis, he offers three qualities of a growing church.

> First, a strong church is strict. The stricter it is, the stronger it is. Second, a church that loses its strictness loses its strength. Third, strictness has a tendency to deteriorate into leniency.[2]

Discipleship training has a tendency to make the church strict. It gives a strong impression of burdening the laity. The fact is, however, these challenging characteristics of discipleship training function positively for church growth. This has been proven through many Korean churches that have been growing steadily through discipleship training.

I say it once again. Do you want a healthy church with natural and continual growth? Go forward with discipleship training. Before long, the vision that Isaiah

---

2. Finke, *The Churching of America, 1776–1990* (Rutgers, 1992, 1975), 143. Chapter 7.

saw will become our reality: 'The least of you will become a thousand, the smallest a mighty nation. I am the Lord; in its time I will do this swiftly' (Isa. 60:22).

Part 1
TODAY'S CHURCH AND THE LAITY
INTRODUCTION

Part 2
MINISTRY PHILOSOPHY
ECCLESIOLOGY

Part 3
MINISTRY STRATEGY
DISCIPLESHIP

Part 4
MINISTRY METHOD
DISCIPLESHIP TRAINING

Part 5
MINISTRY FIELD
DISCIPLES

Chapter 18

The Purpose of Discipleship Training

Once we recognize that discipleship is a biblical answer that can meet the demands of the new era and an important ministry strategy that can change the nature of the church and reform its image, then as the next step, we must find practical ways to apply discipleship to our ministry fields. How can we build up the laity as Jesus' disciples well grounded in discipleship? Discipleship training is a practical ministry method that answers this question.

Clearing Up Misconceptions

In order to do discipleship training correctly, a few misconceptions must first be removed. Otherwise, it will be difficult, for those without clear answers to these common misconceptions, to persist with the training to the end.

To be honest, discipleship training has been greatly misunderstood as a result of leaders who do not know what true disciple making is about and yet claim that they are training disciples. Discipleship training has also suffered from various misunderstandings caused by those leaders who criticize this method in order to defend themselves when they fail to carry out the training.

In addition, some people seem to draw erroneous conclusions based on some abstract phenomenon or notion, without having done any in-depth study or research. In whatever ways these misunderstandings have come about, they need to be corrected.

The primary misconception is to see discipleship training as merely a Bible study. Some say that discipleship training only emphasizes Bible studies, and has brought about depression in Korean churches.

Until now discipleship training played a big part in the growth of the Korean church. However discipleship training is the cause for the recent halt in the Korean church's growth and for its stagnation. Discipleship training makes disciples by training people to listen and to speak. The result is that the Korean church members have become people who listen and speak well. There are indeed many positive effects of the training. However, it cannot be denied that there are more believers who are content with simply learning and gaining knowledge as a result of discipleship training.[1]

It is true that there are many reasons for the rise of such serious misunderstandings. There are churches that have been engaging in poor discipleship training. To give an extreme example, some churches carry out discipleship training that is too pitiful even to be considered a Bible study. In such cases, we have no answer for those who accuse discipleship training of being just another outdated method of Bible study. However, one must be able to distinguish between having a misunderstanding and making a definite assertion. Let's be clear, discipleship training is not just a Bible study! Bible study is only a tool within discipleship training. And discipleship training is not what brought stagnation to the Korean church. There is not a shred of evidence that can link discipleship training to today's stagnation. Instead, it might be more convincing to blame the leaders who remained aloof

1. Sung Hee Lee, *The Great Prediction of the Future* (Korean) 302.

from discipleship training and a large number of the laity who pretended to be faithful whilst evading what they viewed as a burdensome training.

The second misconception about discipleship training is to see it as a course for simply producing people for evangelism and teaching. Discipleship training is more than just training someone to do evangelism.

Of course, the ultimate purpose of making disciples involves producing competent believers who will witness for Jesus in the world and serve others in the church. However, it must not be forgotten that it is very dangerous to take such a narrow and limited view of discipleship by emphasizing only its functional aspect. The focus of discipleship training has to be on learning what it means to be like Jesus and to follow Him.

The lay people must be encouraged to bear in mind the following questions all day long: 'Am I moving toward maturity of character according to the standard demonstrated by Jesus? Do I accept the fact that my calling includes both social and mission responsibilities?' To recognize as disciples of Jesus those who seem to have faith but whose character remains unchanged is to disgrace discipleship. To acknowledge someone as a disciple of Jesus, simply for the reason that he has completed a formal course of discipleship training even though he lives a double life between church and society, is to promote the secularization of the church.

If there are many lay people who complete discipleship training and become competent in leading cell groups and in evangelism but who avoid practicing social justice and helping the poor, then we have to humbly admit that we have gone far astray from the essence of discipleship training.

There is one fact that should be pointed out here. In many evangelical churches over the past half century,

there has been a strong tendency to understand discipleship training within the framework of nationwide
or worldwide evangelization. As a result, discipleship
training became known as a means for training evangelists and promoting church growth.

Consequently, many Christians who loudly proclaimed the gospel took a passive or cynical attitude toward social responsibilities. So what happened? Unfortunately, the churches in Korea experienced the tragedy
of being divided into radically conservative and radically liberal camps. The former emphasized eternal life, the
latter this present life. Ultimately both sides have made
the mistake of losing the good that is in the other.

The root of discipleship training lies in evangelical-
ism, which has a strong tendency toward conservatism.
Accordingly, it must be borne in mind that if we are not
careful, there is a great possibility of developing a passive position about the laity's social responsibility. Genuine discipleship training clearly instructs the lay people
about their calling as priests to offer their lives as living
sacrifices pleasing to God, and not to separate the sacred
and secular in their daily lives.

In the 1974 Lausanne Worldwide Evangelization International Convention, the following declaration was
made about Christianity's social responsibility:

> *Gospel evangelization, politics, and social participation are*
> *obligations for all Christians. Social welfare is both a bridge for*
> *spreading the gospel and at the same time a result of preaching*
> *the gospel. Thus these two can be considered as companions.*
> *Gospel is the root, and thus both sharing the gospel and social*
> *responsibility are its fruits.*[2]

Therefore, one must discern that to regard discipleship
training simply as a course for rearing evangelists or as a
ministry for leading cell groups is a misunderstanding.

A third misconception is that discipleship training is possible only with the lay people from the middle classes or higher – that is, those with a relatively high standard of living. It is strange to me that so many pastors have this misconception. It might be a very convincing pretext for defending oneself for not doing discipleship training. However, one must know that this is an extremely jaundiced perspective. Rather than giving a long explanation here, relating a short episode will be more helpful to remove this misunderstanding.

About ten years ago, I had an opportunity to give a lecture at a seminary in Seoul to a group of young pastors. The requested theme was 'Discipleship Training and Pastoral Ministry'. During the question and answer session after the lecture, a pastor in his early thirties abruptly stood up and said the following: 'From listening to your lecture, it looks like discipleship training is something that can be done in targeted areas, where Christians are college graduates and have a high standard of living. Not long ago, I planted a church in the Inchon slum neighbourhood. I don't think discipleship training has the slightest chance of survival in this church, and I would like to hear your opinion'.

It was a very thoughtful question. However, I could not deny the fact that his thinking was wrong. Jesus never said 'make disciples only of people with a high standard of living'. Before answering the young pastor, I asked him a question. I said, 'Thank you for asking a good question. But before answering you, may I ask you a question? If I were the pastor ministering at your church, do you think I would do discipleship training? Or do you think I wouldn't?'

The young pastor brought his hand up to his head, and for a slight second he seemed embarrassed. Then he

---

2. John Stott, *Issues Facing Christian Today* (Basingstoke: Marshalls), 26.

answered, 'If you were the pastor, then you would'. And he sat down.

The key to discipleship training lies in the kind of person the leader is and not in the kind of people the laity are. Even now there are pastors in farm churches and poor village churches who are bearing much fruit through discipleship training, using creative methods.

Besides those mentioned above, all sorts of misunderstandings are still rampant. To name a few: 'Discipleship training creates fanatics who abandon their family and business.' 'It makes the church into an academy.' 'It takes passion away from the laity.' 'It is weak in prayer and in spiritual training.' 'It makes the pastor ill.' However, misunderstandings are always just misunderstandings. Do you want to do discipleship training? Let's begin by removing the misunderstandings first.

Why Call It Training?
I don't know exactly when making disciples began to be labeled as 'training', but I believe there is a purpose in using the term. Traditional churches have used the word 'education' rather than 'training'. Perhaps that is why there has been a strong negative reaction for some time against the word 'training' itself. Now it seems that the terminology is being accepted as a normal term in most churches. However, understanding why we use the word 'training' will be helpful.

The phrase 'discipleship training' is somewhat coloured by a lack of confidence in the traditional educational methods of the established churches. The phrase seems to contain a strong assertion that the Sunday school format of education (which uses systematic and formal educational environments to convey knowledge) has reached its limit, and thus more constructive and specific educational methods are needed. In other words, the term 'training' has perhaps emerged as a re-action against the education that seems to have failed in established churches.

Hee Seung Lee's Korean Dictionary defines 'training' as: 'A practical action put into practice in order to reach a definite purpose or standard. It is considered to be a part of studying.' According to this definition, several practical features are necessary in order to refer to making disciples as 'training'. First, discipleship training must have a definite goal. Second, it should establish a specific training method. Third, it needs to have trainees who are fit for training. And last, one should be able to expect practical results from the training.

Accordingly, when we begin discipleship training, we must carefully consider the goal, the target, specific training methods, and actual results, in order to carry out proper training.

The term 'training' itself seems so forceful that sometimes we are reluctant to use it. Yet there seems to be no better term in obeying the solemn command of Jesus to make disciples.

> *Training can be another side of discipleship. Discipleship without training is like waiting to run the marathon without ever training for it…. Spiritual training is continually making open time and space for God. Solitude needs training, worship needs training, and serving others requires training, too. All these require that we prepare the time and place to acknowledge and respond to the merciful presence of God with us.*[3]

The Purpose of Discipleship Training

Although the purpose of discipleship training has re-ceived sufficient treatment already, it will be helpful to clarify it once more since it is the subject under discus-sion here.

What is the ultimate purpose of discipleship training? To state it succinctly, it is to ascertain and establish the self-image of a believer who is to be Christ-like in character and in life. It is to make believers who want to be like Jesus and live like Jesus. The disciples we need to make are disciples of Jesus. They are neither disciples of the Apostle Paul nor disciples of the senior pastor. Jesus Christ is the purpose, the standard, and the focus of the training. Without Him remains nothing. To become a disciple of Jesus means to serve Jesus as one's King and Lord, and to follow, obey, and learn from Him. Both the aspects of character and ministry are included here.

Discipleship training must first develop a person's character to be like Jesus. The laity must become like Jesus as the Christians were in the first century church. They even received the nickname 'little Christs'. The importance of the personal commitment of a disciple is found here. Therefore, discipleship training must be the work of transforming a person. It has to make a child of God into a mature person, thoroughly equipped for every good work through the influence of the Word and the Spirit (2 Tim. 3:17).

In this sense, discipleship training can be considered as a kind of spiritual struggle in which both the pastor and the laity partake together.

In this world, where we live in human flesh, no one can become completely Christ-like. We are all on the road together. We have not yet reached the state of perfection that is free from flaws and blemishes. We are in the process of being broken and melted, and remolded into the likeness of Jesus in the hands of the Holy Spirit.

For this reason, discipleship training itself is a labour of rebirth, a closet of contrition and confession. It is hanging onto the grace of God in times of temptation

---

3. Henri Nouwen, *Bread for Journey*, (Harper Collins) February 27.

and suffering. Knowing this, one will not be able to misunderstand discipleship training as just a program of mastering a few Bible studies.

Next, discipleship training is a work that makes the laity into a people with a calling, into those who inherit the ministry of Jesus. Jesus taught and spread the good news, and healed the sick in the world. For this work he dedicated his life completely as a witness to the truth and as a servant of love.

Thus discipleship training must be a process that enables a person to dedicate himself as a witness of the gospel, a teacher of the truth, and a loving healer. One must accept Jesus' vision as one's own. Discipleship training is that which makes a person do his or her best as one called to glorify God's name, and to fulfill God's will, regardless of one's occupation and surrounding circumstances.

Based on Biblical Principles

It is distressing to see many leaders regarding this important work as someone else's task. The Lord gave ministers to the church to be both pastors and teachers at the same time, because (as the Apostle Paul teaches) they are to equip God's people for works of service so that the body of Christ may be built up (Eph. 4:11-12). To equip God's people is to strengthen and build them up for their faith to grow (Heb. 6:2), their character to mature, and for them to live a victorious life each day. In other words, it is a ministry that teaches and trains people to be filled with Christ.

Works of service provide opportunities to dedicate oneself to the ministry Jesus has commanded the church to carry out. When the training is carried out properly, the church will grow both in quality and quantity, and the kingdom of God will continue to expand. So the three elements are as follows: First is to equip God's people. Second is to put them into works of service, and third is to build up the body of Christ. It is an absolute rule of pastoral ministry not to leave out any one of these three or to reverse their order. It is a pity that we often omit whichever we want and change around the order in our pastoral ministry. It is not just a few pastors who consider equipping God's people as someone else's work. Have we not become too accustomed to rushing to put people to work before equipping them first?

This clearly defies the Word. It is the Lord's command not to put people into works of service unless they have gone through an equipping process to some degree. However, we often make the excuse that needs are urgent, and choose a less difficult route. What happens to the church as a result? In the case of Korea, I ask, 'Who is to blame for the suffocation in the life of pastoral ministry? What is causing the bitter roots to grow inside the church?' It is the foolishness of us pastors, who put believers to work before equipping them first. In some ways, we've thrown ourselves into the pit that we have dug with our own hands.

We must return to the Word without delay. A healthy pastoral ministry can be expected when we faithfully follow biblical principles. The reason I call so loudly for discipleship training is because this is the pastoral ministry method closest to the biblical principle.

If the ultimate purpose of discipleship training is for a lay person to adopt the character and life of Jesus Christ to be his own, then there are more than a few practical benefits we can expect. The most important is that we will gain many lay leaders. Moreover, the possibility to mobilize the entire church, as the successor to the apostles who were sent out into the world, will open wide.

In this sense it is correct to say that discipleship training is the method of pastoral ministry that is derived from biblical principle and purpose.

Chapter 19

Who will Lead Discipleship Training?

The Responsibility of the Pastor

It is not just once or twice that we have heard about the importance of discipleship training. For some years now, the challenge has reached most churches. Yet, a sad fact is that those pastors who need to get up and going with discipleship training are not making up their minds to do so. The sobering reality is that it is the pastor's ministry philosophy that determines the kind of lay people we have in the church. A lay person is in effect a mirror image of the senior pastor's ministry philosophy. Thus, discipleship training should be carried out by the senior pastor. It should not be entrusted to someone else. Wouldn't it be difficult to consider a child as one's own if someone else gave birth to him?

A pastor who does his best only for his own personal development and makes no effort to train the laity ought to examine his heart and evaluate for whom he is working. I believe the effectiveness of a local church pastor should be evaluated primarily by the power of the gospel made manifest in the character and life of the lay members.

A pastor should not bury his spirituality, ability, and character within himself, but should use them as the kernel of wheat that dies in the soil of the lay members and bears much fruit. Then the pastor and the laity will be able to build up a healthy church together.

There is an aspect to discipleship training that emphasizes the sacrifice of pastors. But pastors should not avoid or be afraid of it. The Lord entrusted his church to us for this work. I say once again, do not entrust discipleship training to someone else. To give up the yoke of the pastoral ministry is to give up one's happiness.

Become a Disciple First

When we decide to begin discipleship training, there is always a problem that entangles us. Although it may seem like we know everything about it, we can't quite get the feel of it when we actually try to start. A leader can handle a task much more effectively if he acquires a sense of being able to see the whole picture. The same applies to discipleship training. If a pastor is not sure and starts to lose his way from the beginning, it obviously will not last long. Thus, getting a feel for discipleship training is very important.

There are quite a number of men and women pastors who are responsible for discipleship training at SaRang Church. And I often hear from them, 'Pastor Oak, for the first two years, I did discipleship training without really knowing what it was. But I think I'm now finally beginning to get a real sense of what discipleship training is all about.'

That doesn't mean they were making disciples incorrectly for those few years. It means that they were extremely tense and were not confident in what they were doing because they couldn't quite get a feel for it. How can one acquire the sense of it from the beginning? Sharing one or two ideas may prove helpful.

The first recommendation is for the pastor himself to receive the practical training of becoming a disciple. A disciple is made by a disciple. A person cannot make someone else into a disciple without first experiencing the process of becoming a disciple himself. Karl Barth made a statement that cuts through to the heart of Jesus' command to go and make disciples of all peoples: 'Peter, go and make someone who resembles you.'[1]

Peter was already Jesus' disciple, molded in the hands of Jesus. Thus Jesus was able to command, 'Make someone like you'. Paul also states to the same effect, 'Follow my example, as I follow the example of Christ' (1 Cor. 11:1).

There are many opportunities today for a pastor to participate in discipleship training if he will only make up his mind to do so. Disciple Making Ministries International, affiliated with SaRang Church, conducts a mini-training program several times a year for pastors ministering in the rural cities of Korea. Although it cannot be totally satisfactory since the training meets either for 3 nights and 4 days or on every Monday for 8 weeks, it is being well received. One pastor came every week by plane in order to participate in the program.

The following is an actual experience of a pastor who was ecstatic about discipleship training. It was about ten years ago that he came to the seminar and caught the vision for discipleship training. However, once he decided to start, he just felt desolate. Thus he decided to test discipleship training with two young couples he had evangelized and brought to the church recently. They were careful to keep it as a secret from the church. Including the wife of the pastor, the three couples began to meet. The advantage was that these people were new believers, so he was able to lead them without feeling much strain. It was a good opportunity for the pastor to test the possibility of discipleship training and examine his own gifts and spirituality.

---

1. Francis M. Dubose, *Classics of Christian Missions* (Nashville, Broadman, 1979), 44.

A year later that pastor became a discipleship training fanatic. He could not suppress his emotions, because the changes that took place in the trainees and the fruit they bore were far beyond his expectations. He confessed that the grace and blessings he received were so great that he had many regrets for not having known about discipleship training earlier. He naturally gained confidence that he could do discipleship training, and became so passionate about the training that he can no longer think of not doing it. Isn't this indeed a great method?

Examining Ministry Philosophy

Next on the agenda, we need to consider that pastors should not take discipleship training lightly and merely as something to imitate.

Imitation that lacks conviction is like a lifeless statue. A pastoral ministry of imitation has a short life span. A pastor has to re-examine his ministry philosophy and strategy when starting discipleship training. His view of the church is an essential factor in laying the proper foundation.

Let's say that a pastor has a theological opinion which says that he alone has received a calling. Can he make disciples? And if he views the lay people as merely the object of the church and not as the subject, will he be able to feel the need for discipleship training? It would be very difficult under such circumstances. He might be able to give it a try since others are doing it, but he will not have the desire to give his life to the work of awakening the laity.

Only the leader, who has the faith to see his congregation as the heirs of the apostles who were sent out into the world, will be able to put his hand to this work of discipleship training. How can he send them out to the world empty-handed? How can he tell them to go without first equipping them with proper weapons to fight the spiritual battle? From this point of view, one's ministry philosophy is a definite yardstick to assess the success or failure of discipleship training.

The Importance of a Teaching Ministry

Another thing to bear in mind when starting discipleship training is the importance of the teaching ministry. It is rather easy to see that Jesus' ministry consisted of preaching to the crowds, teaching the disciples, and counseling individuals while He was in the world. We pastors are called to be the servants of Jesus. Therefore, following the example of Jesus' ministry would have to be considered the ideal method.

Jesus' disciples were always present among the multitudes when He preached. However, Jesus did not train the disciples with preaching only, but also taught them apart from the crowd. Teaching was much more important for the disciples than sermons. Jesus is referred to as 'rabbi' or 'teacher' over fifty times in the gospels. He was the most excellent educator – a master teacher who knew better than anyone else the effectiveness of teaching face-to-face.

Teaching is the most important skill for a pastor. God gave pastors and teachers to the church. The original text seems to require us to understand these two not as separate offices but as double functions of one office. That is, ministers are to be teachers and pastors at the same time (Eph. 4:11).[2]

This clearly explains the role of a pastor. A pastor is someone who takes care of the believers while at the same time a teacher who trains them. That is why Paul said an overseer must be able to teach (1 Tim. 3:2). Calvin

---

2. John Stott, *One People* (Downers Grove: InterVarsity Press, 1971), 45-46.

says that God designed the church for the purpose of education and explains it in the following way:

> *Despite the fact that God has the power to bring his people to perfection in a second, one can know that he desired them to be nurtured little by little to reach sainthood under the education of the church.*[3]

Nonetheless, the pain we all feel is that in actuality, pastors are too often unable to devote themselves to teaching. They often place all the importance on preaching alone.

Working out the difference between preaching and teaching is an issue that requires further research. Even in the case of Jesus, sometimes these two were clearly distinguishable, but sometimes they were not. The reformers also did not consider the two to be completely different.

> *A great sermon is indeed great teaching. And great teaching contains the preacher's character in it. Both preaching and teaching are for the ministry of spreading the Word of God. It is Jesus Christ we have to teach and Jesus Christ we have to preach to the believers. The contents are the same for both.*[4]

However, what we can say clearly from our experience in pastoral ministry is that preaching cannot fulfill the function of teaching. Moreover, there is a big difference between the sermons preached in the pulpit today and the sermons preached during the Reformation. A sermon can play a huge role in inspiring the congregation and stirring up their reactions. However, it is indeed inadequate to change a person fundamentally and to equip

---

3. John Calvin, *Institutes of the Christian Religion IV.* p. 52
4. John Piet, *The Road Ahead* (Grand Rapids: Eerdmans, 1970), 57.

him with skills and competency to fulfill his calling. In spite of it all, we are still only preaching and not teaching. How can the church not be adversely affected?

A recent survey gathered data from the pastors of traditional American churches that are experiencing a continual decline. The survey explored how these pastors prioritized their ministry activities. It showed the pastors' top priority was preaching and their most neglected ministry was teaching. The specific ranking went in the following order from the highest to the lowest: preaching, pastoral care (counseling, visiting, etc.), organization, administration, and teaching. The ranking of the actual time spent in various ministry activities, starting with the most time spent, was as follows: administration, pastoral care, preaching, organization, and teaching.[5]

This data confirms how current pastors are neglecting a teaching ministry. It is unfortunate that there is no accurate data on Korean churches, but for the most part Korean churches will not be much different from American churches. The development of curricula for practical adult education that deals with the whole person must become an immediate priority in the church. Discipleship training will become an innovative method of pastoral ministry to cure this sickness, for only the pastor whose top priority is teaching can make disciples.

---

5. Oscar Feucht, *Everyone A Minister* (St. Louise: Concordance, 1977), 97.

Chapter 20

How to Start?

Once the pastor decides that he is ready, from then on he must start the specific work of planting the particular seed called discipleship training in the soil of the church. We know well how much effort a farmer puts into cultivating the soil when he goes out to the field in spring to plant seeds. No matter how superior in quality the seed is, it cannot bear fruit if thrown on thorn bushes or on rocky ground.

In order to bear much fruit in discipleship training, the basic ground preparation has to be done wisely. There are some leaders who have neglected this important preparation, quit discipleship training in the middle and are not able to start again. This is very unfortunate. Therefore, it is important to consider a few fundamental things necessary to do this work well.

Share Your Philosophy

A pastor who wants to implement discipleship training must have a definite purpose or goal as to why he must do it. He must have a clear goal as to where his ministry is going. He should have a clear vision about what can be gained from the success of this ministry.

A clear philosophy is bound to become a vision that all can see. Thus in some cases, the philosophy is the vision and the vision is the philosophy. This is not a vision seen at night. It is a vision seen in the daylight. A vision seen while asleep at night disappears the minute one wakes up, but a vision seen during the brightness of the day does not disappear.

The vision for discipleship training must be received from God with eyes wide open and with faith that believes it will certainly become a reality someday. To try discipleship training without such a clear and organized philosophy is in some ways like preparing to fail.

A leader has to share that which he has seen and has assurance about. The greatest thing a human being can do in this world is to see something and clearly tell others what he has seen.[1]

Ministry philosophy is something that a leader has seen with his eyes and has grasped with his hands. He cannot remain silent. It is natural for people to say what fills their hearts. A pastor should leave such a strong impression on the lay people that whenever they see or think about their pastor, they recall his passion for discipleship training. This shows that the church is constantly receiving from the leader a strong challenge that cannot be rejected. But the moment such a challenge weakens or ceases, the vision will begin to disappear.

In order to effectively share the leader's vision of discipleship training, the terminology and the content must be clear, future-oriented, visible, challenging, and at the same time realistic. If the wording is complicated, it loses the power of communication. It must be expressed so that the trainees can always look forward to it. The leader must be able to plant a new hope that a person who is well trained in discipleship will be able to become a competent and a healthy Christian. And the leader should hold out a vision for the church that the laity can see with the eyes of faith.

---

1. Aubrey Malphurs, *Developing a Vision for Ministry* (Grand Rapids: Baker, 1992), 10.

The picture Moses showed his people day and night while wandering through the desolate wilderness for forty years was 'the land of promise, flowing with milk and honey'. This had a visual effect, enabling the listeners to imagine an ecstatic paradise.

A pastor speaking of discipleship training should also draw such a picture. However, it should not sound like riding on a cloud. It needs to be realistic enough to show that it is possible, and to plant the assurance that it will definitely succeed. Perhaps some may feel that sharing the vision of discipleship training is very difficult. However, one must keep in mind that the door will always open for a person who gets on his knees and seeks the wisdom of the Holy Spirit. Obviously, preaching and prayer are the best ways to share the pastor's philosophy and vision. There are plenty of passages in the New Testament one can use to share the philosophy of discipleship training. However, there is one thing to be cautious about: the pastor should preach in a way that the congregation will be able to listen positively in good spirits.

We must keep in mind that the image of discipleship training creates a strong impression, and therefore the listeners may become anxious. The sharper the edge of the sword, the more necessary it is to be kept in a sturdy sheath. Recklessly brandishing it will do more harm than good. It is not difficult at all to speak of the blessedness of discipleship training after wrapping it in the sheath of the gospel of grace.

If, while listening to the pastor's description, the congregation becomes excited with eager anticipation, then that sermon will have been successful. It is also necessary to develop various ideas to utilize the weapon of prayer to the fullest. The pastor should set discipleship training as his top priority in prayer, and should pray about it in every meeting, without ever leaving it out.

Let the prayers be thoroughly saturated with the tears of the pastor. Make discipleship training a prayer request whenever the congregation gathers. A prayer that is offered without ceasing will seize a person's heart and become his desire.

If the cultivation of discipleship training begins this way, people will begin to agree with the pastor's philosophy and vision. At first only a small number may respond, but the existence of this group will be a great encouragement to the leader. They can become the pastor's shields. They can blow the trumpet which proclaims the vision more loudly. The change in the church atmosphere can take place faster. And the number of people devoting themselves to discipleship training will increase.

When such a team is found, the pastor should meet with them often to share with them his thoughts and vision, to pray with them, and to clothe them fully in the garment of discipleship training.

The pastor has to look for the best time to begin discipleship training. He has to be cautious not to pick either an unripe or overripe fruit and miss the right timing. Let's pray that God will give us the spiritual insight to discern the best timing.

Selecting the Trainees

When the atmosphere ripens and the pastor decides that discipleship training can begin, the first thing he needs to do is to choose the trainees. It is good to keep in mind that the success or failure of the future discipleship training sessions depends on the kind of people accepted into the first session. Therefore, selection should be made very carefully.

Follow the principles of Jesus. The first principle Jesus used in making disciples was the principle of 'selection'. Robert Coleman explains this principle clearly:

Jesus began his ministry by calling a few to be his disciples (John 1:35-51). For him, people were the method by which to lead the world to God. His interest was not in a program to lead the multitude. Rather it was with the few disciples, whom the multitude would follow. The people he called were all ordinary people, each with a diverse background.

Jesus, however, saw in these simple people a leader's potential to lead the world to the kingdom of God. They had a desire to learn and had the simple faith to wait for the Messiah and His kingdom. They wanted to be used in the hands of the Lord. Jesus could put into his hands anyone who wanted to be used and remold them into a giant who can move the world.[2]

First, let's consider an established church. An established church refers to a ministry setting whose history goes back many years and where many pastors have ministered. If the congregation consists of a little over a hundred members, then in general there are several elders and deacons. The average age of the lay people in such a church is comparatively older. I would say that over half of all Korean churches fall into this category.

In most cases, the soil of such an established church is unsuitable and inadequate to plant the seed of discipleship training. In the examples of discipleship training in established churches I've seen so far, most of them adopt extreme attitudes of 'do' or 'die'. If successful, the church experiences extraordinary blessings. However if unsuccessful, the church faces a tragic end. This is how complicated and complex the situation often is.

I've already explained earlier how necessary it is for a pastor to share his philosophy and vision in advance. Because it is so important, I want to emphasize it one more

---

2. Robert Coleman, *The Master Plan of Discipleship* (Old Tappan: Fleming Revell Co., 1987), 21-37.

time. One should be careful not to rush into doing disciple-ship training hastily in an established church. It is reckless to press hard with a tone of command before the atmos-phere ripens. I would say that starting discipleship train-ing in an established church may involve altering the tradi-tional direction of ministry in that church by 180 degrees.

There are several reasons for drawing such a conclu-sion. Once the pastor starts discipleship training, he is bound to dedicate much of his time to a few trainees. Then more than likely the rest of the congregation will complain that the pastor is playing favourites. And the pastor will have to live with such criticism. Moreover, pastoral administration and home visits, to which the pastor had been giving much of his time till then, will gradually be pushed into the background. In this event, there may be elders and deacons who will consider such a situation to be a failure on the part of the pastor.

Besides that, as those who have been transformed through discipleship training begin to emerge in the church, an unintended tension may rise between them and the rest of the congregation. This may become a major cause of concern for the pastor.

Judging from these facts, it is clear that beginning discipleship training in an established church is by no means a simple task, and it may become a huge burden for the pastor. Therefore, it is important to handle it very carefully from the start.

In an established church, one does not have to worry about whom to accept as trainees for the first discipleship training. Without question, one must select elders and deacons. Don't make an issue of their age. Their educational background is not a problem either. What is important is that they become disciples who share the pastor's philosophy and vision, for without that the pastor will not be able to take even a step forward.

Thus if a pastor fails to draw this group of leaders into discipleship training, he has to either wait until they are convinced, or give up. Discipleship training should never be used negatively to cause arguments and fights in the church and to divide the church, which is the body of Christ.

Suddenly drawing people in leadership positions in an established church into discipleship training is not an easy task. It is more difficult for people whose ways are already fixed in the traditions and customs of the church. Therefore, it would be helpful to utilize retreat and prayer centres in order to fellowship with elders in comfortable surroundings and develop personal relationships with them. Create opportunities to share the philosophy of pastoral ministry often and naturally.

Pastoral ministry is grounded in personal relationships. It's easy to make time for natural conversations in a quiet environment such as prayer centres. Such surroundings will facilitate having deep spiritual fellowship with each other through the Word and prayer. If a pastor uses such opportunities to communicate his thoughts little by little, then the negative or passive reaction resulting from a lack of understanding on the part of the listeners can be greatly reduced. We can find many instances in which churches were renewed and revived when their session elders completed the discipleship training successfully. We will be able to learn a great deal by visiting such churches.

When the elders are changed through discipleship training and its impact reaches the rest of the church, then many will begin to desire discipleship training. From that point on, the trainees must be selected with much care and composure. The effectiveness of the training will be maximized when fewer empty husks of grain are selected.

Selecting with care does not mean to be secretive in selection. There must be an official door always open for anyone who wants to apply. However, it may be wise to keep the criteria for application a little tough in order to minimize the repercussions caused by drop-outs.

There are various ways to choose people with potential. In order to find out which method would be most effective, you can visit and ask the churches in your vicinity that are excited about discipleship training. There is not a formula or one particular method. So, it is a good idea to examine various examples.

I want to say one more thing about selection. We might think that it would be good if everyone who receives discipleship training has great faith, is obedient, and has a pleasant personality. However in reality, it will be rather difficult for such people to experience a dramatic change, and thus the ripples of change will be too minimal to be acutely felt. Therefore, if one wants to anticipate a radical change like that of Zacchaeus becoming a new person, then it will be a good idea to accept one or two who appear spiritually hopeless. The atmosphere of the class will change immediately when those people experience a dramatic transformation.

Grace is contagious. When the meanest person receives blessing and grace first, it spreads at a tremendous speed. It can be a great adventure for the leader to accept such problematic people. It can also be a catalyst for depending more on God. I would like to recommend that you try it once. If you really want to have exciting discipleship training, don't be afraid. Venture into it.

In the case of a newly founded church with limited human resources, selecting the trainees will not be an issue for the most part. Most likely a newly planted church will consist of only its initial founding members.

However, a pastor should not let such an opportunity slip away. To think that he will start discipleship training after the church has grown somewhat is taboo. It is advisable to plan with all of the church's adult members as the target for the training. It is up to the pastor to decide whether he should begin with men's or women's discipleship classes. He should just keep in mind that the size of the group should be limited to 5-12 people.

It is true that the purpose of the first discipleship training in a newly founded church is to rear a number of lay leaders. However, a greater significance lies in the fact that the pastor has decided discipleship training is to be the church's foundational ministry method. It will not only form the framework for the ongoing ministry, but will also be an important factor in determining the constitution of the church.

In reality, a drawback for discipleship classes that begin this way is that it is difficult to expect great results for the most part. It may seem idealistic for all adult lay members to receive the training. However, among them will always be those who are not quite ready for discipleship training but have been forced into it, which makes it tough to carry out an intensive training.

In the case of SaRang Church's first women's discipleship class, which began with 6 trainees, only one trainee remained till the end and served as a lay leader in the church. The rest gave up after a while or moved to another church. The target members were replaced so often that in the end the class came to a standstill and had to start all over again from the beginning. However, no matter how difficult the training may be in the initial period, the pastor should never stop or give up. If he continues to press on for about three years, he will gain self-confidence and also experience the joy of seeing a number of disciples as a result of his labour. Moreover, he will be able to secure human resources from which to select trainees with better qualifications.

The Principle of Concentration

Once the trainees have been selected and the training starts, the pastor must be resolved to thoroughly follow the principle of 'concentration' that Jesus exemplified in His ministry. Otherwise, he will not be able to succeed. In order to understand the principle of concentration, we need to first examine why Jesus taught a group of twelve, or especially three.

Jesus chose the twelve from among his other followers when He reached the point of two and a half years into his public ministry. These twelve disciples needed more opportunities to remain close to their teacher. They needed to be inspired so as to become like their master, in order to reflect Him and inscribe His teachings on their minds (Mark 3:13-15). Not only that; in order to carry out more intensive training, Jesus had to restrict the number even further.

Perhaps this is the most difficult part for pastors. We are often tempted to teach many people at one sitting whenever possible. The reason for this is simple. It is due to the logic that says the more people we teach the more fruit we can reap. This may work in mathematics or in economics, but not in character education that deals with people.

God blessed Adam and Eve to be fruitful and multiply, but did not permit them to reproduce many young all at once like other animals. To nurture a child is to mold his or her character, and thus one cannot give birth to seven or eight babies at once and raise them well as human beings.

As we know from our experience, we lose all in the end when we try to hold on to too many people at once.

When we are greedy for numbers, the degree of concentration is bound to drop. If even Jesus did not do it this way, what kind of power do we think we have that we gather hundreds of people at once and try to train them to be His disciples? Most of the pastors who give up midway through discipleship training and fail are usually guilty of neglecting the principle of concentration and trying irregular ways. Such calamity results from their ignorance as to what true discipleship training is.

Making disciples can succeed only when the pastor is able to pour much of his time and energy into a few. This is precisely the great principle Jesus taught us. Can we be wiser than Jesus? Only those who think so can ignore this principle.

There is another thing we need to keep in mind in order to be able to concentrate. This applies both to the pastor and the trainees. First, the pastor has to resolutely get rid of anything that interferes with his own concentration. If you decide on every Tuesday morning as the time of your meeting, then that time must be kept even if the sky is about to fall on you. If you change the time or postpone the meeting because of a wedding, your son's first birthday, or a denominational meeting, then the training will lose focus. If such an incident happens more than two or three times, then the trainees start to wind down and their confidence in their leader begins to plunge.

From the beginning, the leader has to pledge himself before God and the trainees, that if he perishes, he perishes. I once heard an inspiring testimony of a pastor who demonstrated that it is possible to do discipleship training in an established church. He had a liver problem and was hospitalized while he was carrying on the training. Yet he continued to conduct the training in his hospital room with an intravenous drip inserted in his body. In the hands of such leaders – willing to give up their lives for the trainees – how can faithful disciples of Jesus not be made?

In the meantime, the trainees must also be prepared to concentrate. After selecting the trainees, one church had them participate in a solemn pledge. They had to sign a commitment paper (this was no joke) that during discipleship training, they'd neither get sick nor die. And wives who had the possibility of getting pregnant during the training period were not accepted from the beginning. As a result, there wasn't a single person absent with sickness throughout the training year. Such events can be anticipated when there is a leader with a clear understanding about the significance of concentration.

The Significance of the First Discipleship Class

Whether in an established church or in a newly planted church, the first discipleship class is highly significant in various ways. There is no guarantee that the first discipleship class will succeed. One should expect some trial and error, and learn from mistakes. But if the first discipleship class fails in an established church, then one can experience a great deal of frustration. Not only will the leader be taken aback, but it could also throw cold water on all expectations for discipleship training. Therefore, it is necessary to pour forth all of one's energy to make sure that the first discipleship class will not fail. When the first class goes well, the news will spread around the church immediately. Let's say that this class is made up of the elders. When they are changed, their families get excited. The elders' prayers during the worship will change. In the case of one church, after completing the training, the elders get together every Saturday to clean the church restrooms. The church board that had been divided and known for severe discord becomes united in love and begins to serve the church in an exemplary manner.

When this happens, how will the congregation look at discipleship training? Won't they think that they too must receive discipleship training? Won't there be requests such as, 'Please accept my husband next time' ? Won't the congregation have confidence in the work of their pastor and a great expectation for discipleship training? Therefore, bear in mind that the first discipleship class holds the key to exerting a decisive influence on all future training ministry.

Chapter 21

Teaching Tools

The Three Training Tools of Jesus

What tools should we use for discipleship training? The three basic tools Jesus used in His teaching were the Word of God, His own example, and the disciples' experiences. The Word of God was the specific educational content. Jesus himself, as the living Word of Truth in the flesh, was the role model for the disciples to follow. The disciples' experiences were the practical application of what they had learned.

The image of a disciple we have is of a mature person whose character resembles that of Jesus Christ. It is also of a new life that is completely distinguishable from the world. For this reason, we must attach great importance to the character building element of the training. Jesus' three training tools comprised: truth of character, a character role model, and an experience of character. These were fundamentally different from the dead knowledge of the Law that the Jewish rabbis taught. Therefore, when we use the Bible in discipleship training, it should always be handled as the living truth through which we have a direct encounter with the living Jesus Christ. The leader should offer himself as a role model for the trainees to see with their eyes what true discipleship looks like. And the truth they have learned and seen should be individually experienced in their lives through obedience.

The Word of God

The Word of God was the most important training tool Jesus used. The Word of God that Jesus taught had two origins: the Old Testament and His own teaching. He was God's final revelation (Heb. 1:2). Only in Him was the Word of Life (John 6:68). Therefore, whoever wanted to be a true disciple of Jesus had to remain in His Word (John 8:31). At the same time He came as the fulfillment of the written Word spoken by the prophets so that 'not the smallest letter, nor the least stroke of a pen, will by any means disappear from the Law' (Matt. 5:17,18). After His resurrection, He explained the Law and the Prophets many times to His disciples to lift them out of their disbelief and discouragement (Luke 24:27, 44-47).

To Jesus, whether in public or private, the Bible was a textbook for teaching the eternal Word of God. In the four gospels, Jesus cited the Old Testament 66 times while conversing with the disciples, and referred to the Old Testament 90 times in His conversations with others.

The paramount work that Jesus did for the disciples while He was in the world was to teach them the words He received from God (John 17:8). The Word gave them eternal life (John 20:31), filled them with joy through the spiritual fellowship of sharing new life (1 John 1:4), and gave them the assurance of salvation (1 John 5:13). The Word also shaped their character and life to become whole as the disciples of Jesus (2 Tim. 3:16, 17).

Therefore, a leader in charge of discipleship training in the church must first prepare his heart so that the words of Christ will dwell richly in him (Col. 3:16). This is much more important than mastering a study guide. The material we truly need to prepare is the Word that we meditate on day and night and that dwells richly in us.

In other words, we have to be captivated by and devoted to the Word, just as was the case with Paul

(Acts 18:5). Only then can we become leaders who hear the voice of God prior to teaching others. When this happens, the Bible is transmitted as the voice of the living God and as food for the souls of the trainees. And the Word will become the channel through which they encounter the living Lord.

The Role Model of the Leader

The second tool Jesus used in training was that of the role model. Jesus was not the kind of teacher who presented the truth merely as a theory to the disciples. He lived out exactly what he taught. Jesus himself was the perfect role model and an object lesson. So what the disciples had to ultimately learn was their teacher Himself. The power of Jesus' teachings came from His authority and His life.

> *Here Jesus' method was more than a continuation of preaching. This was like an object lesson. This was the key to his influential teaching. He did not ask a person to do something unless he showed the example in his own life first and by doing this he showed that it could be done and proved its relation to his life's calling.... All of his words and actions were actually his individual teachings and since the disciples paid attention to it while being there they were learning realistically every moment they had their eyes open.*[1]

Jesus lived with His disciples in order to train them by His own example. The highlight of His training program was His living with them. Their daily encounter with Jesus enabled the disciples to see and confirm all the substance of the truth they had learned from the transparent character of their teacher.

In this sense, Jesus placed His entire self on display as an open training manual. Jesus made the act of living

---

1. Ibid., 82.

together itself, apart from any formality or method, a thing to be known and to be learned. He was always an object of attention for His disciples. Thus, for their benefit He spent His time with them.

When we hear this, we are stunned and challenged. We also may suffer from frustration and discouragement, unable to shake off the thought that perhaps we should quit at once. How many leaders in the world can open themselves up as a perfect role model as Jesus did? That a leader must be a role model is a cross that we must bear. One cannot expect to make disciples unless one becomes a living and walking truth in the eyes of the trainees.

To speak directly, just as we are training others to follow Christ (1 Cor. 11:1), so we have to be prepared for them to follow us.

We are on display (Phil. 3:17ff.; 1 Thess. 2:8; 2 Tim. 1:13). Trainees will act according to what they hear and see from us (Phil. 4:9). Through this kind of leadership, when the opportunity arises, we can share our daily way of life with those who are always with us.

We must accept the truth in our own way of life. We cannot avoid accountability in character. We show the way to the people we train and such an example should come out of a deep fellowship with the Spirit. This is the Lord's method and any other method definitely will not be enough to train other people.[2]

Though we cannot exactly imitate the training style of Jesus by living together with the trainees, we should unquestionably follow the principle it demonstrates in our discipleship training. We are imperfect. Yet as leaders, we need to demonstrate how much sweat and tears we shed in order to follow Jesus, even in our imperfection.

2. Ibid., 83.

The trainees do not ask for a perfect example. They know that we are all human. They only want a leader who is willing to be personally vulnerable and opens the door for them to see him as he is. If the leader doesn't open up and leaves no crack open for them to see what he is thinking or how he copes with family life, the trainees will turn away and close their hearts. We need to bear in mind that disciples of Jesus can never be made under such a leader. Therefore, we must open up our life to be seen by those we are training. The writer of the book of Hebrews warns that a teacher should teach not only with his lips but with his actions. This is making a strong suggestion that a faith that cannot be demonstrated by actions isn't worth learning. 'Remember your leaders, who spoke the word of God to you. Consider the outcome of their way of life and imitate their faith' (Heb. 13:7). Be a role model. This is the key that determines the success or failure of discipleship training.

The Disciples' Experience

Jesus had another training tool that must not be left out. That was providing for the disciples the opportunities to experience ministry settings. 'Open your eyes and look at the fields' (John 4:35). His finger was always pointing to this world's work places. There were many people suffering and wandering about like sheep without a shepherd. There was a Samaritan woman thirsting for living water. There was Jairus, whose daughter was dying in an attic.

Experiential knowledge is gained by having close access to daily living scenes, and by seeing with one's own eyes and listening carefully with one's own ears. Jesus wanted His disciples to know the reality, and to understand correctly the sufferings of life.

After teaching various parables to the multitudes, Jesus explained the parables to His disciples. The contents of these parables were often from common everyday life. What does this signify? Jesus was teaching the disciples that truth is not found somewhere else but in places near to their daily life, if they search carefully with the eyes of wisdom. For this reason Jesus took His disciples everywhere He went.

This was not strange at all. They had to go around and see more of the world. They had to wrestle with actual problems. They had to hear many people's stories. A good understanding of the world and humanity meant that the content of training became that much more realistic and abundant.

'Jesus saw the multitude and had compassion on them' (Matt. 9:36). How was such a pastor's heart possible for Jesus? He had a profound understanding of the world. The disciples following Jesus had to have the same heart. And for that, they had to come into contact with many people who were living in the real world, and had to see and hear for themselves the heavy crosses these people were carrying on their shoulders.

Sometimes our discipleship programs thwart true discipleship. What I mean by this is that we can become so involved with our programs that we isolate ourselves from real life. Jesus called his disciples to him so that he could teach them how to walk with him in the real world. That is true discipleship.[3]

The disciples also needed to personally experience the power of the gospel through practice. 'They went out and preached that people should repent. They drove out many demons and anointed many sick people with oil

---

3. Michael J. Wilkins, *Following the Master* (Grand Rapids: Zondervan, 1992), 22.

and healed them' (Mark 6:12-13). They returned after this practical exercise and reported to Jesus everything they had done (Mark 6:30). There is no doubt from their report that they learned and experienced much through this exercise. The Lord could not hide his joy upon hearing their report (Luke 10:21).

Discipleship training is not something done only in a room. It should be on-the-scene training applied to daily life through practical exercises. Neighbours with many problems can become valuable training materials for us. Sharing the gospel with them and praying for them in earnest will be like igniting flames under the coal of truth in our hearts. Bring before the Word what you have seen in the world, and take back to the world and apply the answer found in the Bible. Such a spiritual experiment becomes a training tool that raises the quality of the training.

When discipleship training approaches the midterm, it is good to incorporate such exercises as frequently as possible. There is nothing in the training content which doesn't need application. Evangelism, prayer life, service – all aspects of the training – need to be experimented with and re-examined in the world in order to become living truths. One should never forget that discipleship training isolated from the real world is not the training Jesus demonstrated.

It is necessary for a leader to examine often whether the discipleship training he leads makes a balanced use of these three tools. If any one of them is being neglected or missing, then it must be supplemented immediately without delay.

A leader who can firmly maintain such vigilance until the end is qualified to do discipleship training.

Chapter 22

Good Teaching Material

Although it is the living Word of God that we teach, it is rather difficult to teach it effectively without suitable teaching materials. It has already been demonstrated through many studies that it is difficult to reap desirable results by teaching only with the Bible. Therefore, systematic and well-balanced teaching materials are necessary in order to do effective discipleship training.

There are plenty of teaching materials with the title 'discipleship training' in the market today. I have found that the teaching materials presented by evangelical mission organizations are effective and helpful. However, many experiences have also proved the fact that training lay people in the church with these materials poses limitations. This is due to the fact that mission organizations and churches are in different environments and thus take different approaches.

A church ministers to a diverse and complex congregation, which comprises different backgrounds, living standards, education, and age. Theological emphases will be slightly different according to the denomination with which each church is affiliated. More importantly, the senior pastors of each local church should want to train the lay members according to their own vision and ministry philosophy. If there is a teaching material that reflects these points to a high degree, then it will definitely be a big help.

Teaching material used in church should have a systematic balance of at least the following elements in order to reap desirable results. Although this is in a large measure my own subjective judgement, I believe it isn't likely to be terribly wrong considering that this is an opinion grounded in many years of experience and study.

Is the Gospel Alive?

First, the gospel must be alive. On this point, I can say that we are very much indebted to evangelical mission organizations. The strength of their teaching materials is that they emphasize the gospel clearly. That is why they are able to continuously celebrate the birth of new lives and enjoy the blessedness of deep gratitude for salvation that does not diminish with time.

Looking at many of the materials that have been used by the traditional churches up to now, we find that the gospel is not alive in most of them. They are excellent in doctrine which can be considered as the backbone of the gospel, but often lack the passion and excitement of the abundant life which results from the gospel. Perhaps that is why the majority of church members do not know the gospel well. There are too many materials that seem to lack the joy of salvation and the happiness that comes from the assurance of salvation. Even more grievous than this is the fact that many pastors are not preaching the gospel. It might sound strange, but pastors often consider gospel preaching to be the most difficult. I've talked with pastors who confess that they feel somewhat awkward when they try to preach the gospel. It is true that many pastors suffer from a vague anxiety that if they say, 'gospel', then the congregation will not listen well but answer instead, 'We already know', or 'Not again!'

Therefore, first and foremost, discipleship training material must be able to teach the gospel. It must have the inspiration to lead anyone, regardless of the length of the years that he or she has been a Christian, to come before the cross and praise God who gave them salvation.

There are more people than we realize in church who need salvation. Those who could live a completely changed life of faith, if only they were touched by the power of the gospel, are spending their days lethargically because they have not had that opportunity. It is indeed a pity when a church is unable to break out of its stagnation because it cannot start the fire. It would be revived at once if only the flames of the gospel would burn in the hearts of the lay members. However, there is no reason for us to just sit and sigh. If we start right now to awaken the lay members with teaching materials that reveal the power of the gospel, then we will soon be able to experience amazing blessings.

Are the Contents Balanced and Systematic?

Secondly, teaching materials should have contents that have an overall system. It is important for the contents to be systematic, because unless we are careful, we could end up overemphasizing only one aspect of faith. For instance, the purpose of making disciples is not to make people who are passionate *only* about evangelism. Teaching material that overemphasizes the importance of evangelism cannot be considered to be good material. Teaching material that is concerned only with personal devotions is also not desirable. If material teaches much about obedience and dedication but neglects the matter of mature faith and character, then this too is definitely not balanced.

We need to keep in mind that the Bible uses rather an extreme expression, 'a perfect person', to refer to a

205

disciple of Jesus. What is being perfect? It refers to a state where nothing is missing. Thus in order to make disciples, we must use balanced materials that teach the whole counsel of God.

Is the Application of the Word Emphasized?
The third qualification of good material is that it should emphasize the application of the Word. I once heard that to study the Bible without applying it is like having a miscarriage. This seems to be an appropriate analogy.

Churches have been teaching the Bible for many years, each in their own earnest way. But many churches have stopped at transmitting knowledge, and have failed to teach how to apply that Word in the family or in society. Jesus said, 'Teach them to obey.' Only then can disciples be made. But it is true that we have often been educating our lay members without seriously contemplating what 'teach them to obey' means.

This has been gradually changing recently. However, the Bible study materials used in traditional churches still leave the impression that they are weak in the application of the Word. On the other hand, it is often true that the teaching materials used by mission organizations have the merit of being strong in the application of the Word.

In order to build up lay members of the church into disciples of Jesus, we have to use materials that will firmly plant this fundamental principle, namely that what has been learned must be lived out. We need materials that take the trainees through the struggles of real-life learning, while at the same time having the power to illuminate each trainee's life in detail by the Word.

Teaching materials must have the strength to prevent both the leader and the trainees from hiding their hypocrisy and lies before the Word, which has the power to penetrate deep into the heart. Teaching materials should also provide opportunities to share the joy of new life that comes from obedience. Teaching materials that are strong in application provide valuable highlights from which the leaders can have a closer look at the transformation and maturity taking place in the trainees.

The Significance of Doctrine

A fourth element of good training material is its doctrinal content. Mission organizations have the tendency to avoid doctrinally sensitive issues in their teaching materials. This is understandable considering their need to minister across denominations. However, it is worthwhile for us to at least consider another side of this issue. Why do mission organizations have a tendency to be anti-doctrinal? It is often a reaction against the traditional churches being too conscious and rigid in their doctrines.

Historically, evangelical mission organizations have their roots in the 17th century pietist movement.[1] At the time when the German church was losing its life by focusing only on dead doctrines, the followers of pietism cried out for the need to rediscover the gospel that emphasizes rebirth and spiritual experience. It was during this time that they became strongly anti-doctrinal.

(The Lutheran church) kept the doctrinal purity and was devoted to preventing the believers from leaving the church. There was absolutely no appeal for emotion. There was no invitational call to the gospel, servanthood or godliness. They only wanted the believers to know the doctrine, attend the worship service and listen to the doctrinal sermon, and

1. Paulus Scharpff, *History of Evangelism* (Grand Rapids: Eerdmans, 1966), 126.

participate in the communion... There was no teaching about inner life and inspiring faith experience.[2]

However, a church is not a mission organization. A church is usually affiliated with a denomination. Consequently, it is bound to have a doctrine that agrees with the denomination's theological background. Doctrines are not always different for each denomination. There are doctrines that are common to and confessed by all churches. Slight differences in opinion are mutually acknowledged. Therefore, although discipleship training materials perhaps should avoid doctrines that may cause disputes or controversy, it would be much more beneficial if the materials appropriately reflected the important doctrines that form the backbone of Christianity.

As an example, the doctrine of predestination arouses a great difference of opinion between the churches following Calvin's theology and the churches upholding Arminian theology. Nevertheless, that doesn't mean we should keep quiet or give an ambiguous explanation while studying God's grace that called us out of the world to be His own.

Therefore, it is better to have a content that is based on the framework of one or other of the two views. In this way, the leader using that material can teach by modifying and supplementing the material according to his stance. It is necessary for the leader doing discipleship training in the church to teach without hesitation the doctrinal content about which he is certain. If a study material has room for such flexibility, then it can be much more useful than the materials which do not.

---

2. B. K. Kuiper, *The Church in History* (Grand Rapids: Eerdmans, 1955), 342-343.

Reflection of the Ministry Philosophy

Fifthly, training material should reflect the pastor's ministry philosophy. We have already discussed what a ministry philosophy is and why it is important. Then is it enough for just the pastor to know his ministry philosophy? No, it is not.

One of the important purposes of discipleship training is to raise up lay leaders in local churches who will be on the same team as their pastor. Therefore, the pastor has the responsibility to teach and instill his philosophy in the lay members. We can work together when our thinking and purpose are the same.

How can we work together with those who do not see the church in the way we do? What can be asked of the lay members who do not have a proper sense of their identity? If the pastor's ministry philosophy has been derived from ecclesiology, then surely the lay members must also know and be convinced of it. Planting a clear ecclesiology in the hearts of the lay members is something that mission organizations cannot do, and therefore, it becomes an important privilege of the church.

To be honest, in its early years SaRang Church was not able to reflect sufficiently the pastor's ministry philosophy in discipleship training. The pastor's thoughts had to be infused gradually into the consciousness of the members. At the time, we were using study materials published by the Navigators, and there was nothing in its content that taught ecclesiology. However, we now teach the doctrine of the church thoroughly in our ministry-training course. As time has passed, I've come to realize more strongly than ever how important it is to equip the members with the pastor's ministry philosophy.

Inductive Method

Sixthly, an effective training material should use the inductive method. (We will explore the inductive method in detail in Ch. 24.) Since discipleship training is most effective in a small group environment with an open atmosphere, we cannot expect to reap desirable results unless the study materials are appropriate for this setting as well. In a small group, everyone can enjoy the freedom of sharing each person's ideology, concept, emotion, attitude, and values.

The Holy Spirit grants the realization of the truth through the leader, but He also makes the truth known through each trainee. Such personal realization is most likely to take place when guided by the inductive method, which uses appropriate questions to observe, interpret, respond to, and finally apply the Word. Such use of the inductive method has been proved through much research and numerous experiences. Thus it is needless to say that study materials which faithfully follow the inductive method are recommendable far more than the materials that do not.

Here we need to think about the theological background in which the inductive Bible study method became an object of attention. First, this method has something in common with the spirit and mentality of lay theology. Lay theology sets a high value on the fact that teaching the Bible is not only for pastors who have completed theological study, but for lay people also. Lay theology claims that lay people can understand the Word on their own and share it with other believers.

Inductive study material leaves half of every page blank. This is tantamount to declaring that anyone who has the anointing of the Holy Spirit can come to an understanding of the truth on his own (1 John 2:20, 27). It can be extremely challenging for a trainee to use various inductive questions about a Bible passage to find answers for himself. It is a challenge to correctly understand the meaning and write out the correct answer. This means that one has to personally come face to face with the Bible. One has to personally knock on the door of the Bible.

Through an inductive Bible study, each trainee tries hard to find the truth on his own, rather than to repeat someone else's interpretation and answer like a parrot. The next time when he is given the opportunity to share that discovery, the trainee gets soaked in the rain of grace once again as he sees other believers being blessed through him. Finally, he will become someone who cannot hide his excitement as he hears the inner voice, 'You too can become a great Bible teacher.'

There is another theological background of the inductive method that we need to consider. Neo-orthodox theology, which was very influential in the study of theology in the early 20th century, emphasized experiencing a personal encounter with God through the Bible. Here, I do not intend to discuss that theology. I merely want to point out the fact that the 'experience of a personal encounter', emphasized in neo-orthodox theology, has played a part in opening the eyes of the traditional churches which have been teaching the Bible doctrinally in a dry and dull manner.

Today church education doesn't focus on experiencing God personally. It stresses doctrinal teaching or sharing the testimony of a third party rather than educating the trainees to personally meet God. [3]

Such criticism became an alarm that awoke many church leaders who, without intention, had been steeped in cere-

3. Lawrence Richards, *Creative Bible Teaching* (Chicago: Moody Press) 31.

monial literalism in their reading of the Bible. In fact, one cannot expect a change of character without a personal encounter with God through the Word. Although we cannot agree with the whole of neo-orthodox theology, it is very important for us to correctly and biblically understand and apply its emphasis on encountering God in the Word. Many popular inductive study materials around us were developed as a result of such endeavours.

Before this, one-way communication was the common pedagogical method, whereby pastors spoke and lay people simply listened. People were filled with knowledge but lacked transformation of lives. This is one of the struggles many churches face. By doing discipleship training inductively, we will be able to overcome this struggle.

Discipleship Training Study Materials

It took a trial period of more than ten years at SaRang Church before completing the material we are using today. This material supplements what we felt was weak in the materials published by mission organizations, and has as its primary objective to properly train the lay members within the church.

In other words, the discipleship training material not only forms a balanced trinity of gospel, doctrine, and life, but also allows the pastor's ministry philosophy to be shared. Its purpose is to thoroughly equip a select few at a time and produce lay leaders who can partner in ministry with the pastor.

SaRang Church's training material uses an inductive approach suitable for a small group setting. This material is divided into two parts: discipleship training and leadership training. It is designed to be completed in 2 years, but can be extended to 3 years depending on those using it.

The Discipleship Training course lays down the foundation of the truth of salvation once more. It is made up of three sections: *Foundation of Discipleship Training*, *My Unshakable Salvation*, and *Become a Little Christ*. These enable the trainee, with a deep gratitude and joy of salvation, to aim for a mature character of faith and a holy life that Jesus desires from believers.

Leadership Training is a course designed for those who, through discipleship training, have been recognized as potential lay leaders to partner in ministry. Accordingly, it aims at transforming the trainees' mentality by focusing on theoretical studies and exercises needed for leaders.

By going through the leadership training, the trainees can learn clearly about the pastor's philosophy and about the status and function of the lay members. Consequently they will accept the pastor's paradigm of the church as their own. For this purpose, they study three books: *The Holy Spirit – the Key to New Life*, *The Church and the Laity's Self-Image*, and *Small Group and Leadership*.

The teaching material is merely a guide. It cannot fully contain every element or every detail. Keep in mind that the way a leader uses the materials will determine whether or not he will reap harvests beyond his expectations. At SaRang Church, many people have experienced a kind of Copernican revolution in their lives through the use of this material. It is my sincere desire that every church will experience the same blessing.

Chapter 23

Small Group Setting

Almost 15 years after its founding, Willow Creek Church in Chicago had grown so big that it began to feel as if it were a giant dinosaur swaying back and forth. It was then that small groups were introduced in earnest and began to form the internal structure of the church. Bill Hybels, who has led the church from the beginning, said that he greatly regrets that he had not implemented small groups from the start.[1]

As a matter of fact, many church leaders still do not understand properly the necessity of small groups and their special and amazing functions. Until recently, most churches operated on the assumption that teacher, student, and study material are enough for Christian education. If the purpose of education is to simply transmit knowledge, then such an assumption is not so wrong. However, when we engage in education which focuses on character formation of the whole person as in the case of discipleship training, we already know from many examples from the past how flawed the above assumption is.

Rediscovering the Early Church
The small group refers to an educational environment where a mutual interaction can develop among the people gathered. For that reason the number of people in the

---

1. Lynne &Bill Hybels, *Rediscovering the Church*, 130.

group should be within the range in which individuals will not be lost. Jesus pioneered this kind of small group. During the three years of his ministry, through His experience and the result of time spent with His disciples, He powerfully demonstrated the possibilities of this structure.

Jesus does not explain why He chose the small group structure, and He has never commanded the church to structure around small groups. Nevertheless, the first century church followed Jesus' precedent and formed a unique community made up of numerous small groups.

The best example is the first Jerusalem church. Although they all met together frequently at the temple, actual fellowship between the believers and tasting the joy of new life took place in small groups gathered in homes (Acts 2:42, 46). We don't know exactly how many small groups were scattered throughout Jerusalem, but it isn't difficult to imagine the importance of their role.

The Corinthian church was not a one-building church like the contemporary churches. It is a well-known fact that it was a community made up of 20 to 30 home churches.[2] Churches after the New Testament period followed the same model and spread like yeast in all directions.

They were having fellowship through high mobility structure(s) like home church or activity centers. They met privately as well as in public. Their small group fellowship penetrated into every level of society. Hence, through the dynamic of the fellowship, those who came into contact with them heard the message of salvation and witnessed the power of the gospel. They slowly multiplied and expanded in an orderly manner.[3]

2. Lawrence Richards, A *Theology of Church Leadership* (Grand Rapids: Zondervan), 319.
3. J. Verkuyl, *The Message of Liberation in Our Age* (Grand Rapids: Eerdmans, 1970), 106.

In the beginning of the twentieth century, small group movements began to spread like wildfire. However, they were a greater object of interest in general society than in the church. Mental hospitals, prisons, social organizations, and educational guilds began to gradually and conspicuously utilize the small group's unit structure in social activities and research, and to treat and counsel mental disorders.

According to Paul Hare's research, from the years 1899–1958, hundreds of academic research theses were written about small groups.[4] Especially before and after World War II, with the knowledge of the effectiveness of the small group structure in increasing productivity, a research team called 'The Test Tube Group' was promoted. Furthermore, it became known that the small group structure is useful not only for increasing production, but also for giving a new meaning to human relationships and consequently, for bringing about the transformation of one's character.

On the other hand, to some, small groups were of more interest not so much for their utilitarian purposes, as because of a quiet belief that small groups could, to an extent, satisfy a strong emotional hunger hidden inside modern man.

People are famished for deep human relationships everywhere. They need relationships that bring security and belonging in the abruptly changing and growing world. Small groups can fill a man's deep craving for love and recognition impossible to attain in an assembly of hundreds and thousands of people.[5]

---

4. Ernest G. Bormann, *Effective Committees and Groups in the Church* (Minneapolis: Augsburg, 1973), 12.
5. Clyde Reid, *Groups Alive – Church Alive* (New York: Harper and Row, 1969), 16.

Some offer the opinion that there is a great interest in small groups, because modern man has failed to overcome loneliness, and therefore try to obtain security and a sense of belonging from anywhere they can. I think this is an opinion that strikes a chord with reality. We cannot deny that it would be natural for the modern church to have been more or less influenced by such a trend. However, it would be somewhat foolish to rush to a conclusion that the church opened its eyes to the significance of small groups due to stimulation from the external environment only. Even if such influence cannot be excluded entirely, a more direct cause has been that the small group is biblical. It is only natural that many, as they agonized over the reality of the church that has grown into a huge granite-like organization, could not remain blind to the spirit of the small group, which permeates the Bible.

'Today the church needs "home churches" like the New Testament period. We need small groups.'[6] Almost anyone can see that in order for the church to recover its function as the body of Christ, it must return to the constitution of the first century church.

The purpose of discipleship training lies not only in producing lay leaders, but also in recovering the organic nature of the church that places a greater emphasis on forming personal relationships. That is why small groups have such immense significance.

An Amazing Healing Element
Small groups play an important role in bringing about changes in people's attitudes, values, and character. This can be referred to as a kind of healing element. When God's children share deep spiritual fellowship in a small

---

6. Lawrence O. Richards, *A New Face for the Church* (Grand Rapids: Zondervan, 1970), 157.

group centred on the Word, the Holy Spirit brings about healing in them. This ministry of healing is entirely up to the Word and the Holy Spirit, but we know that the Holy Spirit does not use only supernatural means.

A small group is a natural channel that the Holy Spirit uses. Things that cannot be expected in large group meetings happen in small groups because of the healing element which is a natural function of the small group. We emphasize small groups because they have the elements that assist the Holy Spirit's work much more effectively than other forms of gathering.

Irvin Yalom identifies eleven elements of healing found in non-Christian healing groups.[7] It would be difficult to incorporate all of these elements into small groups in general, considering the fact that the members of the healing groups used as Yalom's research target were abnormal patients. However, it is difficult to deny that the spiritual changes taking place in discipleship training small groups, or other similar gatherings, have things in common with the discoveries made in Yalom's healing groups. It will be helpful here to introduce a few of the important healing elements discovered by Yalom in order to understand the importance of the small group educational environment in discipleship training.

We are All in the Same Boat
First, let's discuss the element of universality. Each small group participant has a problem that no one else knows. It may be a secret which they just can't tell anyone. Naturally each person thinks that he or she alone possesses and agonizes over such a problem. In some cases they have a deep sense of guilt and belief that they will never be forgiven. Most of the believers taking

---

7. Irvin D. Yalom, *The Theory and Practice of Group Psychotherapy* (New York: Basic Books, 1975), 70-104.

discipleship training suffer from this kind of secret problem, and feel insecure and inferior.

A distinctive feature of the small group is that it is easier to open oneself up there than in other forms of gathering. During the initial period, most participants focus on self-protection. However, after two to three months, they start to feel secure in the group and begin to trust the fellow believers with whom they always meet together. Consequently, after a while they begin to open themselves up without hesitation.

Until this happens, the first two to three months are the most difficult. If the trainees do not disclose their hearts even after a considerable amount of time has passed, then the group may be diagnosed as being dysfunctional. A person who opens himself up usually shares his hidden problems or worries. Then those who hear his stories realize that the problems they have been hiding are not unique to them. 'Now I see that it is not just me who has such problems.' Such sympathetic identification will not only change the atmosphere of the group, but will also bind the personal relationships within the group with deep love and compassion.

Of course, self-disclosure does not mean revealing everything about oneself. When each person reflects upon himself before the Word of God, he finds the Holy Spirit directing him to confess and testify. The Holy Spirit uses the Word as a key to open one's heart. Consequently, each person's statement contains truth and earnestness. It has the power to draw in another person. It is precisely on this point that discipleship training groups differ from other healing groups.

Hence, based on what they have learned and felt from the Word, everyone will come to realize that they are all pilgrims steadily walking toward the distant goal and that there is no one perfect before the Word of God. Then they will approach the Word with a lighter and more cheerful heart, and understand and love one another. We are all in the same boat.

You Are All My Teachers

The second important element of healing is interpersonal learning. This is often considered the most important element in healing groups. In a discipleship training group also, this element is essential in refining each trainee's character. Many psychologists assert that one's individual personality is mostly a product of personal relationships with other people. This element establishes the authenticity of such a view.

Once self-disclosure becomes possible in a group, the group begins to assume the characteristic of a little society in which each person rediscovers and re-forms him/herself. Each person learns more about oneself through other people. They can evaluate what their own words and actions mean to other people. They can learn what is lacking in themselves by comparing themselves with other people. At the same time, they can easily discover their strengths. They can also affirm their spiritual gifts through relationships with others. And perhaps most significantly, they realize the relative importance of their own role in sharing their gifts with others. There is probably nothing more effective, in bringing about a transformation in a person's attitude and character, than to discover that he or she is a very important person to others. The Holy Spirit uses other people to mold our character in the direction that He wants. What an amazing truth! People learn from other people.

It is well known from small groups that character development takes place in training partially through personal and reciprocal relationships. However, forming a new character or amending it does not happen only in small groups. The truth is that it is experienced continually through the whole of church life. However, its possibility is much higher in small groups.

I Want to Try It Too

Thirdly, the element of imitation cannot be left out in a small group. As we have already discussed in the earlier chapters, a role model is one of the important training tools in discipleship training. This refers mostly to 'becoming like the leader'. However, in a small group, the leader is not the only role model. You will be surprised to find in doing discipleship training, that there are many instances where the trainees imitate other trainees in the group as much as they do the leader.

An average lay person does not think it a big deal that a pastor is ahead of others in the life of faith or in Bible knowledge. Whatever is regarded as obvious does not leave a huge impression. However, people are incredibly sensitive to the changes taking place in other trainees within the group. It is rather common to observe a strong will expressed in the trainees' speeches and actions to learn from a member who is recognized to be ahead of others in the group. In a small group where it is easy to observe each other close at hand, each person can become a subject of imitation by others.

I Really Wanted to See It

The fourth element is the cohesiveness of the group. This is a kind of loyalty that is created when the trainees in a group share their hearts with affection, accepting one another as important people in their life. This is expressed more fully as one's acknowledgement of the importance of the small group deepens. The stronger the attachment, the more dependent the person will become on the instructions and decisions obtained from the group. When group cohesiveness is strong, then the meeting is more productive. Morale is high. It is effective in its operation. The atmosphere becomes bright and happy, and attendance also increases.

Developing cohesiveness in the discipleship training group is the key that determines the success or failure of the training. Great results cannot be expected from discipleship training that has to force its members to attend every time it meets.

We need to keep in mind that group cohesiveness is not produced by the uniting work of the Holy Spirit and the power of the Word alone in the absence of human endeavour. How much concern and love is the leader showing? Is each individual considered equally important to the whole group? Is the purpose of the group correctly understood?

Are the special characteristics of the small group being used wisely in managing the group? Constantly examining these various points will raise the trainees' group cohesiveness in discipleship training.

What a Relief after Confession!

Finally, I want to mention the healing element called catharsis. People in general speak of their *thoughts*, but are reluctant to talk about their *feelings*. The exchange of feelings is possible only in an appropriate setting. Small groups have a huge advantage in creating a safe and warm environment for anyone in the group to express their feelings without difficulty.

We find a similar example in the case of Jesus. In general, Jesus did not display his emotions much. However, the three years of personal relationships He maintained with the disciples reached its climax as He went to Gethsemane. At that time the Lord expressed His emotions honestly, to an amazing degree.

'My soul is overwhelmed with sorrow to the point of death. Stay here and keep watch with me' (Matt. 26:37-38). The fact that Jesus, as a perfect man with human nature, disclosed His heart without hesitation when He was with His three beloved disciples is helpful in understanding the function of the small group.

When a comparatively small number of brothers are gathered and their hearts are connected in love, each often expresses his feelings honestly and discloses his hidden worries. For those who had kept their problems to themselves because they did not have anybody to share with, to discover their outlet in a small group is very natural.

In this sense, small groups such as discipleship training can be likened to a sponge that soaks in one another's emotions. Confessing to a person becomes a form of confessing to God. Praising and praying together and reciprocal communication of talking and listening to one another without fault finding, lead to a quick recovery of security and peace of mind.

It is important for the church to be aware when engaging in healing ministry, that the Holy Spirit does not work in a way that contradicts the human being's state of mind, which has been created by God.

Until now we've reviewed the small group's functions and its healing elements. This means that the limitation in the number of people that a leader can effectively handle is not the only reason why discipleship training works best in the small group environment. Discipleship training anticipates spiritual changes taking place as the trainees gather together and reflect upon their hearts and minds in the mirror of the Word. In other words, much importance is placed on the mutual personal relationships through which the Holy Spirit works. The most fitting environment for these purposes is the small group.

The purpose of emphasizing the small group environment for discipleship training is primarily to fill the spiritual needs of those participating. However, taking a step further, the purpose also lies in satisfying the needs of the whole church. The entire church needs to be connected in small groups in order for a large number of believers to be able to make a full use of their gifts without hindrances. And that depends on the lay leaders who have been trained through discipleship training small groups.

For this work the lay leaders must first become used to small groups, and they must first experience a change in their lives in small groups. Through this experience, they will be molded into suitable vessels to serve others and to meet their spiritual needs. In other words, they have to be trained until they are able to share the Word of God with other believers, counsel them about their problems, and show the example of a witness and a servant.

Thus, desired results cannot be expected unless the adult small groups in the church are led by qualified lay leaders. In this sense, the discipleship training small group is the most suitable way to utilize simultaneously both the training and healing functions of a group.

Chapter 24

Understanding the Inductive Method

Inductive Bible study is an effective pedagogical method. Even now it is rapidly being assimilated into more churches, and thus it is no longer an unfamiliar and strange subject, as it used to be in the past. This is truly an encouraging development.

The majority of discipleship training study materials available today use this method, so you can naturally understand what an inductive approach is when you use these study materials. However, study material is only a guide. It does not contain everything needed for an inductive study of the Bible. To compare it to a drawing, the study material is like a sketch. The leader and trainees using the material have to complete the picture together. For this reason, a leader ought to understand the theory of the inductive method and acquire considerable experience in order to lead the study skillfully.

Become an Expert First
Although the inductive method may be applied somewhat differently when individually meditating on the Word than when studying the Word with others as a team in a small group, its principle and process are almost identical.

The most important thing is that the leader must practice this method diligently in his personal devotional time of meditating on the Word. Just as he eats three meals a day, he must constantly go before the counsel of the Word with a pen and a notebook. And when the leader first experiences a great blessing from the use of the method, he will then gain confidence in this method's excellence and also acquire the necessary skills to lead discipleship training effectively.

Observation and practice are the best ways to improve the skills to lead an inductive Bible study. Visit discipleship training classes led by competent leaders, and observe closely. Ask questions such as: 'What would I do in this situation?', 'How is that leader different from me?', 'What are the things I need to learn?', and 'What is my weakest point?'

Keep asking these questions. Continue to observe and learn. Practice what you have learned without delay. Then in a little while, you will be able to see a remarkable development.

You may have some innate weaknesses. For example, you may be impatient and unable to listen well to others. You may be very talkative, so that you cannot stop once you begin to speak. You may be weak in logic, so that you often lose the main point and wander. Your facial features may give a rather hard and stiff impression which makes the other party uncomfortable. If you find that you have these weaknesses, then you need to kneel down before God and pray until your kneeling cushion gets worn out. Weaknesses will not be easily mended until you experience the Holy Spirit's special hand of healing. Therefore, frankly share your weaknesses with the trainees and ask for their prayers and help, always maintaining an attitude of humility.

Understand These Special Features
The inductive method, when compared to the deductive method, has several special features. Leaders must

understand these special features correctly; otherwise they may not be used effectively.

First, every participant is both a teacher and a student. The purpose of the inductive method is not to create a relationship where the leader speaks and others listen. Its purpose is for everyone to share what they think and discover. In many cases a study ends in failure because this characteristic has not been properly understood.

Second, unlike the deductive method which follows the logic of proof, the inductive method follows the logic of discovery. In the deductive method, the leader first decides a certain truth for discussion, and then explains or interprets in order to prove it. And others are persuaded and led to an understanding through the explanation.

By contrast, in the inductive method, the participants verify the truth by allowing each person to discover something in the Word and share with others in the group. Consequently, the leader cannot simply give answers. The leader is only one among many fellow discoverers. The role of the leader in a small group is to encourage and motivate everyone to discover for themselves.

Third, communication is not one-sided, but it has a reciprocal aspect. In an inductive study, communication takes the form of a conversation, so the leader does not monopolize a unilateral conversation. If a leader or any other person within the group monopolizes the conversation, this will shatter the possibility of carrying on meaningful communication.

Fourth, the inductive method focuses on changing character rather than just conveying knowledge. In other words, it emphasizes the importance of a new life that has been given by God so as to develop maturity and Christ-likeness. For this reason, compared to the deductive method, it may be somewhat unstructured and non-academic. However, the fact is that this apparent shortcoming operates as strength in the inductive method. Structured or academic material can take away the freedom of the learner to discover on his own. Once a person's character is transformed, systematic theories can always be supplemented by other readings, lectures and seminars. Let's not forget that our problem does not come from a lack of knowledge, but from our character that is not worthy of the gospel.

Fifthly, the inductive method attaches great importance to the application of the Word.

The deductive method often lets people simply listen, agree, and then leave. However, the inductive method doesn't allow the study to end in such a manner. It demands from the participants a specific decision to apply and practice the truth that each has discovered, realized, and verified in sharing with other believers. No one in the group can evade it.

Approach the Word This Way

The first step is observation. Observation is an attitude by which one intentionally tries to discover something in the passage of the Bible. Most church members are not trained in observation. For a long time the church has depended on the deductive method to teach the Bible. As a result, many people have become accustomed to opening and shutting the Bible with their eyes closed.

People who are accustomed to just hearing a sermon, automatically close the Bible after the reading of the text. Then they wait to hear what the preacher has to say. Thereby they naturally give up the opportunity to observe the Bible for themselves. No one knows the degree of spiritual damage the church has suffered as a result.

The inductive method in essence forces us to see the Bible afresh every time we open it. It guides us to observe the Word as lovers read and re-read love letters. One can observe the text according to the six question principle, asking 'who, what, when, where, how, and why', in order to understand the whole context. Or one can follow a process that begins by getting hold of the entire content as if looking through a zoom lens, and then examines the details. Pay attention to words that are repeated. Search for the content that is emphasized. Also look for any relevant or apparently conflicting content. Then you will be able to see the truths you might not have otherwise discovered.

The second step is interpretation. Interpretation involves research in order to discover the meaning of the text. A Bible study must reach a correct understanding of the content in order to transform lives. You must concentrate in order to understand the meaning.

We accept the Bible, which contains revelations recorded in ancient times, as the Word given to us living in the present age. Therefore, we must engage in appropriate research to overcome any linguistic and cultural barriers. To accomplish this, it would be good to recommend helpful reference books to the trainees. However, there is one thing that we must know. It is the fact that a lay person needs a pastor's help to accurately interpret the Word. Pastors should not let the trainees say, 'I can understand everything without you' (2 Pet. 3:16).

The third step is the process of response. Response is stating what one feels after realizing the meaning. This is the step of internalizing the Word as one's own. It is here that the Bible begins to work within us as the voice of the living God. The deeper the inspiration, the more positive the response will be.

Jesus explained the Old Testament in detail to the two disciples He met on the road to Emmaus. What happened to them? 'Were not our hearts burning within us while he talked with us on the road and opened the Scriptures to us?' (Luke 24:32). They felt burning emotions. So what was their reaction? They strongly urged Jesus to come into the village and stay with them. This was obviously a very positive reaction.

The inductive method always has room to anticipate this kind of response. A leader who keeps this fact in mind will not hesitate to guide and encourage the trainees to express their feelings without pretense.

Application is the fourth step. Once we have been affected by the Word, we must proceed to the next step. This is the step of obeying the Word. We can be moved to tears by the Word, but if an opportunity is not provided for that Word to change our life and character, then that 'inspiration' cannot be considered the blessing of the Holy Spirit. Application is creating an opportunity and space for the burning inspiration of the Word to work freely in us.

There are many people who consider as an application making a statement like, 'From now on I'll love my brothers and sisters'. However, this is nothing more than a mere expression of a general thought. Application must be specific. It must be accompanied by an actual plan to carry it out. If there are things that require repentance, then there must be a decision to fix them. And application must even go so far as making sure that our obedience is carried out properly through subsequent examinations. When that happens, we stand at the place of becoming like Christ.

A leader must lead the trainees so that the application is not done deceptively, simply because they were compelled to do it. Let us, however, be sure of one thing. Responding and application are something that a leader cannot do in place of the trainees. Depending on the situation, the leader may do observation and interpretation for the trainees. However, the leader must guide each trainee to personally and truthfully respond and apply what they have learned before God.

Use Questions

Asking suitable questions is perhaps the most useful tool in leading an inductive Bible study. Therefore, it is necessary for the leader to be trained in the skill of asking appropriate questions. The timing and the kind of questions asked can determine the direction and atmosphere of the study. Therefore in order to become a competent leader, one must always prepare effective questions to open up the hearts of everyone in the discipleship class. The questions should draw each person to the Word and help them to share with one another the truth and the deep emotions that have resulted from the changes taking place in them.

Using questions in Bible study is not a new skill. In the gospels, Jesus asked more than a hundred questions. Someone said that Jesus did not come to answer questions but to ask questions.[1] Jesus gave hints for the kind of answers he wanted, and frequently used loaded questions to help the person being asked to arrive at a conclusion on their own.

When a trainee is asked a question, he should maintain a sincere attitude of waiting for the Holy Spirit's leading as he thinks about an answer. At the same time, the leader should refrain from speaking. Everyone then will concentrate on hearing the answer. In addition, an atmosphere of participating together in the conversation will be created.

Someone made a brilliant remark about the effectiveness of asking a suitable question. 'Asking the right question is like rolling a stone. Even though you're sit-

---

1. Navigator, *Bible Study Methods*, 56.

ting quietly on top of the hill, the stone will roll down and make other stones roll down with it.'[2] Asking a right question can function like rolling a stone to bring everyone into the conversation.

A good question has a clear meaning, is relevant to the text, and is able to stimulate discussion. A question should not be complicated. Its relevance to the content of the study should be clear. It should not be trite and uninteresting. For these reasons, it is advisable for leaders to prepare appropriate questions in advance. However, it is not necessary to disregard effective, well-directed, and impromptu questions that the Holy Spirit gives during the time of discussion. Sometimes they are better than the prepared questions.

A leader has to be careful while asking questions not to create the atmosphere of an oral exam. He should be able to elicit answers with a gentle attitude and lighten the tension with a sense of humor every now and then. He should not demand a hasty answer, but should either wait or turn the question over to someone else. He must listen with a sincere interest in the person answering. And when the leader shows a positive reaction even if the answer is not satisfactory, it will help to raise the trainees' morale.

A competent leader will not try to give an answer to everything as if he were a living encyclopedia. He has to aid the learner to answer on his own. It is better for the leader to avoid immediately answering the trainees' questions if possible. Rather, he should answer a question with another question, and lead the trainees to arrive at the right answer themselves. A discipleship-training leader should avoid closed questions that may be answered with a simple 'yes' or 'no'. This has the danger of ending a discussion. A good question is an open-end-

---

2. Ibid., 22.

ed question that opens a person's mind. Such questions usually begin with 'why', 'what', or 'how'. Furthermore, the leader should avoid clumsy questions with obvious answers.

Benefits of the Inductive Method

There are many benefits that can be gained by a good use of the inductive method, and among them are a few that we must remember. First, the inductive method helps the trainee to recognize the authority of the Scriptures on his own. Even for a person who has been trivializing the authority of the Scriptures secretly in his heart, once he opens the Bible and begins to write answers in the blank spaces of the study material, he will discover that he is beginning to recognize the authority of the Scriptures in spite of himself. And soon he will be overpowered by the absolute authority of God's Word.

Another advantage is that it plants self-confidence in the trainee to study the Bible by himself. Inductive material is designed to help the user look up passages in the Bible, analyse and understand them, and find satisfaction in applying what he has decided in his heart. In other words, the inductive method does not make one feel that studying the Bible is difficult. This plants in the trainee a love for the Word and the self-confidence to study the Scriptures on his own.

An amazing strength of the inductive method is that it enables those studying the Word to receive it quickly, without hesitation. When meditating on the Word inductively, one is bound to record what one discovers and realizes. No one doubts a truth he himself discovers. He will believe at once even the words that he did not believe previously. The Word that has been readily received in this manner can bring about great changes in a person. It is not really surprising for someone who has studied the Scriptures deductively for many years to change into a completely different person in a month, once he starts to study the Word inductively. By keeping in mind these advantages of the inductive method, one will be able to train others in more creative ways.

Chapter 25

Leadership in
Discipleship Training

Leadership that Brings Change

To be honest, the success and health of discipleship training depends entirely on the leader. If it goes well, it is his responsibility; if it goes poorly, it is his responsibility. There is no need to blame the trainees. We shouldn't blame the method either. One has to recognize that 100 percent of the responsibility rests on the shoulders of the leader. Uneducated fishermen of Galilee turned the world upside down when Jesus took a hold of them. Although we cannot dare to compare ourselves to Jesus, we must recognize one thing as a truth. If a leader is excellent, then even if the trainees fall short of the recommended qualification criteria, the training will not be greatly affected. So, did you fail your discipleship training? There is only one reason. The leader was incompetent. If someone who is well equipped begins discipleship training, whether it takes place in the country-side or in the slums will not be a problem. In my country today there are numerous examples, found in various places, to prove that this statement is not an exaggeration.

In this sense, serious research about the kind of leadership we need is an important task that cannot be omitted. I read an article by Leighton Ford in a magazine called *World Evangelization* in which he wrote about Jesus' model of leadership that brings change. After I read the article, I became certain that this is the kind of leadership that needs to be developed by a pastor who wants to do discipleship training. I would like to briefly introduce its content here.[1]

Jesus is the perfect model of 'leadership that transforms' us. The first special feature of leadership that brings change is the knowledge that you are a son of God, and its symbol is an open ear. It was important for Jesus before he began to do anything – before preaching, teaching and healing – to receive baptism and hear from heaven the voice of God the Father saying, 'You are my son, whom I love; with you I am well pleased.' Why? Because leadership comes from a secure self-identity.

Wrong leadership originates from insecurity about self. Everyone has weaknesses and feels insecure about them. The beginning of healthy leadership is overcoming such insecurity, and acquiring and being assured of a secure self identity. How does this become possible? It becomes possible by hearing. In other words it becomes possible when we recognize that God is pleased with us. Such recognition of our secure identity gives us assurance and forms conviction within us.

The second characteristic of Jesus' 'leadership that brings change' is the power to put what has been seen into action. The symbol here is an open eye. A real vision begins with seeing. Immediately after being baptized, Jesus saw Simon and his brother Andrew throwing their fishing net, and told them to follow Him. Later, Jesus saw James and his brother John.

Jesus was a pioneer who had the eyes to see eternity in ordinary, everyday life. He said in the Gospel of John that He was only doing the work He 'saw' the Father

---

1. Leighton Ford, 'Jesus as a Model for Leader,' *World Evangelization* (March/April 1995), 6-10.

doing. For Jesus, vision was seeing what the Father does. Without seeing the Father's will, there can be no leadership that brings about change.

The third characteristic is the power to convey truth in storytelling. Its symbol is an open mouth. Jesus conveyed His vision with stories. When the Word became flesh and was embodied in stories, it was like an explosion of dynamite, manifesting the power of God to transform the hearts and minds of men.

The fourth characteristic is delegated authority. Its symbol is open hands. Not only was Jesus concerned with saving lost sheep, but He was also interested in transforming them into shepherds. The secret of His successful ministry was that He valued the people around him. Thus, He commissioned the disciples with His authority. Open hands mean delegating the authority from oneself to those called by God.

As leaders, we have to ask ourselves whether we have an open ear, an open eye, an open mouth, and open hands. In discipleship training the leader has to be ready to be the first to hear, to see, to say, and to give. Only then can he expect the miracle of change in the character and life of another.

Like Parent, Like Coach

There are other elements besides those I have mentioned above that a leader must have in order to make disciples in a small group environment. These elements can also be easily found in Jesus and the Apostle Paul.

First, the leader has to have an attitude of a parent who loves and nurtures one's children: '...we were gentle among you, like a mother caring for her little children. We loved you so much that we were delighted to share with you not only the gospel of God but our lives as well, because you had become so dear to us' (1 Thess. 2:7-8).

A leader should never stop encouraging the trainees even though they do not meet his expectations. It is important for the trainees to feel that they are being loved. Don't ever show favouritism. Also, give a clear 'yes' or 'no'. One of the most damaging things for the trainees is an ambiguous attitude from the leader. Not only that, a good leader must value each person and take care that personal fellowship is not severed.

One thing that may seem easy but is actually difficult in discipleship training is being honest. A leader should not be afraid to say, 'I don't know'. The more the leader opens up honestly, the more affection the trainees will feel towards him.

A leader who trains with the heart of a parent does not indulge in the attitude of unilateral command or coercion. This doesn't mean it is good to leave trainees to themselves to do whatever they want. It is good to maintain an appropriate tension between leader and trainees. The degree of this tension depends on the selection of communication style.[2] In persuasion style, the leader's authority increases and the group's freedom withers relatively. In a discussion style, the exact opposite occurs. Both of these two types can be very useful depending on the situation.

However, in general, most leaders select the conversational style in discipleship class.

Discipleship class maintains sufficient tension. However, just as comfort and peace should be felt when parents and children sit together affectionately and converse, such tension should feel natural and not stressful. Let love overflow in your speech and expression. This love is the most mysterious power that can change a person.

The leader's role in a small group is often compared to that of a coach. 'Coach' is a term used in sport. However,

2. Clyde Reid, *Groups Alive – Church Alive*, 82.

a coach's function has many similarities to a leader's function in discipleship training. It is a well-known fact that the progress of a soccer or baseball team depends a great deal on the quality of the coaching staff.

A coach's glory is that he is a person who advances and trains other people's ability... A Christian coach has to be someone who is more interested in developing someone else rather than lifting his authority.[3]

The reason we say that a discipleship training leader is like a coach is not only because he finds lay people and trains them to serve. That is also true, but another similarity is the style in which he leads the Bible study. The coach sets up a strategy to win the game. He doesn't appear himself but lets the athletes run on the field. The athletes act as they receive his signals. The outcome of the game depends greatly on the coach's leadership and strategy.

A leader teaching the Bible in discipleship class has a similar role. He can cram the Bible into the heads of the trainees just like a coach who puts the athletes into an intensive training program before the game. However, he hopes, if possible, that the trainees will engage in Bible study firsthand. He wisely thinks it important to help them to understand and apply the truth on their own. This resembles the role of a coach who sends the athletes out into the field while he sits on the bench and gives signals.

Nevertheless, the whole flow of the time depends on the coach. The success of the study depends on the leader's role. In essence he is in the position of leading the whole, but on the surface he behaves as though he is just one of those studying.

---

3. John Stott, *One People*, p. 527.

Good leadership depends on the power to motivate the trainees to run with excitement. However, when we are actually in the midst of doing discipleship training and feel pressured by it, how often do we forget this important principle and taste the bitterness of trying to pull everything off by ourselves?

Chapter 26

First Time Round

Check Before Training

When the time arrives for the pastor to begin discipleship training after long preparation and a careful selection of the target members, something else needs to be done promptly. The pastor or the leader must meet individually with the target members, review the items necessary for the training, and tell them in advance what they need to prepare. In an established church, if the target members are elders or other core members well known by the pastor, then the items of inspection may vary from those for the general membership. It will be necessary for the pastor to make a proper judgement of the situation and make necessary adjustments.

The first is to visit the potential trainees in their homes in advance. It is best if this visit is done about two weeks before the opening worship of discipleship training. Don't forget to pray for them before the individual interview. Pray for each member of the family by name. We know from many experiences that there is a big difference between meeting someone for whom you've prayed and meeting someone for whom you haven't prayed.

Examine the trainees' spiritual condition and background first. If the church structure is small, then it may not be necessary to hold a separate meeting to perform this task, since it is very likely that the leader knows them quite well. However, even though some may be very familiar, it will be better to hold such a meeting in order to give the trainees an opportunity to examine themselves anew, and feel a healthy tension as they go into the training.

Carefully review together how long they have believed, whether they have ever been involved in a pseudo-religious sect or a cult, if they have assurance of salvation, how they are maintaining daily devotional life, how deeply they understand the basics of the Bible, what their spiritual problems are, and so on. These are all vital items that should not be left out. And it is good to find out if there are any conflicts or problems in their family.

Organizing this data in a file will be very helpful in deciding how to deal with each trainee during the training. And one can always add additional information to the file as the training progresses.

Secondly, while visiting the potential trainees at home, tell them the rules and regulations of discipleship training. Explain that they will need to spend about two to three hours a day to prepare for the lesson and to do the homework. Obtain their commitment to do so. Furthermore, it is a good idea to inform them in advance of the general content of the homework.

Explain and have them agree that if they're absent more than three times, then they may not continue with the training. Ask them if they can open their homes as a meeting place when their turn comes to do so. Before leaving, don't forget to bless each family with the Word and prayer. It will be best if the Scripture shared at this time is one that can strengthen the trainees throughout the year and encourage them not to relax or give up even when tempted do so.

When individual home visits and inspections are done, make an announcement in the church and prepare for the opening worship service for discipleship training. The pastor mustn't let discipleship training look like another educational program. He has to make it so important that the congregation will feel, even without a detailed explanation, that the pastor begins this effort with his life on the line and that this is one of the most important ministries in the church.

For this purpose it is necessary to have a special opening service and a completion service which will take place a year or two later. At SaRang Church, from its early years, the services celebrating commencement and completion of discipleship training have taken root as the most passionate and well-attended of all services.

The First Session

At the first session, just meeting together itself is so exciting that it should overflow with grace. The discipleship training pastors should try to leave a good impression. Keep in mind that although the lay people normally do not feel nervous about seeing pastors at a distance, they may find meeting the pastor each week in a limited space with ten or so people to be very stressful. It will be important to create an atmosphere in which the trainees feel comfortable during the first session.

Choose a secretary and a treasurer at the first session to assist the pastor. Select someone whom the pastor thought appropriate when he was visiting individual homes. It is best if the pastor can provide an explanation for his choice, to which all are able to give their consent.

Furthermore, when the membership is more than ten people, I recommend that committees of three or four people be formed according to the trainees' residential locality, and choose a person to be in charge of each committee. This will be very helpful when there is a need to make an urgent call or to examine each other spiritually. In addition, ask each trainee to write down the names of two people who will be a prayer support throughout the training.

At SaRang Church, much information and many assignments are given during the first session. For example, the monthly dues are decided. A hymnal, a Bible, study material, Quiet Time binder and memory cards, coloured pencils, and even a handkerchief are all provided at the first meeting. (Someone may ask, 'Why give a handkerchief?' A handkerchief has a symbolic meaning. It implies that the training will involve many tears. There will never be training where there is only laughter from beginning to end.) And the pastor explains in detail the assignments to be prepared for the next meeting. Everyone might feel overwhelmed at first. Therefore, it is necessary to consider the circumstances and the levels of the trainees. For training to be training, it is better if the demands are slightly imposing. However, if the burden is too heavy, then it can have an adverse effect. If discipleship training ministry is already well established in the church, it will be effective to begin without reviewing everyone's circumstances in the first session. However, for the church just starting out, the pace should match the level of familiarity among the trainees. To obtain good results, the training should be interesting and feel worthwhile despite the difficulties involved. The trainees also should be able to experience the working of the Holy Spirit through the homework. The pastor should seriously consider these matters and handle them with wisdom and prayer.

The pastor should tell the trainees the things to keep in mind when opening their homes. There are many cases where homemakers show a great deal of insecurity and sensitivity in this regard. A trainee from a wealthy home may look forward to opening one's home. However, having guests can be a huge burden for those who are not from as well-to-do homes, and someone may even feel embarrassed if his or her house is small.

Therefore, we need to be careful not to become stumbling blocks to others. Several months into the training, when everyone has visited each other's homes and understands one another's circumstances, they will begin to acquire a right attitude towards each other. This will in turn help them to mature and grow in their Christian character.

When the trainees acknowledge that everything they see and feel becomes a means for growing as disciples of Jesus, the discipleship class will progress into a relationship of loving each other deeply. Boasting will disappear and embarrassment will melt away. Only a community of love shared in Jesus will remain.

Encourage those preparing their home for the meeting to put away anything that can cause distraction. See to it beforehand that phones are turned off and that there will be no unexpected visitors during the study time. Another important matter is the meal time. For some the class may be over lunch, for others over dinner. Naturally, it is expected that the trainee providing the meeting place prepares the meal.

I've come to know from experience that meal times can often become the devil's playground. The homeowner is so busy preparing the meal that he or she can't focus on the training. When the whole house is filled with the aroma of food, the mood is also not right for training. A wealthy home may completely overload the table with food. Others, who are impressed or shamed by this, are discouraged and fall into temptation. Therefore, it is necessary to set up a firm rule right from the start. There are many methods. You may choose to agree on one standard dish, or have a few members to bring a dish at a time. Make sure the quality of the spiritual training does not fall short on account of eating and drinking.

At SaRang Church, whoever is late or absent has to pay a fine. Three or more absences lead to automatic dismissal from the training. Lending or borrowing money among the trainees is absolutely forbidden. If such financial dealings are discovered, then the individuals concerned are asked to leave the group immediately. In addition, the trainees are also strongly advised to avoid conflict with their spouses because of the training. Sometimes we see husbands or wives who are so engrossed in their homework that they study well into the night without going to bed until late. As a result, sometimes the trainees get into a rather embarrassing situation in which they are pressured by their spouses to quit discipleship training.

We have also seen situations where children and family are neglected. There is no other way to achieve a balance between the family and training, or between work and training, than for the trainees to become two or three times more diligent. Repeat this point many times during the early stages of training.

It may also be good for the pastor to make a few predictions before the first session ends. He may tell them in advance, for example, that for a while they may feel the homework is too burdensome and may want to quit. They may be tested with family difficulties that seem hard to bear. There will be times when they are hurt by other trainees. They may suffer from an uneasy conscience for being unable to live out what they have learned, and carry big emotional burdens. For reasons unknown, there may also be times when they don't want to see the pastor anymore. If such warnings are made in advance, then when a forewarned incident actually occurs, the trainees will not be so bewildered.

It is necessary to tell the group these things in advance, because they are actual events that often occur.

We have no need to fear if we know Satan's schemes. Emphasize that we must admit that we are all human, full of flaws, and therefore must have compassion for each other.

Before parting after each meeting, take each other's hand, look at each other, and confess: 'We are a body. We need to help each other. I need your help. Please help me. I love you.' Many will probably want to remain in their seats a little longer saturated in deep emotion. Could anything else bring more joy to a pastor than discipleship training?

Part 1
TODAY'S CHURCH AND THE LAITY
INTRODUCTION

Part 2
MINISTRY PHILOSOPHY
ECCLESIOLOGY

Part 3
MINISTRY STRATEGY
DISCIPLESHIP

Part 4
MINISTRY METHOD
DISCIPLESHIP TRAINING

Part 5
MINISTRY FIELD
DISCIPLES

Chapter 27

A Discipleship Training Ministry Model Church

To what extent is it possible to disciple the laity in a local church? This was the question I had to ask in the latter half of the 1970s as SaRang Church began its ministry. At that time, no one could give any definitive answer. Not one church could be found in which discipleship training had succeeded in changing the church structure in any notable way. Although there were one or two churches that were known for conducting discipleship training through small group Bible studies, it was difficult to view these churches as having their roots firmly planted in the discipleship training philosophy. Therefore, it was only with a great deal of uncertainty that our discipleship training ministry started out. Despite my personal conviction that it could be done, the truth is, no one was able to guarantee its success. Although it was a new church plant, the general church climate was hostile to discipleship training and there were many obstacles to overcome.

Why A Model Church?
Why is a model church for discipleship training necessary? If we were to merely theorize about discipleship training and could not show its fruits in an actual ministry setting, then it would be overly-ambitious to expect

people to show any significant degree of interest. If, on the other hand, discipleship training is indeed consistent with the intrinsic nature of the church, and if it is the most appropriate method of ministry based on biblical principles, then establishing a healthy discipleship training ministry setting for people to come and observe will enable many pastors to take part in the vision of awakening the laity. Furthermore, such model churches can also stimulate a new vision for churches in general.

In order to be a model church, there are several conditions that must be met. First, it must be a church where the pastor has a thorough ministry philosophy of discipleship training. Unless the leader is totally excited and enthusiastic about this ministry, it will be difficult for the church to be recognized as a model church for discipleship training. Churches that are simply imitating or testing it out for a little while on a trial basis will not have the power to convince or inspire anyone else.

Second, a model church must be where discipleship training has been conducted for at least seven years and where it has become the central core of the church's entire ministry. Only then can we examine the changes taking place through discipleship training in the whole of the church and see the ways in which the nature of that church differs from that of the neighbouring churches. The third condition is that there must be some evidence to show that the church is indeed becoming healthy.

Until the middle of the 1980s, model churches could not be found in Korea. It was in 1986 that SaRang Church opened its ministry setting to other churches. The response of many pastors in Korea and abroad was greater than expected. I believe such an overwhelming response was due to the fact that there was no other way to verify the benefits of discipleship training ministry. Since then, SaRang Church has opened its discipleship training ministry setting to thousands of church leaders over sixty-five times to motivate and share the vision for discipleship training. Opening a model church to the public was risky but we knew we had to do it at some point in time.

Perhaps in certain respects, SaRang Church is losing its capacity to serve as an effective ministry setting, mainly because of its size. A ministry setting should be able to provide a sense of identity and encouragement to those who come to observe. It should also be able to stimulate the visitors with the confidence that they can do it also. However, SaRang Church has grown too large over the years to effectively serve that role. It may be able to show that it is possible to grow into a large church through discipleship training. However, there is a fear that visitors may feel rather overwhelmed as when looking at a mountain that cannot be climbed.

However, there is one fact that we should not forget. Whichever church we visit, the things that should interest us and that we need to observe and verify are not just external things. We must be able to discern the things that are not readily visible, hidden behind the external appearance. Everyone knows that when a doctor examines a patient, he or she is not interested in how big or how good-looking the patient is. We must also adopt the same attitude when observing a church and its ministry. We must be able to read the pastor's ministry philosophy from the church environment. We must be able to perceive the spirit that governs the church community. We must be able to examine what is happening in the church. And we must be able to identify the reason for its health and the source of its growth. Only then can we be certain of what we should take back with us to our own respective ministries. In other words, we must be able to hear God's voice, see

His vision, and then return to our respective churches. If the visiting pastors can look at SaRang Church with such discerning eyes, then I believe SaRang Church still has the capacity to serve other churches as a model church for discipleship training.

Model Churches

Today there are many wonderful and healthy model churches. For the past ten years or so, God has blessed these churches amazingly. It is no longer difficult to find examples of the abundant fruit produced through the sweat and tears shed by these pastors day and night in order to awaken the laity. Not only in the big cities of Korea, but in the smaller provincial towns as well, there are many churches that can now boast of discipleship training ministries. Furthermore, even in Japan, a country that has not experienced a revival for the past century, one can now find churches conducting discipleship training and beginning to make an impact. It is difficult to express in words the depths of our gratitude and joy.

Please bear in mind that there are now many exemplary ministry settings to visit and witness the abundant fruit of discipleship training. For the first few years after the CAL (Called to Awaken the Laity) Seminar began, one of the most important objectives for the participating pastors was to see for themselves how discipleship training took place at SaRang Church. However, circumstances have changed since then. Now most of the participants attend the seminar, because they have already been deeply impacted and challenged by the neighbouring churches that have experienced a turning point in their ministry through discipleship training. This development signifies that it is no longer just SaRang Church that provides an effective ministry setting to observe discipleship training, but that there are many sister churches that have come together to take on the responsibility of providing examples of discipleship training ministry.

I would like to introduce several churches that I believe will be of great help to pastors. The New Central Church located in Pusan is an excellent example of how an established church with a long tradition can be changed through discipleship training. When a new pastor was appointed to that church about ten years ago, the pastor emeritus still exerted a strong influence on the church. Most of the congregation was comprised of senior elders who were bound by fixed ideas. There was a significant amount of antagonism between the church members and the full-time church staff. In short, this was the perfect example of a church that possessed all the qualities of a typical established church. No matter how one tried to look at it, this was a church in which discipleship training seemed an impossible goal. However, today in that very same church, great miracles are taking place through discipleship training, and many other established churches are receiving encouragement.

In America, there is a church proclaiming a powerful message about the great potential of discipleship training ministry to the more than 3,000 Korean-American churches, where many Korean-Americans look for spiritual refuge. This is the SaRang Community Church of Southern California. For the past ten years, hundreds of the Korean-American church pastors had been challenged by the vision of discipleship training. Yet most of them gave up halfway through, claiming that the Korean-American churches simply did not have a suitable ground for discipleship training. They claimed that it would do more harm than good to confront Korean-Americans with the concept of 'training', since what they really needed instead was constant care and comfort.

SaRang Community Church of Southern California has overturned such notions, and demonstrated that the Korean-American churches indeed have fertile soil for fruitful discipleship training. Many pastors have been encouraged by this church and have begun to take on the challenge of discipleship training again. That God planted a church overflowing with such inspiration in America is a great blessing for all Korean-American churches.

Another church that deserves our attention is Yeomkwang Church, located in Taean, Korea. Without any actual evidence, it would be difficult to judge whether or not the discipleship training ministry could be successful in the farming villages of remote districts. However for the past ten or so years, Yeomkwang Church has played a big part in removing these fears and uncertainties. Being convinced that there is no royal road to effective ministry apart from discipleship training even for the churches in rural villages, this church advocated discipleship training with greater strength and conviction than any other church. For quite some time now, Yeomkwang Church has become a powerful exemplary ministry setting for discipleship training, attracting the attention of many pastors. I am confident that we will soon witness the miracle of awakening the laity as disciples of Christ even in rural churches.

There are many other churches that are just as wonderful and significant as the ones introduced above. Below are the model churches that are actively involved in discipleship training.

Korea
Hosanna Church, Busan (Rev. H. J. Choi)
Hosanna Church is a model church that shows how even the most conservative churches can successfully adopt

discipleship training ministry. When Rev. Choi came in 1987, the church had 400 members, and now it has grown to more than 7,000 members attending every Sunday.

Jangchung Church, Seoul (Rev. C. W. Nam)
Jangchung Church illustrates how discipleship training ministry can bring about a dramatic change. Though the majority of the members are 60 years of age and older, it also has one of the most vital young adult groups in the city.

Kangnam Church, Seoul (Rev. T. K. Song)
Gangnam Church shows how critical it is for a pastor to carry out his vision consistently and progressively. Rev. Song began discipling the elders for the past 7 years, and now the church has grown by more than 3,500 members.

Hwa Pyung Church, Goyang (Rev. S. T. Choi)
Hwa Pyung mobilizes its lay ministers who have undergone discipleship training, to serve in their house church ministry. Every house church consists of less than 20 members and has its own lay minister as its leader.

Dae Gwang Church, Pyung Taek (Rev. C. D. Bae)
When Rev. Bae planted Dae Gwang, he was determined to equip the laity to be lay ministers, and was convinced that discipleship training ministry was the essence of ministry. Pyung Taek has less than 360,000 residents, and the church has become one of the area's healthiest churches, with over 2,000 members.

Grace Church, Incheon (Rev. J. S. Park)
Grace Church mobilizes its lay ministers to serve in various ministries. All ministries of the church are handled by the lay ministers.

Cheom Dam Church, Kwangju (Rev. D. H. Lim)
Cheom Dam focuses on discipling the laity for trans-formed lives, and implements various ministry models from churches both in Korea and abroad.

Light & Salt Church, Mokpo (Rev. H. Y. Cho)
Rev. Cho was fired from his previous church because he wanted to do discipleship training. He planted Light & Salt in Mokpo which has less than 300 churches with its population of 260,000. Over 90 percent of those 300 churches have less than 100 members. Light & Salt has grown by over 500 members.

Sandol Church, Yeosu (Rev. M. C. Shin)
Sandol was originally planted to commemorate the legacy of Rev. Son who was martyred during the Korean War. Sandol is in the process of producing disciples via discipleship training ministry. It has over 700 members and is the leading healthy church in its area.

Ye An Church, Iksan (Rev. Joo. H. Oh)
Ye An opens its door to the community by sharing ministry resources and its buildings. Pastor Oh believes that this is the way to communicate the gospel today, by allowing the community to see what discipleship ministry is all about.

Saeronam Church, Daejeon (Rev. Jung. H. Oh)
Saeronam Church has overcome the difficulties involved in bringing change to an established traditional church, and has successfully implemented discipleship training and healthy pastoral ministry in a local church. Saeronam Church has focused on raising healthy lay ministers through disciple-ship training, and has become a model church with a Sun-day attendance of over 2,500 adults in the city of Daejeon.

Sansung Church, Busan (Rev. W. K. Huh)
When Rev. Huh became the pastor of Sansung Church upon returning from Chile where he had served as a missionary, he started discipleship training with the elders, who became thoroughly transformed through it. Since then, with the labours of such lay leaders changed through discipleship training, Sansung Church has grown into a healthy church with 1500 members.

Hanbit Church, Changwon (Rev. H. K. Yoon)
Hanbit Church implemented discipleship training in 1987, and has become a healthy church with a Sunday attendance of over 2,000 adults. Rev. Hee Ku Yoon says that the greatest benefit the church has reaped through discipleship training is the lay leaders who partner with him in ministry.

Samsung Church, Daegu (Rev. Jung In Lee)
Despite its disadvantageous location, Samsung Church is known today as a church with the best atmosphere among the churches in the city of Daegoo.

Woolsan Church, Woolsan (Rev. K. C. Chung)
In order to share the church's new vision and ministry plans with the lay leaders reared through discipleship training, Woolsan Church has implemented an additional course called Vision Communion as a follow-up course for discipleship training. The Vision Communion Class has helped Woolsan Church to become a future-oriented and progressive church.

Buksam Jaeil Church, Gumi (Rev. B. S. Woo)
Buksam Jaeil Church is a great model church that has demonstrated that discipleship training can be implemented under any circumstances. Buksam Jaeil Church

even conducted discipleship training on top of a rock in a mountain, because they did not have a suitable place to do the training. Today, Buksam Church has healthy lay leaders who are together carrying out various ministries of the church.

Saechoonchun Church, Choonchun (Rev. J. W. Shin)
Saechoonchun Church has modeled that one can succeed despite experiencing failures, as long as one maintains a conviction about discipleship training and continues to persevere. It took three years to complete the first female discipleship training and five years to complete the first male discipleship training. However, discipleship training took root in the church in spite of much difficulty, and transformed Saechoonchun Church into a healthy and thriving church today.

Seemeen Church, Woolsan (Rev. J. K. Lee)
Seemeen Church has demonstrated that it is possible for a church to experience steady and stable church growth through discipleship training. Seemeen Church was founded 21 years ago, and has grown into a representative church in the city of Woolsan with a Sunday attendance of over 2,000 adults.

Youngan Church, Busan (Rev. J. K. Park)
Youngan Church has demonstrated the synergy that is produced when strong pulpit messages work together with discipleship training. Today, Youngan Church is recognized as one of the fastest growing churches in the city of Pusan along with Hosanna Church and Sansung Church.

Church of Dream, Chungjoo (Rev. K. S. Ban)
Rev. Ban planted Church of Dream in order to make delinquent teenagers on the street into disciples of Jesus.

Today, many young lay leaders have been produced through discipleship training. These lay leaders lead small groups and take care of the lay members of the church. The lay members of the church, made up of people from varying age groups, all admire and desire to become like these young leaders.

Dongsan Church, Ansan (Rev. I. J. Kim)
Dongsan Church was known as one of the most successful and healthy model churches planted in new cities. When Dongsan Church, which has experienced the most epoch-making revival in Korea, began to stagnate, Rev. Kim decided to implement discipleship training. As a result, Dongsan Church experienced a second wave of revival.

Sammool Church, Bundang (Rev. E. J. Park)
Sammool Church offers an example of implementing discipleship training in a church that has been founded by separating from the mother church. It has been 3 years since Sammool Church was founded, and today it is recognized in Bundang region as a leading healthy church with a healthy pastor. Sammool Church took the bold step of limiting the term of office for both the senior pastor and ruling elders in order to implement and maintain healthy and stable ministry.

Japan
Ashiya Gospel Church (Rev. Kamei Tosihiro)
Ashiya Gospel Church is located in Hogohyun, Japan, and has 130 adult members. Forty members have completed discipleship training and there are 13 lay leaders working along with the pastor in the church. Ashiya Gospel Church tried to start discipleship training in 1995, but suffered a major setback due to the Great Kwandong Earthquake. Although the church was thrown into de-

spair by the earthquake, the pastor and the lay members earnestly prayed and launched discipleship training with the determination that this was indeed the time when 'nothing else would do other than discipleship training.' Ahiya Gospel Church aspires to become a model church for discipleship training in Japan as SaRang Church is in Korea.

Niitu Gospel Church (Rev. Matsunaga Yasutomo)
Niitu Gospel Church is located in Nigatahyun, Japan, and has 100 adult members and 10 lay leaders working alongside the pastor. Rev. Matsunaga Yasutomo graduated from the Called to Awaken the Laity Seminar twelve years ago, and after having read *Called to Awaken the Laity* several times, he implemented discipleship training in his church. However, still feeling inadequate, he recently attended the Discipleship Training Experiential School. His passion and determination were renewed to return to the starting point of discipleship training and carry out authentic discipleship training in earnest.

Oomiya Church (Rev. Kunimaro)
Oomiya Church is located in Citamasi, on the outskirts of Tokyo. It has 200 adult members and 102 years of history behind it. In order to implement discipleship training in this traditional, established church, Rev. Kunimaro attended the Called to Awaken the Laity Seminar with the church elders who were against discipleship training. The church experienced losing a half of its members in the beginning. However, the church has now become a model church where 50 lay leaders are serving the church alongside the pastor. Rev. Kunimaro is also a professor at Christ Theological Seminary, a leading seminary in Japan, and is promoting discipleship training at the seminary by using *Called To Awaken the Laity* as a textbook.

America
SaRang Church of Southern California

SaRang Church of Southern California was planted 18 years ago, and has now grown to be a mega-church with 7,000 adult members. SaRang Church was founded upon the ministry philosophy of raising healthy lay leaders through discipleship training. The founding pastor left the church in 2002 in order to serve as the senior pastor at SaRang Church in Seoul, Korea. However, it was possible for the church to remain solid and to prepare for a new stage, because there were healthy lay leaders who had been trained through discipleship training.

New York Bayside Presbyterian Church

New York Bayside Presbyterian Church has shown that there is no such thing as an impossible condition for discipleship training. The church has attained healthy church growth and spiritual transformation of the laity through carrying out discipleship training even in the midst of the barren reality of hectic immigrant life.

Hanbit Church, San Diego

San Diego Hanbit Church was a traditional immigrant church that had been barely maintaining its life due to endless problems peculiar to immigrant society. However, Hanbit Church has become a vibrant church through discipleship training and family ministry. Currently, nonbelievers and new believers make up 60 percent of the church. Hanbit Church has exemplified how spiritually immature Christians can be nurtured and built up through nurturing and discipleship training.

Yangeuimoon Church, Philadelphia

Philadelphia Yangeuimoon Church has demonstrated that even the immigrant life that has been simplified due to the cultural barriers and ruptures can be a favourable condition to train a person, and later, for the trained person to minister. The church has faithfully treaded on the straight and narrow path even in the midst of difficult circumstances, and has remained true to the essence of discipleship training. As a result, the church continues to enjoy a steady growth.

Oceania
Hanwoori Church, New Zealand
Hanwoori Church has demonstrated how important it is for leaders to have a healthy ministry philosophy that builds people up. The church continues to grow both in quantity and in quality. Furthermore, Hanwoori Church considers serving the local churches and pastors to be part of its mission, and therefore conducts diverse seminars that are open to other churches and pastors.

Siloam Church, Sydney
Sydney Siloam Church consisted of mostly students who were very mobile. Thus the church lacked stable membership, making it difficult to focus on discipleship training. Yet in spite of such adverse conditions, the church did not give up the ministry philosophy of discipleship training and continued to labour to build up healthy lay leaders. As a result, Sydney Siloam Church has become a healthy church, acknowledged even by the Presbyterian Church of Australia.

Chapter 28

Heritage of the Korean Church

When the Korean church was first being established, it was greatly influenced by the Nevius ministry method. In 1890, foreign missionaries in Korea invited Reverend John Nevius and his wife, who were ministering in Chifu, China, to come to Korea. For two weeks, the missionaries in Korea spent time with the couple, learning the principles that would guide the future of missions in Korea. Among the Nevius principles, one in particular draws our attention. This is the first principle, which essentially teaches that every believer must become a minister for Christ – *where they are* – and must also work diligently in their given occupation, living lives that reflect Christ to all those around them.[1]

It is necessary to pay attention to a few important implications contained in this principle, because this became the spirit that made making disciples of the laity possible, through which the entire congregation of the early Korean church was mobilized.

First, it made an education-centred ministry possible. The basic principle of the Nevius method had as its goal not only nurturing and training individual lay believers, but also raising the productivity of the entire church. Declaring that all lay people must become individual

---

1. Nak-Jun Baik, *The history of Protestant Missions in Korea* (Korean), 151.

ministers for Christ was premised on the fact that lay people have interdependent ministry responsibilities. Furthermore, it emphasized that each individual believer must live so as to reflect Christ in their lives. This was based on the understanding that the whole church has been called to be a gospel witness in the world. Consequently, it was natural that the churches at that time prioritized teaching over preaching. However, this is not to say that preaching did not play an important role. Rather, the ministry in those days emphasized the importance of training the laity in the Word *as much as* preaching. It is quite well known how prevalent the gatherings akin to Bible study groups were in those days. They were a kind of discipleship training which greatly influenced individual spiritual growth and personal evangelism.

The first Bible study class was formed in Seoul in 1890 at the private study of Dr. Horace Underwood, with seven students. In 1901, a general mission policy was adopted with the aim of establishing Bible study groups everywhere the missionaries went. Four years later, 60 percent of the entire nation's church population was attending one or two Bible studies. Statistics also show that in 1909, there were approximately 800 Bible study groups in the Northern Presbyterian Mission District alone, with over 50,000 people studying the Bible.[2]

In essence, teaching has a wider sphere and a more precise character than preaching. While preaching may be the superior method for proclaiming the gospel to the world, the strength of teaching lies in being able to minister to both the church and the world, meeting their needs through the Word. Preaching appeals to the listeners' response, while teaching requires intellectual interaction and widens the listeners' thinking in the

2. J. Herbert Kane. *A Global View of Christian Missions*, 265.

process.[3] Therefore, those who desire to grow in wisdom and maturity, so as to be able to discern good from evil, must be trained to eat solid food through the teaching of the Word (Heb 5:14).

During the early days of the Korean church, men and women, and even children were all students and teachers at the same time. Each was personally nurtured by those more mature in faith than they, and in turn, each taught those with weaker faith than they.[4]

As Nevius has pointed out, through engaging in this kind of interdependent ministry, the laity in the early church were able to use and develop their gifts, and so matured in knowledge, strength and efficiency.[5]

Second, it made the house church ministry possible. The church in its early years could not avoid using a house as a base for missions and ministry in their given circumstances. Since all the early churches appearing in the Bible were house churches, there was no reason why it should have been any different for the early churches in Korea. However, it would be misleading to conclude that the early Korean churches were house churches and family-centred simply due to their circumstances. In fact, most of the churches did have their own facilities, though meager, a short while after being established. Through centring on family meetings, the church leaders at the time seem to have been aware of the many spiritual changes and influences that were taking place in the world of the laity. 'Living room' meetings for men spread with vigor, and 'inner room' meetings for women were being pursued with interest. Whenever they gathered together, they were able to receive spiritual training through the Bible studies and

---

3. John Piet, *The Road Ahead* (Grand Rapids: Eerdmans, 1970), 57.
4. Suk-San Chung, *The Evangelization of Korea and the Neveius Principles* (Korean), 68.
5. Ibid., 68.

were able to create opportunities for sharing the gospel by inviting their unbelieving neighbours.[6]

Thirdly, the Nevius method made the personal evangelism-centred ministry possible. In the early days, the lay people of the church were all evangelists. They did not evangelize with any specific mission strategy or under the compulsion of leaders. Rather, their enthusiasm for evangelism was the natural expression of the potential that had been accumulating through the training-centred and house-centred ministries. Herbert Kane describes this phenomenon as follows:

> *Beginning in 1895 and for the 10 years following, there was consistent and continual growth in over half the mission districts. In the year 1900 alone, the number of churchgoers increased by 30 percent. New believers continued to emerge, even after the missionaries had already reached their limit in the ability to teach them, and the doors to evangelism were opened as far as even the remote areas where missionaries could not otherwise have set foot. For the most part, these phenomena did not arise through any form of organized evangelistic movement, but rather, it was the result of the personal evangelism of believers, who shared the gospel with everyone in a simple and sincere way in the course of their daily lives.* [7]

There were, of course, more than one or two methods of evangelism that the early Korean churches used. It is clear, however, that the most effective method of evangelism was through personal contacts.[8]

From 1909–1910, a movement developed to save one million souls. Each individual devoted a day during the

---

6. Nak-Jun Baik, T*he History of Protestant Missions in Korea* (Korean), 151.

7. J. Herbert Kane. *A Global View of Christian Missions*, 265.

8. Nak-Jun Baik, *The History of Protestant Missions in Korea* (Korean), 151.

week to personal evangelism, and statistics show that the total number of days that the laity devoted to personal evangelism was over 100,000 days nationwide. [9]

We need to have a clear understanding of the above three characteristics in order to know more about the ministry of the early churches in Korea. Behind the fact that the Korean churches have become one of the most successful examples of world missions lies their spirit of ministry, centred on the training of the laity. The fundamental spirit of the early churches in Korea was neither to establish missionary-centred nor staff-centred church, but rather to establish a laity-centred church. They maintained a biblical spirit, emphasizing the training of the laity in order that they might serve one another within the church and go into the world and witness for Christ through their words and deeds. With such intentions, small group meetings such as the living room and inner room meetings were used as the cradle for raising disciples.

Our present environment is vastly different from that of those early churches. From a methodological perspective alone, we probably will not be able to exactly imitate the methods used by those early churches. However, we are more than able to inherit at least the basic ministry spirit of the early churches. Indeed, now is the time for us to rediscover the spiritual heritage left behind by our great predecessors of faith, and rekindle the fire in our own ministries.

---

9. Hee Keun Jang, *The Korean Church History* (Korean), 118.

Chapter 29

SaRang Church's Discipleship Training Takes Root

Yesterday and Today

When SaRang Church opened in July 1978, it possessed only one thing: the pastor's thorough determination to venture his life on discipleship training. Although the ten church members who were there at the time did not understand the details of their pastor's vision, they had already identified themselves with the vision and were zealous to give their support as the body of Christ.

While the pastors of the surrounding churches were ministering according to the methods taught by their predecessors, SaRang Church alone took on a different approach. It wasn't because following others is bad in itself, but rather because of the conviction that God had something better in store for SaRang Church. It was also a reflection of a crisis of sorts – awareness that existing ministries had reached their limit.

During the first few years of its history, SaRang Church had to overcome many trials and tribulations: various difficulties such as worshipping in a rented space of a small commercial building, the terrible pain of seeing people leave the church because they could not adjust to the changes brought about by a growing church membership, the times of extreme financial hardship when the church members could only gaze at their pastor's face during consultation, and more.

However, there were more jubilant and encouraging moments than difficult ones. Time flew by quickly. The fruits of discipleship training were so wonderful that it was difficult to remain still for even an hour of rest. That is why even when a staged demonstration opposing the construction of SaRang Church was taking place on blistering hot summer days, even when the construction site collapsed and things appeared so black, even when the church had to stop the construction midway through because the construction company went bankrupt, and even when there were Sunday worshippers packed like sardines in the church and struggling to breathe properly in the extreme summer heat, we just could not let go of the vision for discipleship training. 'Where would be the joy of ministering if I were to stop discipleship training?' There was never a day that passed without hearing such a cry of the heart.

There was a time when I became severely ill due to exhaustion and overwork, and walked through the valley of the shadow of death. I had to let go of every ministry for over a year. However, God in His grace lifted me up again, and the pulse of discipleship training at SaRang Church still pounds with vigour, continuing to grow as a body of Christ.

One thing that changed after my recovery is that I no longer led discipleship training small groups. I concluded that it is not advisable for the senior pastor of a mega-church to train what could appear as a privileged few around him in a small group on a regular basis. It may leave the impression that the senior pastor is showing favouritism.

As a result of that decision, now over forty associate pastors are responsible for leading discipleship training groups. All of my energy is invested in training the associate pastors and educating the lay leaders of the church. And just as faithful (or perhaps more so) disciples of Jesus are being made through the leadership of the associate pastors.

Over 20 years have passed since SaRang Church began discipleship training, and discipleship training has not merely taken root in SaRang Church. It may be compared to a large cedar tree that has been growing for more than 20 years. It produces a forest of cedar trees that constantly provides the pillars for the temple of God. For discipleship training to have become the foundation of the church ministry and to play such a productive role, there were several background factors which cannot be underestimated. In ministry, every fruit has a reason for its existence, as does every stage of development and growth. One thing is certain: it is God who enables us to labour with His energy which works powerfully in us (Col. 1:29). There are several principles which have been followed during the past 20 years of ministry at SaRang Church. These had to be faithfully adhered to in order for discipleship training to take root and serve the church in mighty ways. There are quite a number of principles, but I will mention just a few that the pastors who share the vision of discipleship training will find helpful.

Do Not Change Course

Discipleship training is not just one of many ministry methods that we can choose. Discipleship training corresponds to the essence of the visible church and is the sole model that Jesus Himself exemplified and commanded. Therefore, a pastor who decides to do discipleship training must finish the race and complete the training. He should not show any sign of regret even when he tastes failure due to a lack of experience, especially when he hears criticism, doesn't see immediate fruit, suffers exhaustion, and even when there appears to be an easier way. Discipleship training is the ministry method taught by Jesus Christ our Lord, the head of the church. It may not be disregarded or abandoned. Saying that we are not qualified cannot be an excuse for abandoning God's work.

The members of SaRang Church know that their pastor's desire and passion is nothing but to do discipleship training. In order to become a leader who creates such a deep impression, he must maintain an unfaltering attitude towards the work that he has begun.

One day, less than a year after SaRang Church was planted, a male deacon whom I had known since my student days asked, 'Pastor, are you going to continue doing ministry this way? The surrounding churches are holding revival meetings and already have hundreds of people worshipping at their churches, while we lead a handful of people day and night in discipleship training. At this rate, when are we going to catch up with other churches?' My answer was brief and straightforward: 'Yes, I will continue to minister in this way'. I had forgotten that this conversation took place. However, it had such a powerful impact on the deacon that he kept it in mind and reminded me of it three years ago. This episode shows the resolute nature of my vision for discipleship training with no room for compromise. By the grace of God, I am happy to say that I am still the same and nothing has changed – as SaRang church well knows!

In ministry, there are numerous temptations. It is especially true for the pastors who continue to think laboriously and question, 'Will things work out if they're done this way or that way?' The most detrimental are those that tempt pastors not to venture into discipleship training. There is also a common temptation to turn discipleship training small groups into a huge, lecture-like class. The idea that quitting discipleship training and developing an inspirational worship service will revive the lay people is another challenging temptation.

Examples of successes and new information that we hear through various seminars are valuable in themselves. However, they must serve as a sort of tonic to reinforce discipleship training, and should not become an alternative to discipleship training. No matter how good a tonic is, no mother would substitute it for meals. Running from seminar to seminar to hunt for a better and more successful ministry method is useless. Unfortunately, there are some pastors who minister by piling up the seminar binders and making a copious display of them on their bookshelves. Frankly speaking, when we are totally immersed in discipleship training, there is no room to turn our attention to other ministry strategies or methods. In such a short life span of ministry when we do not seem to have enough time to even do one thing well, how can we find the time to wrestle with two or three things?

Up to the present day, SaRang Church has never looked for an alternative nor has it lost its course nor strayed from its path. It is because the pastor has never shown room for such variation. It certainly is not easy to maintain such an unfaltering and consistent attitude. However, that is the only way for discipleship training to take root. The most important thing of all is that the congregation trusts the pastor who steadily walks on one path with perseverance. Redirecting the course and constantly changing methodologies may provide temporary stimulation and excitement among the church members. However, no church member will be able to trust and follow such a leader. They will ask, 'How long will this one last?' I dare to say that pastors who cannot eradicate such uneasiness are not qualified to take on the responsibility of discipleship training.

Managing Time and Energy

One of the most difficult things that I had to do as I was serving SaRang Church was declining many outside teaching and preaching invitations. The most difficult thing was to refuse the requests to speak at churches and Christian organizations that were interested in discipleship training. The main reason for turning down such requests was that a pastor should not vacate his place often if he wants to press on with intensive discipleship training. It would be a violation of the concentration principle for pastors to begin spending time outside their respective churches in order to give lectures and hold seminars. Even if there is a capable group of associate pastors who can carry on discipleship training, if the senior pastor who has the overall responsibility fails to give his undivided attention to discipleship training, then the church might soon face a crisis of divided attention. One should comply with outside requests to a certain degree. However, there is a principle. The outside requests must be accepted only within the bounds of maintaining the quality and intensity of the church's discipleship training ministry.

To date, I have kept the principle of refusing nine out of ten outside requests. I'm told this has earned me the reputation of being a man who digs his hole and stays in it. Needless to say, I am not insisting that this attitude is always right. Here and there I see that at times this practice surfaces as a self-centred approach that only cares for one's own church and even as a stumbling block to the expansion of God's kingdom. However, except for special cases, focusing and faithfully ministering to one's own church is the best way to serve the entire kingdom of God. And I believe this is especially true of discipleship training ministry.

There is another principle I adhere to in order to be more faithful to discipleship training. Some may view this as being rather extreme. Nonetheless, it is important in its own way. When SaRang Church first began, I made a tacit agreement with the church elders. We agreed not to hold any positions and to limit our involvement in denominational gatherings or other Christian organizations for pastors and elders. The purpose was to avoid things which would take away our time, and to remain focused, giving ourselves to training and taking care of the church members. Surprisingly even up to this present day, our promise has not been broken. The message I would like to convey here is that in order for discipleship training to function as the heart that makes the church vibrant and healthy, church leaders must first focus on discipleship training. How can anything good come out of a place where thoughts and hearts are divided?

Strive for Self-Development
Let's think for a moment. Is there anything in this world that would put more pressure on the pastor than to cry out to others to become disciples of Jesus Christ? The more one understands what it means to become a disciple of Christ, the more one may want to avoid speaking about it. Consequently, pastors who start discipleship training must be determined to minister with chains on their feet. How can someone teach another to become a disciple of Jesus Christ if he himself doesn't make any effort to live and be like Christ? If the leader is not able to model any changes while conducting discipleship training, then it will become a dead education and the training may as well not exist. Therefore, one should keep in mind that discipleship training may place a tremendous burden and stress on the leader.

A pastor cannot open up his feathers like an extravagant peacock in order to express himself. This should not be allowed either in his sermons or in small groups. A pastor is a lonely combatant. Only before the Lord does a pastor whip himself, wet with tears and sweat. Strangely enough, however, the church perceives accurately how diligent the pastor is, how hard he tries, and how much effort he makes in order to develop himself. A positive image of the pastor in the eyes of the church members will lead him to the place of proper authority.

The pastor of SaRang Church lives in an environment in which he cannot afford to maintain the *status quo*. He must continue to run ahead and take a forward step, even against his own will at times. How can the pastor sit back while the lay people are running forward? How can the pastor relax and rest when things that daunt him are happening almost everyday in the world of the laity? Such a climate is a strong stimulus for pastors not to rest but continue to wrestle in order to improve. Therefore, the determination – to run with all his might, to grow and mature even a bit more – has sort of unconsciously become the pastor's nature.

There were moments when things were so burdensome that I felt an urge to run away from them all. At times there were impulses to let go of everything due to exhaustion. However, I believe the strength to persevere without giving in to such temptations and difficulties came from the unique environment of SaRang Church. It would be frightening if someone were to ask, 'Then how satisfied are you with your own self-development?' The fact is that there would be nothing for me to say. However, I can say this - an insistent idea that I must press on kept its eye on me as though it were a harsh master. Therefore, once discipleship training establishes itself, it creates a healthy environment for both the pastor and the lay people to move forward. I have no doubt that I have been abundantly blessed by God in this sense. As long as one does not refuse such blessings, he will certainly experience an overflowing abundance of God's grace.

No Training, No Work

From the beginning, we have adhered to the principle that lay people must receive proper training in order to partake in important ministries of the church. And I believe our adherence to the principle has contributed greatly to establishing the discipleship training ministry of SaRang Church on a solid rock. The important ministry referred to here is first of all the teaching of God's Word to others. For the first two to three years, SaRang Church had to recruit lay people to teach small group Bible studies *while* they were receiving discipleship training, due to the shortage of teachers. After those early years, however, there have been no such cases. We chose not to put a person to work unless he or she had been trained and was ready. Even though a person appeared to be qualified outwardly, we never assigned to a ministry anyone who had not gone through discipleship training. There were some who came from other churches and complained. In unfortunate cases, some people even left the church altogether. Nonetheless, SaRang Church remains steadfast to this principle.

With the firm principle of not allowing anyone without verifiable training to minister to others, SaRang Church has been able to plan and provide timely and suitable responsibilities for those who complete the training. Consequently, people have learned to acknowledge that regardless of one's ability and impressive spiritual background, one cannot partake in ministry at SaRang Church without humbly learning from the beginning.

This eventually became an unwritten law at SaRang Church.

Accordingly, more people stepped forward to receive discipleship training, and the quality and intensity of discipleship training were also heightened. What I wish to particularly point out here is that as a result of this principle, we were able to prevent many mishaps and trials that churches often undergo by giving important ministry responsibilities to unprepared and wrong people.

Looking over our past experiences, I think those with problems or bad intentions find it difficult to set foot in churches with a thorough discipleship training ministry. They seem to know that although they may be able to enter wearing a sheepskin, it will be difficult for them to play a trick and cause mishap. Also they seem to sense that once they begin discipleship training, that there is a high risk of exposing their true identity.

How important this is in securing peace and stability within the church! Up to this day, SaRang Church has not encountered any significant problems to shake the church. Looking from the outside, one might think that it is because SaRang Church has many high quality lay people. However, I believe it is due to the extra grace which we received as we remained steadfast to the fundamental principles in order to carry out discipleship training faithfully.

Maintain Balance and Rhythm

The church must take care to avoid making excessive demands on lay people or causing them to lose balance in discipleship training or in ministry. We must not neglect the fact that as there is the natural law in which there are days and nights and a time to work and a time to sleep, the same applies to spiritual training and ministry. No one can go through the entire day with tightly clenched fists. There is a time to clench and a time to relax. A proper balance of toil and rest is the rhythmic sense of ministry.

When discipleship training first begins, it is novel and exciting. And often for twelve straight months, pastors just keep on going without taking any rest. The lay leaders also, unable to control their zeal when they are given the responsibility to take care of a small group, are busy running here and there all year long. However, a person who runs like a short distance runner cannot last long. In order to continue on with the race, there must be a harmonious balance between work and rest. This is a matter that depends on the guidance of the leader.

Preventing an imbalance in training is also extremely important. Continuously meeting in a small room behind closed doors to study the Bible is not desirable. Once in a while it is advisable to meet outdoors and go to places like a retreat centre to share love and to spend time in prayer. Furthermore, it is good to develop diverse programs designed to further the growth of those who have completed discipleship training and are partaking in ministry, in order to supplement their weak points. For example, as mentioned earlier, inductive study is not as systematic or theoretical as some other types of study. Accordingly, it is possible for a person to become lopsided if he or she insists only on inductive study of the Bible. Thus, opportunities for systematic study of the Bible should be provided. This will prevent discipleship training or ministry from becoming lopsided.

SaRang Church has been deliberately placing great importance on maintaining balance and rhythm. As a result, we have implemented various extra-curricular programs in addition to discipleship training. To replenish and fully meet the on-going needs of the lay leaders, we have established a Bible college. The church also holds seminars on family life and offers special lectures by inviting well known speakers. In addition, over the summer and fall seasons, leaders and trainees are given four months of vacation for rest and leisure. Those who at first protested about such a long break are now the ones who eagerly look forward to this vacation period. In addition, SaRang Church also provides opportunities for lay leaders to participate in social service.

At one time, while trying to promote rhythm and balance, training suddenly became loose and the church suffered some spiritual ailments as an adverse side-effect. However, it has again become a recharging channel that maintains steady training and steady ministry.

The principles mentioned above made great contributions to the fact that discipleship training took firm root in SaRang Church. I believe these are important principles for the churches or the pastors who are serious about discipleship training to know and put into practice. Stated again, the blessings that flow from focused discipleship training are great, but they do not come by chance to those who sit around and wait. With the principle – we reap what we sow – before us, from the very beginning, we should not even entertain the idea of compromise.

Chapter 30

Moving from Discipleship Training to Leadership Training

The beginning stage of our discipleship training was like an experimental cultivation in a new ground called the church. Unlike many parachurch organizations, a church does not have a homogeneous group comprised of (say) all college students. Thus, it was difficult at first to assess the outcome of discipleship training since the group consisted of a small number of a mixed group – men and women, old and young, rich and poor, and educated and uneducated. In addition, my ministry philosophy was not yet organized in a systematic manner at the time. Borrowing materials from mission organizations was common.

However, the most important thing was that I began to apply discipleship training to a general church ministry situation. And in order to do that, it was essential that I remain open-minded. During the experimental period, one must maintain a flexible and elastic attitude. While holding fast to the basic framework of discipleship training, I had to be ready to modify it without hesitation and resolutely give up when necessary. The purpose was to let only the best remain. As a result, we were able to come up with the framework of the training program that is now producing an abundant harvest for SaRang Church.

Starting Men's and Women's Discipleship Training Groups

The first women's group met a crisis in less than six months. Only my wife remained out of the six original members. But a new group was soon formed when several married women with appropriate qualifications joined the church. From that time on, women's groups proliferated rapidly and never met another similar crisis.

When the church membership grew, I had to form four classes with ten or so trainees in each class and teach them with all my energy. The Holy Spirit worked so mightily that whether they had been Christians all their lives or had just become Christians, they all experienced being broken by the Word of God and the reshaping of their lives. The diligence and dedication of these women became a driving force that brought about the revival of the church. We soon had to create small groups called Darak Bang (Upper Room in Korean) in order to teach and nurture the increasing number of new members. There were no trained lay leaders then, only those in training.

However, taking into account the special circumstance of this embryonic stage, we chose suitable female deacons among those who had been receiving discipleship training for eight months. These deacons were to serve as small group Bible study leaders even as they continued on with discipleship training. It is regrettable that I am not able to relate all the amazing things that happened in those small groups. These lay leaders are still serving faithfully. Most of them are now in their fifties, but their fervor and dedication still remain the same.

I am truly grateful that at any time I can always confirm the potential and the greatness of the laity by observing them. Today there are thousands of other female leaders who are developing God's purpose in the world together with the pastor.

A men's group began a year later than the women's group, because there weren't enough men to start a group at first. Eight out of the first twelve chosen for the training were those coerced by their wives to participate. In other words, what these men needed was a course on basic Christianity more than discipleship training. Consequently, I had to exercise much patience with these men. For the first few months, in order to make certain of their attendance, I would personally go and pick them up by car. Many times our study ended in frustration because their hearts were not open. They had no experience of God's saving grace, even though most of them had come from Christian families with quite impressive spiritual backgrounds. These men were proud and confident, and did not seem to lack anything. They were bold and imposing even when they were giving the reasons for their unbelief and disobedience. They saw no problem in considering themselves more righteous than God.

After about six months, from the most obstinate and discouraging, God started to touch each one. From then on, the group atmosphere changed as if it had entered into light from darkness. Their expressions were full of joy and peace, and their conversations were laced with thanksgiving and love. As their lives were being transformed, changes began to take place in their family and social life. We often heard many beautiful testimonies of what they had experienced during the week. Within four and a half years of the inception of the church, many from this original group were appointed as elders.

Subsequent to them, hundreds of men at SaRang Church became faithful lay leaders through discipleship training and are now working for the kingdom of God.

CALLED TO AWAKEN THE LAITY

Only Jesus knows what is happening in the small group meetings led by them and what God is doing through them in their workplaces. However, it is not hard to meet wonderful brothers in the church who were saved through these lay leaders or who are growing in the Lord through their efforts. Even today, Jesus as the head of the Church is using their mouths to teach and proclaim, and their hands to heal.

There were many obstacles to overcome in order to train the men. They were in a sense far more unyielding and difficult than the women. The initial women's group failed at the first attempt, and the second men's group experienced similar setbacks soon after it started. The most difficult problem was that there were not very many men to choose from compared to the women. In the early years of SaRang Church, men comprised less than 20 percent of the entire church membership. Most were coming to church for the first time, so it was only natural for women to lead the way.

My desire to forcefully continue the men's discipleship program at the same pace as the women's brought on disaster. The men apparently were too busy. It was tough to decide the best time to meet together. We tried evenings and also early mornings. When that didn't work, we tried Sunday afternoons. However, the men who were baby Christians soon gave up. Men are generally not as spiritually sensitive as women, some to the point of being incorrigible. In order to train men, the leader must be ready to face a greater spiritual warfare. If the leader loses his spiritual power, he will not be able to continue for long. On the other hand, once men taste the grace of God and experience the transforming power of God, they tend not to cause problems with frivolous matters or by impulsively changing their minds.

Discipleship training now plays the role of the central nervous system at SaRang Church. It has become the gateway to discovering lay leaders. Each year hundreds are selected, but the number of candidates is almost always double the number of the fixed quota. Selection criteria are stringent. Moreover once they are in the program, the intensity of the training is so high, it sometimes feels like a boot camp. But even so, their faces are full of joy and dignity. I receive an overwhelming number of personal letters from the trainees every year. The letters are all about the grace they experienced through discipleship training. They invariably express their heartfelt thanks to God and to the leaders for giving them the opportunity to receive discipleship training. I don't think I can express in words, how rewarding it has been and how I am filled with overflowing praise to God for what He has done and is doing through discipleship training.

Leadership Training

When the church became somewhat settled and discipleship training was on track, I started to develop our own training materials appropriate for the church. After having gone through dozens of revisions and additions over a period of many years, they were finally developed into the current study materials, *Called to Awaken the Laity: Discipleship Training and Leadership Training*. These new materials brought about an epoch-making change to the training program of SaRang Church. Formerly, the emphasis was on strengthening the foundation of the gospel and faith, and on pursuing holy living and a mature character in Christ. However, when we were changing the materials, Leadership Training (at first it was called Advanced Discipleship Training) was added as a follow-up to discipleship training.

In order for the lay members to co-minister with the clergy, they need to have more than simply good faith and character. These are: a sense of identity that comes from the correct understanding of self, a new paradigm that comes from sharing the ministry philosophy of the pastor, and the self-examination by which one discovers one's spiritual gifts and confirms the appropriate areas of ministry to use those gifts. All of these are too much to be included in the one-year discipleship training course. That is the reason why we added leadership training, which is another year-long course. Since the full development of our leadership training materials at SaRang Church, those who complete discipleship training always move on to the second year of training unless there are special circumstances.

As the church grew and the number of applicants continued to increase, I handed over discipleship training to a team of assistant pastors and concentrated solely on leadership training. Because three discipleship groups merged into one leadership training group, it was slightly unsatisfactory as an organic educational environment. However, the members were those who had already become accustomed to small group settings through discipleship training and, therefore, it was not too difficult to manage the entire group. The number of trainees in the class was not as critical because, unlike discipleship training, leadership training consists more of teaching and instruction than discussion and conversation. However, the number of trainees in a group should not be over 25. Otherwise, individuals can get lost in the group.

With every passing year, the effectiveness of the leadership training for making lay leaders became increasingly evident. We were able to verify that a lay person convinced of his calling can indeed become a competent minister both in the church and society. We were also able to confirm that a lay person who shares the pastor's ministry philosophy can fortify the church with a healthy doctrine of the church. Through the countless number of brothers and sisters who have gone through our leadership training course, we were also able to confirm that a layman who learns specific theories and methods of serving other believers with the Word can effectively lead a small group. Furthermore, we have also learned that a lay person who feels the need to learn God's Word more systematically and in depth will diligently develop himself.

Evangelism Explosion Training
Both discipleship training and leadership training do, however, have a decisive weakness in evangelism. It is true that the courses teach that lay people are called to proclaim the gospel and that the church exists to save the world. However, there is a danger that evangelism might end up as an empty theory unless the trainees are given opportunities and places to evangelize. Jesus took the disciples with Him, showed them how He proclaimed the gospel, and instructed them to do likewise.

The pastor of SaRang Church does not have the necessary strength to imitate Jesus' pattern. Yet, the fact of the matter is that evangelism training in which the pastor does not go out himself into the streets is meaningless. To overcome this weakness, the Evangelism Explosion program was introduced. Anyone who finishes the leadership training has to then complete this four month program.

For over ten years, SaRang Church has received abundant blessings through the Evangelism Explosion program. The celebration of the birth of new believers never ceases because these trained lay leaders continue to run

CALLED TO AWAKEN THE LAITY

the race of faith with a passion to share the gospel. There are some who even cross national boundaries to ignite the fire of the gospel in different countries. This method has the power to open people's mouths and is a spring from which the joy of salvation constantly overflows. I am confident that an astonishing number of souls will continue to return to the heart of God through this training.

Educating Small Group Leaders

Once the lay people complete the training courses and dive into ministry, their spiritual demands continue to increase. In some ways, the pastor begins to carry a greater burden than before. In order for the lay leaders to serve effectively in their ministries, the pastor has to continuously provide them with necessary resources. He must continually replenish their spiritual needs.

Spiritual ministry is a type of warfare. The power of darkness, which remained dormant when a person was not doing anything, persistently approaches him to challenge and tempt, once he devotes himself to ministry. As a result, it follows that those who are active in ministry may experience a greater spiritual depression. It is easy to mislead other people when the first passion dampens and habit replaces authenticity. Lay leaders must possess a conviction that they cannot remain at the same level as others if they want to have the spiritual authority necessary for leaders. And they want to continue to grow.

Furthermore, the lay leaders are often involved in counseling others. Consequently, they have to possess a degree of spiritual discernment and counseling skills in order to carry out their ministry. The program we have launched to meet such needs is the weekly small group leadership education. This is a life-long educational program for small group leaders. As long as a person is in ministry, he or she must continue on with the weekly small group leadership class.

The small group leaders program offers separate classes for men and women. For the last twenty years, female small group leaders have been meeting every Tuesday from ten to twelve in the morning. I personally consider this as the most important time and carefully prepare for it. It is not easy to instruct thousands of small group leaders gathered in one place, but there is a unique sense of spirit, unity, and inspiration in this meeting that cannot be found in any other meeting at SaRang Church.

Depending on the circumstances, we spend about an hour in concerted prayer. There are times when we are so immersed in the grace of worshipping God that we even forget the time.

During the session, we summarize the main point of the Scripture passage, using the small group materials I've written. It is rather regrettable that, due to the time factor, I am not able to give them more ideas in detail that could help the inductive study. However it is not desirable to spoon-feed these lay leaders. Sometimes they are admonished. What a blessing it is that a leader can admonish the laity without worrying about how they will respond. This would not be possible if they were not the leader's spiritual children. I always yearn for this time with the small group leaders. It has become a time of refreshment for me and a time of catching the vision once again.

The men's small group leaders class is still somewhat unstable. The senior pastor is responsible for the small group leaders and he must teach them. Yet because of their work schedule, it is difficult to find a proper time to meet. Given these concerns, our men's small group leaders class is not able to meet every week. Thus, male small group leaders prepare by listening to the recording of the teaching given to the female small group leaders. And the first Sunday afternoon of every month is reserved for the male leaders to meet and pray with the assistant pastors, and to share appropriate information. I often come in during this time to give a short lecture and to encourage them. It is not a totally satisfactory solution. However, it is comforting to witness the increasing number of men's groups and to hear that many men are experiencing amazing transformations through these groups.

When well-trained lay people dedicate themselves as able ministers, most of them do not want to relinquish their ministries. Sometimes they are fearful that the pastor might ask them to step down. If their family situation does not allow them to continue with their ministry, they usually want to get back into it when the situation improves. I often hear them saying, 'What joy is there in the Christian life, if you are not involved in ministry?' Perhaps this is why many of the church members who emigrate, or are appointed to a foreign office, witness to people around them and start small groups. Sometimes this creates a friction with the local Korean churches. Most of the time, however, they become a source of encouragement for the local pastors.

Supplemental Programs
SaRang Church operates a diversity of supplemental programs to aid the small group leaders and other lay leaders in ministry. There is a general tendency to want to learn more as one works. Studying only the small group materials is often not enough to become a competent small group leader. It takes much effort to use these materials correctly. The Old and the New Testament surveys, systematic theology, counseling techniques, and more are all needed. As a result, SaRang Church offers

many lay college classes. They are extremely beneficial courses which use the Crossway materials in order to study the Bible in a systematic and interesting manner. Lay leaders and other lay members alike may register for the class at any time according to their convenience. Special speakers are also invited during the Winter Break to give a series of counseling lectures for a week. In addition, seminars on family and marriage problems are conducted by professional counselors. Consistent prayer training is done through an intercessory prayer group that meets every Thursday evening.

Although SaRang Church is doing everything it can to awaken the laity, we do recognize that there are still areas of weakness that the church has not been able to cover yet. We know that the visible church will always be in a state of imperfection till Christ returns. Therefore, even though we still lack many things, we remain thankful and content.

I would also add a note of caution. Because these are the programs of a mega-church, imitating them just as they are might prove difficult for other sister churches. However, it should not be too difficult to discern a basic program that can be applied to all churches regardless of their size.

Chapter 31

Harvesting with Joy

It has been more than twenty years since discipleship training began in SaRang Church. As a result, we have been privileged to see both the positives and the negatives of awakening the laity. Nothing can be hidden and everything is in the open. I would like to first share with you some of the abundant fruit being harvested with joy.

Honestly, I did not know at first the extent of the laity's potential. I could not have predicted that discipleship training would harvest such amazing fruit in ministry. This speaks eloquently of God's overflowing grace that gives us immeasurably more than all we ask and wish for. It is not only SaRang Church that enjoys such grace. As mentioned earlier, the same grace is witnessed in many other churches doing discipleship training. Thus I even dare to say, 'Please do discipleship training. You will harvest the same fruit with joy.'

Chapter 17 describes in detail the changes that occur in the nature of the church when discipleship training takes healthy root. However, in the case of SaRang Church, it does not seem appropriate to say that the nature of the church changed since SaRang Church was founded with discipleship training at its very core from the beginning. Thus, many of the changes in the nature of the church that take place through discipleship training in the established churches were already embedded in SaRang

Church from its early years. I will, therefore, introduce just a few that seem most important.

A Powerful Spirit Leading the Community of Believers

As the years pass by in the life of a church, it is natural that it develops a mindset or a spirit that guides the church. Not all churches develop the same spirit. The spirit of each church is determined by the ministry philosophy of the pastor, the number of people influenced by it, and the depth and the breadth of the impression it leaves. Thus there can be quite a difference from church to church.

Discipleship training plants a strong sense of calling in the laity as those sent into the world. It gives them a clear self-awareness of being the principal body of the church. It makes them unable to doubt that they are stewards, along with the clergy, who must give an account of their life before the judgement seat of Christ at the end of the age.

Consequently, they do not consider any title or position given to them by the church as something to boast of, but as a ministry of service. They don't forget that mutual accountability between all brothers and sisters in Christ is necessary for a healthy Christian life. Nor do they forget that they are debtors to their fellow believers for this. At the same time, they always keep in mind the fact that they exist for other brothers and sisters in Christ. Furthermore, they always bear in mind that their church and social life cannot be separated for they are both holy sacrifices unto God, so they behave accordingly. It is when such convictions formed whether consciously or subconsciously are cohesively brought together, that they become a powerful mindset or spirit that leads that particular community.

Recently we surveyed 652 lay leaders and 157 of the general lay members of SaRang Church. 93 percent of the lay leaders described themselves as those who have been called to ministry on an equal footing with the clergy. More than 67 percent said that they acquired the sense of their calling through discipleship training and leadership training. And eight out of ten point to the atmosphere of the SaRang Church as the impetus that led them to become a lay leader. In other words, they dived into training and ministry because they sensed from the church atmosphere that if they didn't, they would remain as outsiders. This seems to suggest that they were not so much motivated to join the laity training programs by a sense of calling, as they were stimulated by the general spirit and the climate of the church that had caused them to think that they could not remain still.

There is another statistic which proves the prevalence and persistency of such a mindset in SaRang Church. 70 percent of the survey respondents answered that they are mentoring people around them to become lay leaders in their footsteps. This demonstrates a dynamic mindset that is being transmitted to the next generation.

The quickest way to find out the influence this mindset has on the general membership of SaRang Church is to ask those who have just joined the church and are taking the new membership class. This group consists of both new believers and Christians who have transferred from other churches. Of these, 72 percent said that they want to receive discipleship training. Only 7 percent answered that they feel burdened by the atmosphere of the church that emphasizes the training, and 25 percent said that they are ambivalent. Thus, above 70 percent accept the spiritual climate of the church as being natural and reasonable. I believe this data gives a glimpse of how influential such an unspoken and unseen mindset stemming from the pastor's philosophy of ministry can be on the collective consciousness of lay people.

Why is it that being a small group leader or a Sunday school teacher imparts more spiritual authority than the office of an elder or a deacon? Why do the meetings that share the Word and encourage one another prosper more than the meetings that discuss administrative matters? Why do people prefer to devote more time to evangelism, serving, and learning than to any other events often found in other churches? Why are their words so full of confidence? Why is the worship climate so unique? How is it that the church has not suffered from any exhaustive and destructive problems within? Why is it that nine out of ten have a strong sense of pride in being a member of the church?

There is only one possible answer to these questions. It is because an invisible inward conviction formed due to discipleship training governs the entire community. SaRang Church is a church that insists on discipleship training. And as such, SaRang Church wants to share this mindset prior to any other, because it firmly believes that this is indeed a precious inheritance that can sustain the life and health of the church.

Healthy and Consistent Church Growth
When we talk about church growth, there are several other growth factors. SaRang Church is no exception. I do not insist that discipleship training is the only reason for the church's growth. For instance, for the most part, discipleship training is not the reason why people who come to church for the first time return the next Sunday. No matter how well trained the lay members are, if the church is careless about those who set their foot in the church for the first time, it will surely hamper their growth. However, we should not overlook the fact that there is one element that plays a dominant role in church growth.

In the case of SaRang Church, this leading factor has clearly been discipleship training. The training itself awakens the laity as those who have been called. Therefore, as long as discipleship training is carried out properly, the church will not be able to remain mute. The more trainees there are and the greater their influence on other believers, the more the life force of the church is bound to explode towards the outside world.

For the first seven years of SaRang Church, until the opening service in the new church building, the average annual growth rate of the Sunday adult attendance had been 40.2 percent. Then until 1998, the Sunday adult attendance had stayed at an average growth rate of 24.7 percent. And from then on until 2004, the average growth rate remained at 12.2 percent. In 2004, as an example, the number of the new adult members from college age and up was 10,297. Of those, 26.4 percent or 2,710, were first time believers who joined the church via evangelism. Although this number is lower than the number of transferees from other churches, the fact that the church has the energy to bring 2.6 out of 10 people to salvation should certainly not be underestimated. Everyone would agree that this could not have been realized if it were not for the trained laity who play a key role in the life of the church. SaRang Church has a major lack of spaces for worship, education and ministries. Still, I believe it is able to sustain its growth because the seeds which were sown in tears have grown and are bearing fruit a hundredfold. Healthy growth takes place gradually and continuously. I don't know of any factor that could guarantee such growth other than discipleship training.

Expansion and Diversification of the Ministry Field
Trained people must work. Otherwise they will become like marathon runners who practice for many years

without ever running a race. Thus, a leader must not only train but must also make an equal effort to provide ministry fields for the trained laity. If the leader is unable to provide appropriate ministry fields for the trained laity, then it is better to discontinue the training for a while. It is better to eat less than to become spiritually obese by just sitting around and studying the Bible. SaRang Church has been able to continue running on the single path of discipleship training without growing weary, because the church leaders have persistently provided ministry fields for the trained laity to run to their fullest measure.

Our most basic ministry field is the small group. This is a small group Bible study led by a small group leader. It is open for anyone to attend. The life of the small group lies in its continuous growth and multiplication. A small group with about ten people is like a small church. The leader is like a pastor and the group members are like the young sheep left in the care of the leader. We can always witness how Jesus uses these small groups for teaching, proclaiming, and healing.

A survey was conducted among the small group members to find out the extent of the spiritual influence the lay leaders exert on them through the small groups. Nine out of ten answered without hesitation that they considered their leaders to be their spiritual parents. Accordingly, most of them replied that they are deeply grateful to the leaders for their dedication and service. With such an open heart toward the leader, it is no wonder that 85 percent of the group members acknowledge that they look forward to and enjoy their small group meetings. Most of them feel very much loved in the group. And they sense a healthy obligation towards the small group for the systematic study of the Bible and for the prayer support. On top of that, 92 percent of the members admitted that their love for SaRang Church began through these small groups. What more is needed to prove the enormous value of the work the trained lay leaders are doing?

The health of the small group affects the health of the church. The purpose of the group is not Bible study alone. Rather, it is another arena where Jesus' disciples are made. It is also a place of love where each serves the other as different parts of the body to build up the body of Christ. There, new lives are born. There, young lives are nurtured. Multiplication of the small group has a direct connection with church growth. The demand for lay leaders surpasses the number we can provide, partly due to those who step down as leaders because of their personal circumstances, but mostly due to the proliferation of the small groups. Presently, 65 percent of the entire church membership, from college age and up, is enrolled in the small groups.

At times, it is beneficial to assign only one or two members to a leader in order for the group to start out like a new church plant. SaRang Church often assigns this type of ministry especially to the male lay leaders.

The following is an incident from the early years of SaRang Church. A male deacon, who had just finished discipleship training back then, started the first small group with seven members. However, the members continued to drop off until the only person left was a drunkard, who was out to make trouble. This battle continued for two months. The leader could have taken over another group but he refused, and he continued to pray and witness diligently. He often said that it was a precious opportunity for God to work on his pride and endurance. Amazingly, he overcame the spiritual warfare and his small group was then able to multiply into four other groups within a year. The leader now serves as an elder at SaRang Church. SaRang Church is full of such

303

stories. God sometimes works on the leader rather than the group. At times, a small group might have to be sacrificed in order to train a leader. A competent leader is not made overnight.

Just as important as the small group ministry is the mercy ministry in which trained laity can serve with love. For the first ten years of SaRang Church, we could not develop the mercy ministry because we did not have enough leaders to send. Almost everyone was invested in the small group ministries where they served by teaching the Word. However, now SaRang Church offers extensive mercy ministries. There is a constant increase in the number of members who prefer to be part of the mercy ministry, according to their gifts. Also, the number of the lay leaders serving both as small group leaders and in mercy ministry simultaneously is on the rise.

If the small group members get used to studying the Word and partaking in fellowship amongst themselves for a prolonged period of time, then their Christian life could become stagnant. Both leaders and members, therefore, should be encouraged to go out periodically and serve others who are in difficult circumstances. For these reasons, many of our leaders and their members are involved in mercy ministries - working with the physically impaired, in the slums, with delinquent juveniles, with the elderly and homeless, with homosexuals, and in rural and hospice ministries. None of these ministries can be carried on without the love of Christ. Without question, I believe these are the services that must be accomplished by the church that has been sent into the world. A church that is apathetic or powerless about being the salt and light in society is not a church that Jesus desires. SaRang Church will continue to develop mercy ministries. Last year, the district of SeoCho (where SaRang meets) commissioned SaRang Church with the operation of a local community welfare office. SaRang Church is also working with the city government and has launched a volunteer organization that can penetrate deep into the local community.

A Rise in Lay Leadership

As discipleship training continues on steadily, the number of the trained lay leaders is bound to increase. Even taking into account several natural factors of decline, a moderate increase in the number of trained leaders is still expected. SaRang Church takes nearly two and a half years to train a lay leader. Unexpected circumstances can crop up during this training period. Also the number of applicants for the training could diminish. There could be no more people to train, or people might avoid the training because of the long commitment it involves. All these things could be stumbling blocks to the continual development of lay leaders. However, gratefully, SaRang Church has not yet encountered such problems.

Approximately 10 percent of the adult membership at SaRang Church is currently serving in lay leadership. In other words, nearly 3,000 disciples are working together with the pastor. This percentage is not trivial, compared to the total size of the church. Any church, regardless of its size, that has one out of ten serving as a trained leader should be considered to be a healthy church.

A surprising fact is that in many churches, those who are making up the workforce of 10 percent have not received proper training. We must bear in mind that what matters is not the numbers, but that these are the spiritual children and the co-workers of the pastor who has thoroughly trained them.

A distinguishing feature of the trained lay leaders is that they are thoroughly equipped with the pastor's ministry philosophy. Therefore, the pastor can assign them to ministries with peace of mind. More importantly, because they are prepared leaders, they will bear much fruit and many of them will find ministry to be rewarding and worthwhile.

According to the survey previously mentioned, 98 percent of the leaders in SaRang Church perceive themselves as God's instruments in building up the church. 80 percent of them said they have maintained a healthy balance between their church ministry and family life. Furthermore, 78 percent of them said there is a balance between their work life and their church ministry. It is amazing that 59 percent consider serving others with the Word as a small group leader to be the most appropriate ministry for them. Close to 88 percent replied that their ministry is bearing fruit and testified that God is working through them. And almost 93 percent said that they find much joy and worth in their ministry. These statistics demonstrate how beneficial the trained laity can be to the life of the church and how strong and healthy their spiritual life can be.

Building Mutual Understanding in Ministry
It is distressing for pastors to encounter various misunderstandings and complaints of elders and lay leaders who lack sufficient understanding about spiritual ministry.

There is a vast difference between dealing with precious souls and dealing with administrative work such as signing a document, or between serving the body by nurturing the weak and settling a matter at the church board meeting or deacons' meeting. Administering or governing in the church ought to be interpreted as a spiritual ministry whose purpose is to strengthen and nurture believers. However, the reality seems to be otherwise. Most churches generally do not have a firm foundation for understanding spiritual ministry.

From its inception, SaRang Church did its best to train the laity to partner with the pastor in spiritual ministry. Thus SaRang Church has laid a firm foundation for understanding what it means to care for the souls. This is not only a great blessing for the pastor, but also a precious asset for the church as a whole.

The attitude of an elder who gives himself as a small group leader to care for and nurture ten or more souls that are in his charge would clearly be different from that of an elder who sits in a board meeting, killing time by looking through the minutes. I often hear these words at our church: 'Pastor, how exhausted you must be caring for so many souls. We are having a hard time just taking care of the few in our small groups. Take heart. We are praying for you.' It might sound insignificant, but these are words that can be exchanged only among those who understand what spiritual ministry is all about. When the level of understanding and empathy between the pastor and the laity deepens, the church will surely be able to manifest a greater power. In this sense, as the senior pastor of SaRang Church, I am not lonely. I feel secure and confident. What an amazing grace this is!

Trust and Love Towards the Pastor
Unless there is a particular reason, lay people in any church love and trust their pastor. This subject matter might, therefore, appear slightly redundant. Nevertheless what matters is the kind of love and trust. Imagine a hard working pastor who does not hold back sweat and tears to make each person whole in Christ. This is the image of a pastor who does discipleship training. Of course, other pastors who are not doing discipleship training are also just as dedicated in caring for their sheep. However, compared to the sweat of a pastor as worship leader, preacher, visitation pastor, or senior administrator,

I believe the sweat and tears of a pastor who intimately shares sorrows and joys through discipleship training touch the hearts of the laity more deeply. Every pastor labours and sweats for the lay people. The truth is that a pastor who does discipleship training moves the hearts of the believers in a more profound way and gains their affection more than those who do not. It is the same principle as that of a son feeling more love and gratitude to a mother who worked hard to send him to school than if she did so out of material affluence.

Although it might seem impertinent, I would really like to mention this. Any pastor who does discipleship training ends up exposing himself quite plainly before the lay people. He cannot pretend even if he wants to, and he cannot just roll along even if he wants to. Truth is transmitted as truth, and a lie is transmitted as a lie. Therefore, in order to develop his sheep into disciples of Jesus, he must exert all his strength, fully concentrate, and willingly sacrifice himself. This attitude of honesty will move the people. A pastor is not respected because he wants to be. Instead, respect should come to him naturally. He should not have to beg for love or harden his neck to show his authority. Even if he does none of this, he will be loved. I would venture to say that this is an overflowing bonus that can be enjoyed by a pastor who does discipleship training.

People often anxiously say that if the lay members become too smart, the clergy will get hurt. But SaRang Church can clearly show that the opposite is true. At SaRang Church, not only the senior pastor but also many associate pastors invariably receive trust and love from the members. This is not a phenomenon without a reason. I would dare to say, 'Do you want to receive trust and love? Humbly go to a lower place and make disciples.'

Chapter 32

Remaining Problems

Can a church become an ideal church if discipleship training is carried out properly? Will there be other problems beneath the surface? The answer is simple. A church will not become perfect or exist without any problem by carrying out discipleship training. Discipleship training might solve many problems, but implementing it could also bring in new problems and challenges. I believe SaRang Church can offer a number of examples from which pastors can catch a glimpse of such issues.

Endless Challenge and Responsibility

When the lay people are spiritually awakened, they expect more from the pastor. People who are growing in their faith and who want to dedicate themselves need proper nourishment to support their spiritual growth. This remains a responsibility that pastors must bear. Yet, this might not be too much of a burden. A more difficult concern is that those who pursue spiritual maturity to become like Christ look to their pastor as a model of Christian living. To be frank, it is difficult to know where to draw the line regarding the level one must reach to be more like Jesus or the stage one must arrive at to be considered mature.

People who are naive want something a little more visible. This is an extremely heavy burden for the pastor.

They do not verbally demand specific things, but through the teaching of the pastor, people end up forming standards by which they measure one's level of maturity and practice of good deeds. However, just because a person is a pastor does not mean that he always practices everything he teaches, or that he has already reached a certain level. Consequently, a difficulty for a pastor is that the more he does discipleship training, the more obligated he feels. Where the Spirit of God is, there is peace, but it is not going to be easy to shake off the yoke that comes from carrying out discipleship training. Perhaps we will gain complete freedom from that burden when the time comes for us to leave this world behind.

Higher Demand on the Role of the Clergy
Theoretically speaking, one may think that the need for professional clergy will diminish as the number of lay leaders increases through discipleship training. It is like asking what else there is for the clergy to do when there are so many active lay people in the church. I had naively thought like this when SaRang Church was first planted. There was even a vague expectation that discipleship training might reduce the church expenses. However, now we acknowledge that such thoughts were far from reality. The reality is that as the number of lay leaders increases, there is a higher demand for pastors.

Why is this? Well, as stated earlier, lay leaders can be exorbitant spiritual gluttons that are not easily satisfied. They also pass through the various swamps of spiritual depression that all pastors pass through as they engage in ministry. This means that they often require more help and care from the pastor than regular believers. Of course, lay leaders do encourage and support one another, but other lay leaders still cannot take the place of the pastor. This is the first factor that places a greater demand on the clergy.

Moreover, when a church continues to grow through lay ministries, there is often an increase in the number of ministry spots that lay leaders are unable to cover. Pastors or staff members must often fill in these voids, until properly trained lay leaders become available. Accordingly, there is a need for more pastors to run discipleship training. If an adequate number of clergy is not assigned to carry out team ministries, the senior pastor will end up collapsing before long.

There are about seventy full time pastors working at SaRang Church. We would like to reduce that number if possible. However, the prospect is that the number will continue to increase. This may continue to remain as a challenge.

Idealism Addiction
The focus and the goal of discipleship training is Jesus Himself. This makes those involved in discipleship training vulnerable to idealism in their theory and standards. And they will naturally have an idealistic view of the church. Then is idealism bad? No, it is not that idealism is bad, but its adverse side effects are bad. The visible church is definitely not perfect. No matter how hard a leader challenges others to become disciples of Jesus, he himself is only an imperfect example. Nevertheless, many lay people unwittingly view the pastor and evaluate the church through an idealistic lens. This is indeed a dangerous matter.

A person who is immersed in idealism has a tendency to react hysterically whenever his standards are not met. Idealism always demands perfection instead of showing tolerance that embraces things that are insufficient, weak, or even things that appear slightly wicked. Consequently, idealists are shocked if a pastor makes a mistake or shows a slight imperfection. They also take fright at trifling matters that occasionally happen in the church, as if there had been an earthquake. Idealism weakens people. It takes away the energy needed to adapt to reality. As we are well aware, when a person stays in a germ-free environment for a long time, his immune system weakens and he will quickly contract the cold virus or other germs as soon as he comes out. In some ways, idealism functions similarly to the germ free environment. Idealistic theory ought to remain as a goal toward which we run; it should not become a drug that poisons us.

It is sad to see some in SaRang Church who seem to have become addicted to idealism. They will be okay during times when the church is sailing under a favourable wind, as at present. However, I am anxious that these idealists might be knocked down when the time comes to fight a massive spiritual battle. Believers who have experienced various trials during their long spiritual journey have already developed a strong immunity, and thus are not easily shaken even when faced with disappointments in the church. On the other hand, the members of SaRang Church have yet to be immunized. As their pastor, at times I am worried about whether or not they will be victorious as strong soldiers of Christ.

A High Threshold
A church that uses the word 'training' will naturally create a strong image of itself. This was one of the problems SaRang Church had to wrestle with from its beginning. We tried various ways to soften the church image. Sometimes new members are intimidated by it. However, this does not necessarily have negative effects only. For example, a person who joins SaRang Church having heard of its training ministry is more likely to be challenged and dedicate himself. Such a strong image is

also effective in preventing people with bad or impure intentions from joining the church. Moreover once a person joins the church, he is more likely to submit to the authority of the church. Above all, a new believer in Christ will be nurtured to become a strong believer from the beginning. These are some of the positive aspects of a strong image.

However, we cannot neglect its negative effects. For example, such a strong image has a tendency to create a difficult climate for so-called successful people of the world to adapt to. It is not that they don't want to participate, but their conditions do not seem to allow them to receive discipleship training. However, the church cannot take their situation into special consideration and treat them on an equal footing with the trained leaders. Thus naturally, they have a difficult time setting their foot in the church. This does not mean that people from such a class never join the church. It is just that, in general compared to other large churches, there are not as many people from the upper class at SaRang Church.

Although about half of the high ranking people in Korean society identify themselves as Christians, in reality most of them fail to influence society as Christians. Quite the opposite, many actually hide the glory of God by being involved in all kinds of scandals. It is heartbreaking to think that they cannot easily enter the church because of its high threshold. If it is indeed a responsibility of the church to train these people in whatever ways possible, so that they can exert a positive impact in their social arenas as Christians, then SaRang Church has yet to overcome a significant weakness.

The visible church cannot be perfect. And just as the presence of bad germs in the air builds up strong immunity in our bodies, I believe the presence of some weaknesses which may be difficult to overcome in the church will help strengthen it and enhance the quality of its ministry. No matter how high the obstacles, they cannot be compared to the fruit of discipleship training. Thus even today, SaRang Church continues to do its utmost to awaken the laity.

Chapter 33

21st Century: Ministry Opportunity

Discipleship Training is the Key to Tomorrow's Church
What should the church be like in the 21st century? It is the question I hear all the time. Many plausible prognoses are pouring in. Undoubtedly the church in the information age will not look the same as the church in the industrial age. The essence is the same, but the appearance will differ.

Some people humorously compare it to a DC-3 plane – which uses propellers – and a Boeing 747. At a quick glance, the two planes appear to be alike. They both have wings, windows, seats and wheels. But the two are vastly different in many points such as in speed, capacity, expense, complexity, and noise level.

By the same token, the 21st century church will be different from the latest model of the previous century. From its expense to its complexity, it will be different in many ways. Be that as it may, both models are the body of Christ and both exist to bring glory to God.[1]

Someone may ask whether discipleship training will be effective in the 21st century. A person could ask such a question if he views it merely as one of the ministry tools. Discipleship training, however, is the essence of biblical ministry. Thankfully, many scholars are anticipating that

1. Leith Anderson, *A Church for the 21st Century* (Korean Translation) (Bethany House Publishers, 1992), 32.

the ministry of making disciples will be the decisive key affecting the life of the church in the 21st century.

Pastor Sung Hee Lee, a prominent leader in the Korean church, has warned that in the 21st century, the church must convert its visitation ministry into an education ministry; its mass ministry into small group ministry; Sunday church into everyday church; a gathering church into a sending church; clergy-centred to laity-centred; the authority of the pastor into leadership of the pastor; and discipleship training into apostolic training.[2]

I think the reason he distinguishes discipleship training from apostolic training comes from an incomplete understanding of the concept of a disciple. We must not lose sight of the fact that Jesus' command to make disciples includes the apostolic calling of being sent into the world. Nonetheless, we must pay heed to the need for transformation that Rev. Lee forecasted for the sake of future ministry. We must note that the content of the changes proposed by Rev. Lee indirectly suggests the necessity and importance of discipleship training. In other words, the church in the information age needs a resolute ministry philosophy to build up the lay people as disciples of Christ more than ever before.

There is another amazing fact that supports the opinion that discipleship training will indeed be the basis of the 21st century church ministry. Recently, a survey was conducted with 5,000 pastors in America. The questionnaire asked what they thought was the most needed element to strengthen, equip, and revive the church of the 21st century. The results were stunning. Almost 100 percent of the pastors replied that their first or second priority is to find the laity and train them to become partners in ministry. How could such urgency be applied only to the American churches?

2. Sung Hee Lee, *The Great Prediction of the Future* (Korean), 109-313

PART 5: MINSTRY FIELD

Just as training children at home gets tougher as time goes by, so there is a possibility that training lay members will become more challenging. As parents lose their power to control their children, so a pastor can gradually lose his influence over the laity. Under these conditions, the first thing a pastor must do is to restore the laity to their proper biblical position and role. If the laity could be properly taught, they will become a source of strength rather than an obstacle. But if we miss the opportunity, then they may become difficult to handle. Rather than to teach them as one of the audience in a large group, we need to teach them in a small group. I believe there is no better way to build up the lay people than through personal encounters. This will become even more so as time passes.

During one of his missionary journeys, Paul had an opportunity to stop over briefly in Troas before he moved his ministry setting from Asia to Europe. The door was open for the gospel, but when he could not meet with Titus, his co-worker, his heart was grieved and he left the place (2 Cor. 2:13). Much as it was difficult for Paul to carry on his mission without Titus, it will be difficult for pastors from now on to have powerful ministries without lay leaders.

Before trying to save many souls at once, we should turn our eyes to developing one person as a disciple. Before installing the state of the art multimedia systems in the church, we should have the vision of finding lay people who can partake in ministry. Lay members who are properly trained in the hands of the Holy Spirit through the Word of God will not stumble, no matter how much the world changes. They will not leave the pastor's side even if many others fall away. If we fail to devote ourselves to raising lay co-workers like Priscilla

---

3. Frank R. Tillapaugh, *Unleashing the Church* (Regal, 1982), 20.

and Aquila, who did not hesitate to give their lives for Paul, no one can know the kind of crisis churches will face in the future.

It Is Not Too Late to Begin
SaRang Church conducts the 'Discipleship Training Leaders' Seminar' annually in order to assist and encourage those who have the vision for discipleship training. Over ten thousand pastors serving Korean churches and Korean emigrant churches around the world were able to gain a new vision from these seminars for the past twenty years. In addition, hundreds of churches in Japan are turning to discipleship training ministry. Pastors from India, China, Brazil were impressed with the seminar.

Although the seminar is only a week long, it is an intensive program that offers theory, practice, and field studies. This seminar does not hand down discipleship training methodology in an encyclopedic fashion. Although methodology is important, priority is given to changing the paradigms of the pastors. The seminar aims to firmly plant in the hearts and minds of the pastors the fact that renewal in the pastoral ministry begins with paradigm transformation, and not with a methodology. Above all, a distinctive character of this seminar is to provide several opportunities for the participating pastors to visit and see for themselves SaRang Church's actual ministry situations where the lay people serve.

Quite a number of pastors who returned to their churches with the vision of discipleship training after attending the seminar have experienced great success. This suggests that the possibility of Korean churches to succeed in discipleship training is very high.

I believe discipleship training is possible in any church in any nation as long as the pastor is willing to change the old paradigm with which he might feel comfortable now. Thus, it seems wise for the pastor to start discipleship training when the lay people are still willing to listen to him.

As the door of evangelism was wide open for Paul when he arrived at Troas, the door to awaken the laity is also wide open before us today. Each pastor must decide. If he desires a ministry that is healthy, productive and that can lead society in the 21st century, then he should not dream of doing ministry all by himself. Pastoral leadership is no longer what a pastor can do *for* the laity. No, now is the time to develop a leadership that focuses on what a pastor can do *with* the laity. Opportunities do not always come. Now is the time to establish a ministry philosophy for making lay people into disciples of Christ.

'Lord, may your disciples rise up like swarms of bees in this nation. Amen.'

Christian Focus Publications
publishes books for all ages

STAYING FAITHFUL

In dependence upon God we seek to impact the world through literature faithful to His infallible Word, the Bible. Our aim is to ensure that the LORD Jesus Christ is presented as the only hope to obtain forgiveness of sin, live a useful life and look forward to heaven with Him.

REACHING OUT

Christ's last command requires us to reach out to our world with His gospel. We seek to help fulfill that by publishing books that point people towards Jesus and help them develop a Christ-like maturity. We aim to equip all levels of readers for life, work, ministry and mission.

Books in our adult range are published in three imprints.

Christian Focus contains popular works including biographies, commentaries, basic doctrine and Christian living. Our children's books are also published in this imprint.

Mentor focuses on books written at a level suitable for Bible College and seminary students, pastors, and other serious readers. The imprint includes commentaries, doctrinal studies, examination of current issues and church history.

Christian Heritage contains classic writings from the past.

Christian Focus Publications, Ltd
Geanies House, Fearn, Ross-shire,
IV20 1TW, Scotland, United Kingdom
info@christianfocus.com

For details of our titles visit us on our website
www.christianfocus.com